THE OXFORD INTERNATIONAL RELATIONS IN SOUTH ASIA SERIES

SERIES EDITORS
Sumit Ganguly and E. Sridharan

After a long period of relative isolation during the Cold War years, contemporary South Asia has grown immensely in its significance in the global political and economic order. This ascendancy has two key dimensions. First, the emergence of India as a potential economic and political power that follows its acquisition of nuclear weapons and its fitful embrace of economic liberalization. Second, the persistent instability along India's borders continues to undermine any attempts at achieving political harmony in the region: fellow nuclear-armed state Pakistan is beset with chronic domestic political upheavals; Afghanistan is paralysed and trapped with internecine warfare and weak political institutions; Sri Lanka is confronted by an uncertain future with a disenchanted Tamil minority; Nepal is caught in a vortex of political and legal uncertainty as it forges a new constitution; and Bangladesh is overwhelmed by a tumultuous political climate.

India's rising position as an important player in global economic and political affairs warrants extra-regional and international attention. The rapidly evolving strategic role and importance of South Asia in the world demands focused analyses of foreign and security policies within and towards the region. The present series addresses these concerns. It consists of original, theoretically grounded, empirically rich, timely, and topical volumes oriented towards contemporary and future developments in one of the most populous and diverse corners of the world.

Sumit Ganguly is Professor of Political Science and Rabindranath Tagore Chair in Indian Cultures and Civilizations, Indiana University, Bloomington, USA.

E. Sridharan is Academic Director, University of Pennsylvania Institute for the Advanced Study of India, New Delhi.

THE OXFORD INTERNATIONAL RELATIONS IN SOUTH ASIA SERIES

Globalization and Deregulation

Ideas, Interests, and Institutional
Change in India

Rahul Mukherji

OXFORD

UNIVERSITY PRESS

Oxford University Press is a department of the University of Oxford.
It furthers the University's objective of excellence in research, scholarship,
and education by publishing worldwide. Oxford is a registered trademark of
Oxford University Press in the UK and in certain other countries

Published in India by
Oxford University Press
YMCA Library Building, 1 Jai Singh Road, New Delhi 110 001, India

ISBN-13: 978-0-19-809617-7
ISBN-10: 0-19-809617-8

Typeset in Adobe Jenson Pro 10.5/13
by The Graphics Solution, New Delhi 110 092
Printed and bound in India at Repro India Ltd., Mumbai

This book is dedicated to the three musketeers and the Almighty who presented them; who fought against the odds to ensure that the book sees the light of day—Anjali Mukherji, Ayon Mukherji, and Adheesh Mukherji. The shortcomings, nevertheless, belong to the author alone.

Contents

Tables

Acknowledgements

THIS BOOK HAS BEEN a long time in the making. Its journey began as a doctoral project on comparative responses to financial crises at Columbia's political science department many years ago. Along the way, I have edited two books, co-authored a book, and published numerous papers in scholarly journals and edited volumes. It is impossible, therefore, to thank all those who passionately believed in this project.

I am sincerely grateful to professional colleagues who helped shape the project in a number of ways. Pre-eminent among the well-wishers of the project are Jack Snyder, Sumit Ganguly, Mark Blyth, John Harriss, Ashutosh Varshney, T.N. Srinivasan, Jagdish N. Bhagwati, C.P. Bhambri, Sudha Pai, Balveer Arora, Zoya Hasan, Gurpreet Mahajan, David Baldwin, Helen Milner, Tan Tai Yong, Yong Mun Cheong, Vikram Chand, Gyanesh Kudaisya, Vineeta Sinha, Medha M. Kudaisya, Chua Beng Huat, Francine Frankel, Robert Jervis, Montek Singh Ahluwalia, Mukul Asher, Rahul Sagar, Kurtulus Gemici, Baldev Raj Nayar, Pratap Bhanu Mehta, Sunil Khilnani, Prasenjit Duara, E. Sridharan, Pradeep Chhibber, Premachandra Athukorala, Sanjaya Baru, Rakesh Mohan, Raghbendra Jha, Kanti Bajpai, Juliet Johnson, and Hal Hill.

I am especially grateful to Sumit Ganguly and E. Sridharan for encouraging me to submit this book for the IRSA series with Oxford University Press. The support of the team at Oxford University Press was invaluable. The referees chipped in with valuable comments. John Grennan did an excellent job of copy editing the book.

The manuscript was supported by an Academic Research Committee Tier 1 grant made available by the Faculty of Arts and Social Sciences, National University of Singapore (R-123-000-013-112). This book has enjoyed the support of two deans of the Faculty of Arts and Social Sciences—Tan Tai Yong and Brenda Yeoh.

The manuscript benefited from presentations at Columbia University, the University of Michigan (Ann Arbor), the University of

California at Berkeley, the Australian National University, the School of Advanced International Studies—Johns Hopkins University, the International Studies Association's Annual Convention in Montreal (2011), the Indian Institute of Management in Bangalore, the Centre for Multilevel Federalism at the Institute of Social Sciences (New Delhi), and the Indian Institute of Technology Bombay.

It gives me the greatest pleasure to acknowledge students who cheerfully kept the project moving. They include: Sitaram Kumbhar, Siddhartha Mukerji, Ajoy Lywait, Taberez Ahmed Neyazi, Priscilla Ann Vincent, Wee Shi Chen, Vasudha Dhingra, Sojin Shin, and Yogaananthan. I hope they, too, learned something about research in the process.

The book has involved acquiring area competence on a number of issues. Tarun Das, Amit Mitra, and D.H. Pai Panandiker explained the business response to the reforms of 1991 and helped obtain valuable primary materials. I have learned much about Indian telecommunications from T.V. Ramachandran, Pradip Baijal, Nripendra Misra, Vinod Vaish, Dilip Chenoy, Virat Bhatia, Arun Thiruvengadam, Mahesh Uppal, and Vikram Raghavan. On power sector reforms in Andhra Pradesh, I have benefited from conversations with T.L. Shankar, S. Malla Reddy, Venugopal Rao, Srikumar, Rachel Chatterjee, Gajendra Haldea, Umesh Sharraf, and Sutirtha Bhattacharya. Prakash Sarangi, Amit Misra, and K.C. Suri made my stays at the University of Hyderabad a memorable experience.

The historical richness of the manuscript owes it to various libraries and data sources: The Parliament Library (New Delhi), the library of the Indian Institute of Public Administration (New Delhi), the Nehru Memorial Museum and Library (New Delhi), the Central Library at the National University of Singapore (Singapore), the World Bank archives (Washington), the International Monetary Fund archives (Washington), the Confederation of Indian Industry (New Delhi), the Federation of Indian Chambers of Commerce and Industry (New Delhi), the Cellular Operators Association of India (COAI, New Delhi), Prayas (Hyderabad), the Andhra Pradesh Electricity Regulatory Commission, and journals located in various trade union offices in New Delhi.

The World Bank archives played a seminal role by helping with the declassification of the Bell Mission Report (1965), which was the basis of the lending conditions faced by India in 1966. The Oral History of the

World Bank was a critical resource for understanding the crisis of 1966. The International Monetary Fund archives made available the minutes of the Meetings of the Executive Board from 1990 to 1992. The commitment of these organizations to transparency and access is commendable. Thanks to the aforementioned organizations, the arguments in this book are based on substantial primary material.

I must especially thank colleagues and friends in Singapore and Delhi who endured me during the past five years. They include, Yong Mun Cheong, Gyanesh Kudaisya, Vineeta Sinha, Medha Malik Kudaisya, Kurtulus Gemici, Manjusha Nair, Indivar Kamtekar, Vidhu Verma, Pralay Kanungo, Rajesh Rai, Andrea Pinkney, Bishnu Mohapatra, Ted Hopf, Nur Jannah Mohamed, and Hamidah.

I would have lost faith in this project without the love and affection of my family. They include, my father (Professor Partha Nath Mukherji), mother (late Goparani Mukherji), grandparents (late Bijoya and Narendra Nath Mukherji), late Basudeb Ghosal, Deepa Mukherjee, Indra Nath Mukherji, Subhadra Mukherji, Shantanu Mukherji, Probhati Mukherji, Debabrata Mukhopadhyay, John Vincent, Christie Vincent, Atul Sarma, Nibha Sarma, Suman Kumar Mukherji, Dhiman Mukherji, Abhimanyu Mukherji, Alpana Sarma, Navnita Sarma, Pradeep K. Chakravarty, Abhinaba Chakravarti, Kalyan Ganguly, Tarun Kumar Roy, and Satyendranath Mukherjee.

I have drawn inspiration and spiritual solace from the Ramakrishna Mission, especially from Late Swami Vireshwarananda and Swami Tathagatananda of the Vedanta Society of New York, Pravrajika Prabuddhaprana of the Sarada Math in Dakshineshwar, West Bengal, and Swami Muktirupananda and Swami Samachittananda of the Ramakrishna Mission in Singapore. I concur with Albert Einstein, when he said, 'Science without religion is lame, religion without science is blind.'

Abbreviations

AIEI	Association of Indian Engineering Industry
AP	Andhra Pradesh
APERC	AP Electricity Regulatory Commission
APGENCO	Andhra Pradesh Power Generation Company
APTRANSCO	Transmission Corporation of Andhra Pradesh Limited
ASEAN	Association of Southeast Asian Nations
ASSOCHAM	Associated Chambers of Commerce and Industry
BC	backward caste
BICP	Bureau of Industrial Costs and Prices
BJP	Bharatiya Janata Party
BPL	British Physical Laboratories
BSNL	Bharat Sanchar Nigam Limited
CAG	Comptroller and Auditor General
CDMA	code division multiple access
C-DOT	Centre for Development of Telematics
CEI	Confederation of Engineering Industry
CII	Confederation of Indian Industry
COAI	Cellular Operators Association of India
CPI	Communist Party of India
CPM	Communist Party of India–Marxist
DMK	Dravida Munnetra Kazhagam
DoT	Department of Telecommunications
FERA	Foreign Exchange Regulation Act
FICCI	Federation of Indian Chambers of Commerce and Industry
FOB	free on board
GDP	Gross Domestic Product
GoT	Group on Telecommunications

HDPE	high-density polyethylene pipes
ICICI	Industrial Credit and Investment Corporation of India
IDA	International Development Association
IMF	International Monetary Fund
ISI	import substitution industrialization
JD	Janata Dal
JS	Jan Sangh
MGNREGA	Mahatma Gandhi National Rural Employment Guarantee Act
MNC	Multinational Company
MOCIT	Ministry of Communications and Information Technology
MP	Member of Parliament
MRTP	Monopolistic and Restrictive Trade Practice
MTNL	Mahanagar Telephone Nigam Limited
NDA	National Democratic Alliance
NTP	National Telecom Policy
PL	Public Law
PMO	Prime Minister's Office
PSP	Praja Socialist Party
QR	Quantitative Restrictions
RAX	Rural Automatic Exchange Switches
RBI	Reserve Bank of India
Rs	Rupees
SC	scheduled caste
SDR	special drawing right
SEBI	Securities and Exchange Board of India
SSP	Samyukta Socialist Party
TDP	Telugu Desam Party
TDSAT	Telecom Dispute Settlement Appellate Tribunal
TRAI	Telecom Regulatory Authority of India
UC	upper caste
UPA	United Progressive Alliance
USAID	United States Agency for International Development
VSNL	Videsh Sanchar Nigam Limited
WLLM	Wireless in Local Loop with Limited Mobility

Introduction

From Market Failure to Government Failure

IN 1991, WHEN A PERSON would want to make a phone call in India, he/ she would use the government phone company's line, travel on the country's national airlines, and mail letters through the government-controlled post office. By 2011, all these modes of communication were dominated by private companies. This book discusses the significant role that private companies have played in the Indian economy since 1991.[1] Rather than focusing on entrepreneurship, this book examines how India transformed its regulatory structure and promoted Indian enterprise in the global economy. Twenty-five years ago, India's economic institutions presumed markets would fail and that the government needed to intervene. Today, these institutions reflect a much greater faith in private initiative, trade, and foreign investment. Identifying how these changes happened helps explain India's economic successes and offers potential lessons for other countries.

Institutions facilitate certain modes of economic behaviour and inhibit others. Economic institutions had discouraged entrepreneurship in India. Airlines, iron and steel, mining, banks, telecommunications, power generation, and a variety of other economic activities were almost entirely state-controlled before 1990.[2] Successful private companies in car and scooter manufacturing—such as Hindustan Motors, Premier Automobiles, and Bajaj Auto—depended on permissions, monopolistic privileges, and government protection. The fate of the Indian multinational Infosys, which was ranked as one of the world's 15 most innovative companies in 2011 by *Forbes*, looked quite bleak in 1990 under this government-controlled regime.[3] Foreign investment was minuscule at this time. The ratio of India's annual trade to its gross domestic product (GDP) hovered around 16 per cent all through the 1980s, whereas the same figure ranged between 25 and 29 per cent for China.[4] During this period, India's economic institutions and policies placed significant constraints on the country's entrepreneurial talent.

The framework of India's economic institutions changed quite dramatically after 1991, building on the gradual deregulation of private companies that began in 1975. The state actively promoted this transformation. The paradigmatic shift in policy in 1991 (discussed in Chapter 3) has substantially enhanced the role of private and foreign companies in India's economy. For example, there was no private investment in the telecom sector in 1991. In contrast, more than 84 per cent of the investment in Indian telecom companies came from private sources in December 2010.[5] In 2004, the country had only 76.5 million telephone connections. In the quarter that ended in February 2013, India had 892 million telephone lines—one of the world's largest and most competitive telecom sectors.[6] India also boasts of the world-class telecom company Airtel, which is the largest telecom service provider in India and the fifth largest in the world with a footprint in 19 countries. Competition has driven down prices and mobile phones have penetrated rural areas, becoming more accessible to the poor. The process of promoting competition has withstood numerous attempts to derail it by rent-seeking firms that wish to kill competition (as can be seen in Chapter 4). Like private telecom companies, private airlines have also revolutionized air travel since 1991, even though the national carrier has been stifled by unnecessary political interference.[7]

The Indian automobile industry provides another dramatic example of the country's economic transformation over the past two decades. Cars that ruled the roads in India's era of dirigisme—from the 1950s till the 1980s—such as Fiat and Ambassador, have all but vanished. Today, India is one of the world's most fiercely competitive markets for small cars. In 2009, the sales from Suzuki's Indian operation, Maruti Suzuki, had exceeded the revenue of its Japanese parent company, which is now investing Rs 15 billion (USD 300 million) in a research and development facility in India.[8] As the state withdrew from investment decisions, India experienced rapid economic growth after 1991, which accelerated even more dramatically after 2003. The infamous Hindu rate of average annual economic growth between 3.5 per cent and 3.7 per cent till the 1970s accelerated to 5.7 per cent in the 1980s. This was in stark contrast to rapidly growing parts of Asia in the 1970s and 1980s. The average growth rate exceeded 6 per cent after 1992 and accelerated to 8.8 per cent between 2003 and 2007. Even with the global financial crisis, India's economy has continued to grow at an annual rate of more than 5 per cent, making it the world's second-fastest growing major economy after China. India's achievements in human development leave a lot to be desired but growth has had a positive effect on the country's overall development.[9]

And yet, the transition to a market-based economy has not cured the infrastructure deficit. India's roads, ports, and the power sector (see Conclusion) are far from being a model of private sector participation that has engendered efficiency.[10] In addition to examining the economic changes that have promoted private sector participation and efficiency in India, this book addresses the obstacles that persist within India's democratic political economy. Economic reforms have been especially challenging in areas such as the power sector, where India's numerous and politically powerful farmers refuse to pay electricity bills.

This book proposes a 'tipping-point model' of economic change, where new economic ideas and politics are equally important for understanding the slow-moving processes of change. Rather than arguing that either politics or ideas explain economic change,[11] this book proposes that both matter equally. Gradual and endogenous changes in ideas— resulting from policy failures in India, the international demonstration effect of rapid economic growth in Asia and the collapse of the Soviet Union—made an impact on Indian policymakers in the 1980s and led to small, but demonstrable, policy changes. India was at a tipping point in 1991, when a balance of payments crisis spawned a paradigm shift in the country's economic policies (see Chapter 3). India had faced a similar crisis in 1966, but the economic ideas and government policies had not evolved in the direction of change at that time (see Chapter 2). The tipping-point model of change, discussed at length in Chapter 1, emphasizes the importance of endogenous and slow-moving processes that can bring a system to the brink of change.

Economic ideas within the government and politics are equally germane to this tipping-point line of explanation. The balance of payments crisis in 1991 upended Indian politics, enabling Indian technocrats to negotiate a deal with the International Monetary Fund (IMF), which implemented some of their home-grown ideas about conditional lending. The agreement with IMF shifted the domestic balance of power in favour of those who believed that the Indian economy had been excessively regulated and self-contained. Even though the technocrats agreed with the IMF and the World Bank on many issues, they were able to negotiate a deal that worked within India's democratic political system and did not constitute a bitter pill for its citizens.[12]

The discussion on telecommunications and electricity in this book also highlights the salience of politics in India's tumultuous democracy. For example, the Prime Minister's Office (PMO) supported the regulatory reforms that promoted private sector participation in the telecom sector and led to the industry's rapid expansion, but faced fierce opposition from the Department of Telecommunications (DoT) (see Chapter 4). India's power sector, meanwhile, could not be significantly reformed.

Chapter 5, on power sector reforms in the relatively well-governed state of Andhra Pradesh (AP), demonstrates the political power of farmers who would not pay for electricity, and who have largely scuttled the reform process. This chapter describes how Western and developing countries shifted their emphasis from the economic idea of 'market failure' to the idea of 'government failure'. It then engages with the economic scholarship that is relevant for understanding India's transformation.

Finally, a case is made for the tipping-point model of economic change that stresses the importance of both ideas and politics in an attempt to understand economic change in India.

A Tale of Two Economic Ideas: Market Failure and Government Failure

This section describes the advent of two important sets of policy questions pertaining to economic development. First, what were the economic reasons for the rise of regulation in the West, and in the developing countries through the 1970s? Why did governments think markets were likely to fail and require government intervention? Second, why did government intervention subsequently become unpopular in the West and in developing countries? What were the economic reasons for the rise of deregulation, beginning in the 1980s?

Market Failure

Economists have pointed to the possibility that markets may not allocate resources efficiently. Spontaneously operating markets, after all, are premised on assumptions such as low transactions cost, perfect information, and respect for contracts. Transactions cost is the price paid for specifying, monitoring, or enforcing a contract.[13] If an economy is characterized by high transactions cost, knowledge about market conditions is poor, and contracts are not respected, the markets will fail to deliver an efficient outcome. The possibility of such an environment becomes the rationale for government intervention. This section will discuss the reasons why the governments of developed and developing countries favoured the idea of government intervention over market determination in the allocation of resources prior to 1980.[14]

The challenge of reducing transactions cost is quite substantial in the political arena. The state often makes decisions that can hurt investors but cannot be challenged by them.[15] For example, foreign investors in India in the 1960s had made business decisions based on the view that Indian laws would permit them to have 51 per cent foreign equity in Indian firms. This level of equity was associated certain powers over the decisions of a company's board. Yet the Indian government's decision to reduce the maximum permissible foreign equity in Indian firms to 40 per cent with the enactment of the Foreign Exchange Regulation Act (FERA), 1973, suddenly and unpredictably increased these investors' costs of doing business in India.[16] No foreign company could challenge this Act in court. Given scenarios like this one, investors worry whether governments can make credible commitments that are essential for long-term investments.

There were additional reasons why postcolonial developing countries regulated their foreign and domestic economic activity. First, these countries did not possess an advanced industrial base. Their competitive advantage in unprocessed primary commodities was considered a handicap. Indian economists believed that the demand for these commodities did not respond either to a rise in income or a decline in price.[17] While a few liberal economists emphasized that promoting comparative advantage in trade was the path to economic development,[18] influential dependency theorists argued that this was a sure way for a country to remain consigned to the periphery of the world economy.[19]

Before the 1980s, import substitution with state intervention was the developing world's preferred economic path. This policy followed from the assumption that a country with a poor manufacturing base would face market failure in an open global economy because it could not modernize its manufacturing base when faced with competition from more advanced industrial countries.[20] In India and other developing countries, import substitution industrialization (ISI) relied on high tariffs and import quotas, an overvalued exchange rate, and guided industrialization. The overvalued exchange rate reduced the price of imports required for manufacturing goods and other essential items. The high tariff wall and import quotas protected domestic industry. Governments concentrated industrial production in the hands of a few licensed private companies and publicly owned industries in order to coordinate industrialization and achieve economies of scale. Large-scale production within a protected domestic market was considered essential for industrial development during the early stages of industrialization. The view that markets fail in both developed and developing countries produced an era of heightened industrial regulation in the 1960s and 1970s.

The Rise of Government Failure as a Policy Idea

Policies emphasizing market failure generated dilemmas that led many economists to argue that governments were rather inefficient. It became apparent to economists that industrial regulation largely served private, rather than public, interest. These regulations perpetuated monopolies, circumvented the forces of competition and productivity, and produced extraordinary profits or rents for certain privileged parties.

The failure of governments to regulate markets in the US generated an influential literature on regulatory capture. George Stigler demonstrated that US corporations benefited from the systematic capture of industrial policy by private companies. Powerful lobbies benefited from regulation in a number of ways. These companies sought subsidies that would privilege them in the market. Domestic airlines, for example, received 'air mail' subsidies that amounted to USD 1.5 billion in 1968. The beneficiaries lobbied successfully against the competitive bidding of 'air mail' contracts to preserve their exclusive financial benefits.[21]

Stigler lamented that a small and concentrated group of industrialists in the US could obtain substantial rents by providing resources to politicians. These resources helped politicians remain in power and allowed party workers to gain access to government jobs. Moreover, the average voter did not have the time or the information to judge what was beneficial. Richard Posner reinforced this view by suggesting that regulatory agencies were not mismanaged—they deliberately operated in ways to maximize the inefficient goals of the executive branch.[22] Economists were, therefore, puzzled when industrial deregulation occurred in the US, starting in the mid-1970s. Why would the US government give up its regulatory privileges when it was locked in a relationship with powerful companies? Did the government pursue public interest in opposing private rent-seeking corporations that could provide politicians with valuable resources? Industrial lobbying could not explain deregulation in telecom, airline, and the trucking industry between 1975 and 1980. In a classic book, Martha Derthick and Paul Quirk demonstrated why these cases signalled the triumph of public interest as the factor driving deregulation, rather than the capture of regulation by powerful interested companies.[23]

Technological change during the 1980s could have created new business opportunities that considerably increased the economic cost of protecting government and private monopolies. Advances in information technology reduced transaction costs in the financial services sector, and the revolution in digital technology transformed mobile telecommunications. The promotion of competition, now, became an even greater economic imperative than in the past. The new regulatory structures that emerged in the 1980s were closely aligned with a state's particular institutional inheritance and existing institutions. 'Pro-competitive re-regulation' and new juridical structures emerged in the UK, where the state became actively involved with reorientating regulatory processes.[24]

As predatory industrial regulation in the US attracted criticism by the 1970s, so did industrial regulation in developing countries. Autarkic state-directed industrialization in India and other developing countries, such as Turkey, Brazil, and Mexico, also inspired critical theorizing associated with the idea of rent-seeking industrialization. Rent-seeking industrialization—conceptualized and analysed by economists such as Anne Krueger, Jagdish Bhagwati and T.N. Srinivasan—resembled the analysis of regulatory capture of agencies in the US. These economists argued against the virtues of state control in the context of a developing country.[25] They demonstrated that ISI had evolved as a regime of controls where the government interfered with all kinds of industrial activities— such as the permission to produce, the scale of production, and obtaining financing for imports. Under these circumstances, industrialists could not make decisions based on considerations of profitability in a competitive environment. The incentives offered by these economic institutions forced industrialists to expend resources on lobbying for production licences that would protect their monopolies. They had no incentive to invest in innovation and productivity, as these investments were a deadweight loss to the economy.

The theory of rent-seeking industrialization emphasized the government's failure to allocate resources efficiently. Import substitution—the protection and nurturing of an infant industry in a backward economy—was supposed to facilitate an industry's maturation to a point where it could compete globally. The theory, however, was silent on a number of critical issues. First, it was not easy to locate an industry fit for protection. Moreover, economists could not define the duration of protection that an infant industry needed in order to mature into a globally competitive entity.[26] In addition, the 'infants' often behaved like spoiled children who charmed their parents into treating them as infants forever. Owners of secure monopolies became the new princes of modern India, whose privileges depended on their relationship with the ruling party rather than on their ability to compete in the Indian or global market.

Under these circumstances, government intervention stifled competition in India. A symbiotic relationship evolved between the country's business class and politicians. Then prime minister Indira Gandhi unleashed the most stringent system of economic controls after 1969, after a spate of government takeovers of private businesses. It is reported that underground or illegal wealth—famously known as 'black money' in India—became the main source of party-funding at this time. The bargain was for an industrialist was to give 'black money' to governmental officials, in exchange for rents accruing to private monopolies created by government control. This phenomenon was aptly called 'briefcase politics' by the leading scholar of business and politics in contemporary India, Kochanek. In the mid-1970s, a briefcase full of Indian currency notes of a certain denomination became a unit of value for the corporate sector in its dealings with government officials in India. These investments in procuring licences constituted a deadweight loss to the economy.[27]

ISI was dealt a major blow when several East and Southeast Asian countries grew quite rapidly in the 1980s by promoting their exports. Even though state-direction had played a major role in the industrialization of these countries, they grew by competing with the world economy rather than by restricting economic activity within the confines of the domestic market. Moreover, the Soviet Union's economic strategy of autarkic industrialization, which had inspired the Indian model of development, had collapsed. These experiences suggested that there were 'pathways from the periphery' that became possible by engaging with the world economy.[28]

The Politics of Globalization and Deregulation in India

The previous section described evolution in economic thought about development policy. But how did economic ideas about globalization and deregulation become embedded in politics? It is one thing for economists to be puzzled by development outcomes, but policy change that involves politics is quite a different matter. This section explores the significance of various explanations of deregulation and globalization and assesses their value for the Indian experience. It proposes a path-dependent, tipping-point model for India that will be further developed in Chapter 1.

In the 1980s, India's political economy was locked in a state-driven, import-substituting equilibrium that resisted transformation. The state behaved as a balancer of class interests, which did not lie in globalization or promoting competitiveness. Indian industry was comfortable with rent-seeking industrialization, which assured it a large domestic market and monopoly production privileges in return for rents.[29] The pro-business reforms of the 1980s only increased the privileges for the big Indian business houses without subjecting them to competition.[30] The farming community, which has grown into the largest voting block since the green revolution of the early 1970s—was clamouring for ever-increasing subsidies, free power, and no taxation.[31] In addition, the middle class extracted privileges from the state in the form of subsidized higher education and guaranteed government jobs.[32] The state was seen as an actor that could balance the interests of these classes but not transform them substantially to favour globalization and deregulation. These classes depended on regulation and the comfort of a closed economy to secure their privileges.

India's transformation poses a puzzle for the developmental state model of institutional transformation from import substitution to export-led growth. Developmental states or hard states possess the capacity to deal with social actors that oppose economic reform. Import substituting industrialists and labour unions are squashed if they come in the way of export promotion. Yet, India was a relatively weak state in an environment inhabited by powerful social actors.[33] Peter Evans pointed this out quite clearly on in his work on embedded autonomy, where he held that the best developmental states were the ones that were embedded with social actors but autonomous from them.[34] India did not possess the characteristics of a developmental state that could easily engineer a transition toward economic reform.

How, then, did the transformation occur?[35] Did economic reforms favouring private sector participation and global competitiveness occur as a result of foreign pressure during the balance of payments crisis in 1991?[36] This argument suggests that states can make a transition because donors have coercive power to direct development when foreign exchange is scarce. The evidence presented in this book suggests that India would not have undertaken comprehensive and holistic economic reforms in the absence of a technocratic consensus in favour of reforms. Chapter 2 demonstrates that when the weight of economic ideas within India's technocracy favoured import substitution in 1966, the World Bank and IMF could not coerce the country into making the transition from import substitution to globalization. Moreover, Chapter 3 traces the paradigm shift in policy that occurred in India in 1991. It demonstrates that a majority of the technocrats were in favour of change, and ideas and politics of the 1980s had pointed towards it. Economic change favouring globalization and deregulation, without the support of powerful politicians and technocrats, would not succeed in India.

Another explanation for India's economic reforms focuses on the rise of business associations, such as the Confederation of Indian Industry (CII). Did the CII capture the state and guide it toward economic reform? Did the rising power of a professional business class interested in deregulation propel the state toward economic liberalization in 1991?[37] While it is true that the CII emerged as a powerful lobby post 1984 (especially after 1991) and played a significant role in advocating reforms, it was not the prime mover of economic reforms in 1991. That CII was not a critical player in 1991 is evident from the fact that it did not lobby for trade reforms in the 1980s. But CII actually wanted access to markets in India and abroad, without subjecting Indian industry to competition. Also, when India's financial crisis ended in 1992, CII did not object to the creation of a 'Bombay Club' of Indian industrialists who opposed the entry of foreign investment in India.[38]

Chapter 3 demonstrates that while the support of industry organizations like CII was essential during the 1991 financial crisis, the Indian state—which persuaded the country's business class to adjust to globalization—was the primary author of the reform strategy. The government did not receive support from India's other leading industrial lobby, the Federation of Indian Chambers of Commerce and Industry (FICCI), because the captains of Indian industry were habituated to the comforts of a large and protected market. The state directed India's industrialists towards reform at a time when they indirectly depended on the IMF for foreign exchange that would finance their imports.

Did economic change in India occur by 'stealth'—which implies change in policies and institutions under the pretence of continuity? Scholars have pointed out that gradual economic reforms in the 1960s and 1980s occurred furtively. According to this line of argument, politicians with short-time horizons in a democracy can ill afford to take long-term political risks. Rather than claim to promote change, Indian politicians promoted change in the garb of continuity.[39] While gradual changes in industrial policies favouring the private sector in the 1980s may have occurred stealthily, the change in policy direction in 1991 was debated and criticized quite openly. Chapter 3 details how the reforms of 1991 were debated in Parliament and were opposed—in no uncertain terms—both inside and outside it. Moreover, regulatory evolution in telecommunications (Chapter 4), which promoted private sector participation, was opposed by the powerful DoT housed within the Ministry of Communications and Information Technology. Telecom reforms were debated in Parliament, the Supreme Court, and later within the Telecom Regulatory Authority of India (TRAI) and the Telecom Dispute Settlement Appellate Tribunal (TDSAT). None of this very public debate could be characterized as stealthy.

Nor could the power sector be reformed stealthily.[40] Chapter 5, dealing with power sector reforms in the state of AP, testifies to the political power of numerous farmers who blocked all efforts to make farmers pay for the electricity they consumed. The establishment of an electricity regulatory agency and the unbundling of the state electricity board into generating, transmission, and distribution companies did not occur stealthily. The regulator held periodic public hearings where civil society groups took the government to task.

Finally, what is the relationship between democracy and economic reform in India? The Stolper-Samuelson Theorem in international trade suggests a democracy such as India should promote free trade. According to this theorem, a sector of the economy where production factors are abundant should demand free trade because the price paid to these factors will be low. Since labour as an input is priced competitively, countries where labour is abundant should be globally competitive in labour-intensive forms of production.[41] In populous and poor countries like India, labour should demand free trade; and a democratic political framework should aid the majority of the workforce to express this view. Yet, we find no evidence of labour demanding a freer trade regime in India. Trade unions have successfully protected their rights, but haven't expressed a preference for either tariff liberalization or the freer entry of foreign investment into the country.

Are democracies more likely to make credible commitments to investors because these political regimes need to produce economic growth to keep winning elections? According to this argument, democratic rulers do not enjoy the luxury of autocratic rulers, whose position in power is assured for long periods of time. This makes it imperative for democratic rulers to produce the public goods and legal framework essential for economic growth.[42] Charles R. Hankla has argued that over-regulation of the Indian economy occurred during periods when the ruling Congress party was losing its mass base and resorting to patronage politics.[43] Irfan Nooruddin has contended that coalition governments are best at making credible commitments to investors because of the checks and balances in place owing to the presence of numerous veto players in the governing coalition. And in India, economic deregulation and growth since the 1980s has coincided with a period of greater political competition and party fragmentation.[44]

Our story of India's path to reform clearly shows that successful economic transitions are possible within democratic states that have to take their social actors seriously. One needs to go deeper than regime type, however, to understand the process of change.[45] India was no less a democracy in 1990 than in 1991, when the paradigm shift in economic policies occurred. Moreover, if coalition politics was driving the story, India had already entered an era of party fragmentation and coalitions in the 1980s.[46] One cannot ignore the interplay of ideas and interests, which need to be traced by analysing the process of economic change.

The tipping-point model of economic change proposed in this book and developed further in the next chapter holds that slow-moving endogenous changes in policy ideas and economic practice drove India to the tipping point for reform in 1991. India's response to the balance of payments shock in 1991 was quite different from the crisis in 1966, because the policy elite was well-prepared in 1991 to harness the country's dependence on IMF to initiate the transition to deregulation and globalization. In 1966, however, India's policy elite was not convinced of the need for fundamental reform. The country's leaders made a brief and tactical retreat to reforms, while countries such as Indonesia and Singapore chose to pursue the path of globalization.

This book advances the literature that suggests that explanations of economic reform based on ideas and those based on politics need to be integrated. The defining role of ideas does not undermine the salience of interests and politics. India's 1991 reforms are a story of both liberal economic ideas and the ways that the Indian government utilized dependence on IMF to usher in far-reaching changes in economic institutions and policies. The country's dependence on IMF helped nudge Indian industry to accept a more competitive economic order. The PMO took on the DoT to gradually promote competition in the telecom sector, which would expand dramatically in the next two decades. At the same time, chief ministers in numerous Indian states have been unsuccessful in taking on the lobby of powerful farmers, and free electricity in rural areas has ensured that reforms have not produced meaningful results in the power sector.

Chapter 1 situates the tipping-point model of economic change, which integrates economic ideas and politics, in the comparative political economy literature. The chapter contrasts the punctuated equilibrium model of change with the model. It also delineates paths in the tipping-point model and the punctuated equilibrium model to show where economic ideas matter and where they do not. This exercise theorizes India's transition and locates it within a comparative framework.

Notes

1. On the role of entrepreneurship, see Damodaran (2008); Narayana Murthy (2012: 462–72); Nilekani 2008; Nirmallya Kumar 2009; Majumdar 2012; Tripathy and Jumani (2007: 207–32).

2. On the problems faced by Indian business groups at the height of regulation, see Kochanek (2007: 417–24); Tripathy and Jumani (2007: 182–206).

3. See Narayana Murthy (2011: 467–9). For the *Forbes* ranking, see http://www.infosys.com/newsroom/features/innovation-rankings/Pages/index.aspx (accessed 9 November 2013).

4. See World Bank (2010).

5. See Department of Telecommunications, *Annual Report 2010–2011* (New Delhi: Government of India, 2011): 3, 139.

6. See Telecom Regulatory Authority of India (2013) (http://www.trai.gov.in/WriteReadData/WhatsNew/Documents/Monthly_press_release_February_2013_16april2013.pdf (accessed 9 November 2013).

7. See Mukherji and Kankanhalli (2009: 1–18).

8. A Factiva search for news between February and June 2010 in October 2010 revealed this trend.

9. On India's rapid growth, see Nayar 2006; Rodrik and Subramanian (2004: 3–39); Srinivasan (2011: 33, 60); Wallach 2003. On growth and development, see Ganguly and Mukherji (2011: 60–118). On the relationship between growth and development, also see Dreze and Sen 2011.

10. See Mukherji (2010: 184–93); Panagariya (2008: 370–414).

11. This debate is dealt with at some length in the Chapter 1.

12. These matters are discussed in greater detail in Chapters 1 and 3.

13. See Dixit (1996: 38). On why transactions costs are often neglected in economic theorizing, see Coase 1998.

14. See Dixit (1996: 40–1). On the reasons why small groups may lobby with greater ease than larger groups, see Olson (1965: 5–65). More generally, on market failure and the need for regulation, see Noll (1989: 1,254–87).

15. See Dixit (1996: 37–60).

16. On FERA, see Ganguly and Mukherji (2011: 88–9); Panagariya (2008: 62–3); Tendulkar and Bhavani (2007: 106–16).

17. On the pessimism about primary product exports, see Bhagwati 1958 and Krueger (1993: 45–7).

18. See Bhagwati (1967); Johnson (1967); Lewis (1978); Reynolds (1983).

19. See Wallerstein (1979).

20. On imports substitution, see Gerschenkron 1962; Hirschman 1980; Krueger (1993: 44–5); Rodan 1943.

21. See Stigler (1971).

22. Posner (1974). For a defence of regulation, see Becker 1983.

23. See Derthick and Quirk (1985).

24. On the relationship between technological evolution and changes in the business and regulatory environment, see Bronckers and Larouche 1997; Cowhey 1990; Kranser 1991; and Vogel 1996. On institutional inheritance and regulation, see Levy and Spiller 1994.

25. See Bhagwati and Srinivasan (1980); Krueger (1974). For a review on rent-seeking and why trade policies changed, see Krueger (1997). The Indian case was important, and Bhagwati and Srinivasan were Indian economists. See Bhagwati and Desai (1970); Bhagwati and Srinivasan (1975).

26. See Dasgupta (1974); Todaro (1981: 453–4).

27. See Kochanek (1974, 2007).

28. See Haggard (1990); Naughton (1995); Shirk (1993); Tsiang (1985: 27–56); Wade (1990). On the economic impact on the collapse of USSR, see Aggarwal and Mukherji (2008: 125–58); Thakur (1994: 116–23).

29. See Bardhan (1984); Chibber (2003); Rubin (1985); Vanaik (1990).

30. On the pro-business orientation in the 1980s, see Kohli (2004, 2006); Panagariya (2008: 78–94); Sinha (2005); Tendulkar and Bhavani (2007: 58–71).

31. See Gupta, A. (1998); Rudolph and Rudolph (1987: 211–44, 333–92); Varshney (1998: 81–145).

32. See Bardhan (1984); Weiner (1986).

33. See Amsden (1989); Haggard (1990); Wade (1990); Woo-Cummings (1999).

34. See Evans (1995).

35. There are very few scholarly writings that reflect deeply on the structural transformation in India's political economy. See Chatterjee (2011: 22–5).

36. See Simmons and Elkins (2003: 275–304); Stallings (1992: 41–88).

37. See Kochanek (2007: 424–5); Pederson (2000: 265–82); Sinha (2005).

38. See Kochanek (2007: 425–8).

39. See Jenkins (1999); Kudaisya (2002: 216–20); Panagariya (2008: 78–94).

40. For a mid-term appraisal of the 11th Five-year Plan, see the Planning Commission (2011: 312–21).

41. See Milner and Kubota (2005).

42. See Olson (1993).

43. See Hankla (2006).

44. See Nooruddin (2011).

45. See, for example, Murillo (2009).

46. See Ganguly and Mukherji (2011: 109–40); Gowda and Sridharan (2007).

1   Ideas, Interests, and the Tipping Point

Understanding Economic Change in India

THIS CHAPTER DEALS WITH institutional change and suggests
a path for economic change in India. Economic institutions are
normative orders based on formal and informal rules backed by a legal
and administrative framework. Institutions encourage certain modes
of economic behaviour and proscribe others.[1] One institutional setting
might allow private investors a free hand, while another economic
order might highlight the salience of market failure and the need for
governments to intervene in economic activity. Each of these economic
arrangements has different consequences for the nature of economic
activity that it engenders.

It is not easy to bring about change in economic institutions.
Economic ideas are central for understanding why new economic orders
are born and sustained. The Introduction dealt with the economic
considerations that gave rise to the view that market failure generated
the need for government intervention. But these changes in economic
ideas needed political support behind them in order to alter economic
institutions.

This next section briefly describes the general reasons for the stickiness
of institutions and the logic of change. Institutions are biased in favour of
the status quo for a number of reasons. First, vested interests that benefit
from existing institutions may block institutional evolution. Second,
institutional orders may have a complementary set of institutions that
are locked into each other. Deregulating financial markets, for example,
may not correspond well with long-term employment. Third, institutions
may be supported by shared understandings about what is good. For

instance, some societies may view lifetime employment as a greater benefit than higher incomes. Finally, institutions, rules, and standards may be endowed with network externalities. If Indian telecom companies had, for instance, learned to live as government monopolies with the International Telecommunications Union fixing rates for international calls, they may find a new regulatory environment of competition and foreign investment quite perplexing. Why would they want to adjust to new rules of the game?[2]

Institutional change is not an easy process, because institutions structure social life in a society over long periods of time. This chapter suggests that we pay heed to incremental change and offers two ways of thinking about it. First, ideas can shape interests in a tipping-point or gradual model of change. Old policies become puzzling when they do not deliver results. Over time, these riddles can lead economic technocrats to rethink their policies and introduce incremental changes. Institutional change or a shift in a policy paradigm, however, may be affected by an exogenous event that builds upon incremental changes of the past. This is the India story, which is similar to the account of the rise of neo-liberalism in Great Britain, as described by Peter Hall.[3] Endogenous factors drive this account of change, even though the impact of an external factor may have a role in the transformation.

Second, conflicts of interest among powerful social groups over time may produce a tipping point and institutional change. Douglass North and Barry Weingast demonstrated that the rising power of the capitalist class represented in the British Parliament during the seventeenth century may have empowered the Parliament, produced the Glorious Revolution, and given birth to the Bank of England.[4] This is an evolutionary story where incremental changes in social power led to social eruptions after they reached a tipping point. I argue that that a combination of the tipping-point model of ideational change needs to be complemented with an account of political conflict between social groups to understand the process of economic change in India.

Some abrupt economic changes can be driven by externally induced economic shocks, and these social phenomena cannot be understood within a tipping-point model of change. Scholars have often described such changes as a 'punctuated equilibrium'.[5] There can be two different ways of thinking about abrupt economic change that is significantly affected by exogenous events. First, the persuasive power of economic ideas during a severe and cognitively challenging economic shock can engender a change. Under these circumstances, policymakers cannot make rational calculations, but are persuaded by the appeal of new ideas.[6] Second, an external shock may also change domestic constituencies' interests during an economic crisis if multilateral organizations or powerful donors have the power to rescue the country.[7]

This chapter introduces four historical cases that will be used to understand the relationships between new ideas, economic crises, conflicts among interest groups, and institutional change. The first two cases deal with India's balance of payments crises in 1966 and 1991. Why did India respond to the balance of payments crisis of 1966 by reverting to government intervention and autarky, but then embraced globalization and deregulation after the 1991 crisis? Changes in the Indian technocracy's economic ideas help explain the differences between the government's responses to these two crises.

The third and the fourth cases deal with India's success and failure, respectively, in engendering competition in infrastructure provision after 1991. Why has India's booming telecom sector been successful in promoting competition and private investment, while the power sector, even in the relatively well-governed state of AP, remains saddled with investment pessimism and losses? Both cases involved challenges to established interests, but the oppositional coalition of farmers in AP— who are far more electorally significant than workers in state-owned telecom companies—were much more successful in resisting change. These cases bring to light the challenges that India's mass politics presents to the economic reform process.[8]

What Do We Know about Institutional Change?

India's transition from a country with high-degree government intervention to one with a freer hand for private companies constituted a comprehensive transformation in its economic institutions. This section begins by first taking note of the reasons for institutional persistence. Why do institutions structure behaviour over long periods of time? Thereafter, the section turns to the issue of institutional change, examining different scholarly traditions such as historical institutionalism, rational choice traditions such as game theory, and sociological approaches. The section argues for a tipping-point model of change for India's economic reforms that places the explanatory focus on policy puzzles and ideational change, where exogenous events can lead to a paradigm shift when substantial ideational change has occurred within the technocracy. Resolving conflicts of interest is central to this story of economic change in a democratic polity.

Institutional Persistence

Why are institutions so 'sticky' and why do they resist change? Scholars argue that institutions are characterized by increasing returns after they are established. This makes institutional persistence more likely than change. A number of reasons have been offered to explain the bias in favour of the status quo. First, establishing an institution is an expensive process. In addition, there are learning benefits from institutional persistence. The QWERTY-style typewriter, for example, may not have been the most efficient keyboard, but after people became accustomed to this style, popularizing a new keyboard became expensive. Second, in an environment of positive externalities where complementary activities and resources reinforce each other, there is a high likelihood that a particular type of activity is more likely to occur in a certain location.[9] To give some examples, London and New York are financial hubs, while Silicon Valley is the computing capital of the world. Auto manufacturing in India is more likely in Pune or Chennai, but advanced software production is located in Bangalore and Hyderabad.

If economic processes and institutions are sticky and are likely to progress along a certain path, it can be argued that political processes are even stickier. Political scientists have pointed to a number of reasons for this. Why would some political actors pay for the provision of public goods, such as new institutions, when everyone else will benefit from them? Every economic regime has powerful beneficiaries whose short-term interests may trump the larger population's long-term interests over a longer period of time. Why would the ruling elite confront the dominant interest groups?[10]

The classic case for institutional persistence is found in the literature on varieties of capitalism, which argues that capitalism in the industrialized world is of two distinct types—liberal market capitalism and coordinated market capitalism. As institutional persistence theory would predict, the pressures of globalization have not produced any significant convergence among these economic systems. The liberal market variety of capitalism associated with the United States (US) and Great Britain depends largely on market coordination and a legal system that supports contracts. Coordinated market capitalism, on the other hand, relies on strategic interaction among firms and between business associations and trade unions, creating an economic environment of coordination rather than spontaneous exchange. Firms train their workers and then provide them with long-term employment. They do not poach workers from other firms. The economies of countries such as Germany, Japan, Switzerland, the Netherlands, Belgium, Sweden, Norway, Denmark, Finland, and Austria operate within such an economic environment.[11]

Scholarship on India's political economy suggests that the dominant coalition comprising rich farmers, industrialists, and the middle class thwarted the country's globalization and deregulation efforts. These politically mobilized dominant classes demanded more and more from the state, thereby, contributing to the fiscal crisis of the 1980s. Industrialists and farmers demanded subsidies and the middle class (comprising largely of government employees) enjoyed the privilege of cheap access to government-funded higher education. These groups remained quite comfortable within the confines of a protected economy. The dominant coalition was, thus, locked in a state-directed import-substituting equilibrium.[12] What could be the route to institutional and economic change in India?

Ways of Thinking about Change

The theoretical and empirical factors discussed in the previous section pose challenges while explaining institutional change. Yet, such changes characterize social life. Why, for example, did the monarch surrender to the checks and balances of a parliamentary system in seventeenth-century England? What explains the industrialized countries' shift from Keynesian economic policies with a high degree of state intervention and social spending, to monetarism during the 1980s? Why was there a rush to international trade and globalization in the developing world after years of regulated, state-controlled industrialization? And, in the case of India, why did the equilibrium of state-directed import substitution become unlocked as the country opted for globalization and deregulation? When and how do such institutional changes occur?

This section will review punctuated equilibrium and the tipping point—two models to help understand social change. It will map social processes that deal with the interaction of these two models of change and their relationship with economic ideas and conflicts of interest among powerful interest groups. This exercise will also situate the Indian case within scholarly debates on economic change in comparative political economy.

Punctuated Equilibrium

First, the punctuated equilibrium model of change is characterized by critical junctures when an exogenous shock brings about a drastic change in continuous processes or institutional patterns.[13] This can be likened to a meteor that makes a quick impact. A meteor may also have a long-term effect, depending on the impact that you want to study. If you buy the theory that a meteor that hit the earth led to the death of dinosaurs and the subsequent evolution of mammals, then the evolution of mammals is a long-term process whose origin can be traced to the meteor. The duration of the critical juncture is relatively short in comparison to the evolutionary period. A new evolutionary period could begin with the end of a critical juncture that produces a change in equilibrium conditions.[14]

The authors of the punctuated equilibrium idea of abrupt change, evolutionary biologists Stephen Jay Gould and Niles Eldridge, argued against an evolutionary view of biological and social change. In their view, Charles Darwin was so deeply affected by the liberal values of Victorian society that he had stressed gradualism over abrupt change. During this era, European rulers desired harmony and continuity. Ideas they valued— such as laissez-faire, liberalism, and political conservatism—aligned well with Darwin's approach of a hereditary past. Gould and Eldridge quote Marx suggesting that Darwin used elements of the capitalist system, such as division of labour, competition, innovation, and Malthusian struggle in his account of evolution. Punctuated equilibrium, on the other hand, involves abrupt and revolutionary change, a view that is closer to the philosophy of Hegel.[15]

What do arguments about social and economic change based on the notion of punctuated equilibrium look like? In one case, Albert Hirschman has argued that the Second World War played an important role in the adoption of Keynesian ideas across the European continent. According to Hirschman, this occurred because the US had benefited from the successful application of Keynesian ideas during the Great Depression. American technocrats and economists had been won over by Keynesian ideas. During the Great Depression, American technocrats learned that overproduction can exist, that deficit spending by the government can activate the economy, and that the imposition of import duties and export subsidies can improve a country's trade balance and domestic employment. The US victory in the Second World War played an important role in exporting Keynesian ideas to the rest of world through post-war aid agencies and multilateral institutions that reflected American power and its commitment to Keynesianism.[16]

Other scholars have made a similar argument about the exporting of economic deregulation as a policy idea to the developing world. Scholars such as Barbara Stallings, Stephan Haggard, and Sylvia Maxfield have argued that countries in the developing world facing balance of payments crises reduced their fiscal deficit, deregulated trade and investment, and promoted private companies largely because of pressure from the IMF.[17] In both these cases, the critical junctures—the end of the Second World War and balance of payments crises in the developing world— were relatively short compared with the new processes that these critical periods unleashed.

We now turn to another set of historically grounded social science arguments that make a compelling case for the power of economic ideas during a critical juncture. For example, Blyth argues that when an exogenous shock like a Great Depression hits economic institutions, it can lead to a specific kind of uncertainty for policymakers. This type of uncertainty is different from rationalist accounts of uncertainty, where cognitive limitations produce suboptimal results. In rational accounts, interests are well-known and problems arise due to actors' limited mental capacities that impede the realization of interests. In Frank Knight's conception of uncertainty deployed by Blyth, on the other hand, grave and unprecedented crises produce situations where people do not have fixed interests because they suddenly need to re-evaluate their understanding of cause-and-effect relationships about the real world. In such a situation, the sociological appeal of an idea—rather than a rational assessment of its utility—brings about institutional change. In this vein, Blyth argues that Keynesian ideas inspired the US' economic policies during the Great Depression because of their sociological appeal rather than any rational assessment of their ability to solve America's policy woes. According to this sociological view, ideas (and not institutions) reduce uncertainty, make collective action possible, become the protagonists' weapon in their struggle to replace existing institutions, act as blueprints for new institutions, and ultimately engender institutional stability.[18]

The punctuated equilibrium model is an especially convenient tool in social science, which is replete with theories that suggest that institutions are locked into a status quo and cannot be changed easily. For game theorists, the punctuated equilibrium idea is useful because a meteor-like disruption can help explain why a game has fundamentally changed away from previously existing patterns. In the case of a punctuated equilibrium, game theorists do not need an endogenous reason to explain certain processes that change over time that cannot be understood in the context of a static game. Punctuated equilibrium also provides a convenient tool for historical institutionalism, because scholars in this tradition often argue that institutions reflect asymmetries of power. In historical institutionalism, a punctuated equilibrium model suggests that dramatic changes in the balance of social power can occur due to a sudden exogenous event. Unpredictable and sudden exogenous events such as a war, secession, or a balance of payments crisis can transform the balance of power within a society and usher in change.

The Tipping Point

While the punctuated equilibrium model explains how a sudden exogenous shock can produce far-reaching social change, a great deal of social change is evolutionary in character—especially in countries that evolved as liberal democracies such as the US, Great Britain, and India. Recent economic change in India evolved gradually since the mid-1970s, and cannot be understood appropriately by invoking the metaphor of a meteor causing a dramatic, exogenous shock.

What tools in qualitative social science, then, can help explain the evolutionary economic change in India? The second idea of evolutionary change is that of a tipping point. This is a rather unexplored area in the study of institutional change, which has the potential to illuminate many aspects of gradual social and economic change. The metaphor of a tipping point is homologous to the idea of an earthquake, although this may not perfectly characterize all slow-moving endogenous changes. Incremental, slow-moving processes may not produce incremental changes when pressure for change builds up internally over time.[19] For example, seismologists sometimes tell us that an earthquake is imminent over a certain period of time. They knew, for instance, that Fukushima,

Japan, was due for an earthquake in recent years because of the pressures building up below the earth's surface, even though they could not predict exactly when it would occur. Similarly, demographic changes over time can reach a threshold or tipping point after which there may be a revolution.[20] What the tipping-point model of change suggests is that endogenous and continuous processes, rather than external shocks, are important for understanding dramatic change. Moreover, the change can look quite drastic after an internally driven process has brought the system to the threshold of change.

The logic of the tipping-point model of change hinges on the characteristics of a system that ultimately undermines it. The Fukushima earthquake, for instance, occurred because of the tectonic pressures that built up over time. Similarly, a bridge collapses not because of the last motorcycle that crossed it but because of problems in the structure that undermined its carrying capacity over time. Some social structures can undermine themselves when small upheavals are suppressed and discontent is not allowed to surface.[21] To further increase the utility of the tipping-point model, we can consider the idea that an exogenous shock may further activate endogenous, slow-moving processes of change. A tipping point may be a situation driven largely by endogenous processes, but one where a small exogenous shock produces a big change that builds on the momentum of the slow-moving, internal processes. A system may become more susceptible to change after an exogenous shock, if slow-moving internal processes undermine the old system or institutions.[22] This model of change asserts that exogenous shocks have an impact, but history matters and change is path-dependent, building upon important elements of the past.

For example, one can argue that Bangladesh (previously East Pakistan) obtained freedom from Pakistan (previously West Pakistan) in 1971 not because of the involvement of the Indian Army in the conflict, but because the people of East Pakistan desired it. In this analysis, discontent in Bangladesh built up over a period of time owing to its cultural and economic exploitation by West Pakistan. This discontent was the reason why an intervention by the Indian Army in 1971 had such a dramatic effect. India's intervention may have helped Bangladesh's emancipation from Pakistan, but it was clearly not a sufficient condition.[23]

Social scientists and historians have shown that material factors often drive slow-moving endogenous social change. For instance, Charles

Tilly's account of state formation in Europe is an evolutionary account, where the technology-driven increase in the cost of waging war ultimately culminated in taxation, social welfare, and the consolidation of the modern European state. It was easier and less expensive to tax willing citizens in return for social welfare than to coercively extract resources from royal subjects to wage expensive wars.[24] For Barrington Moore, commercial farming and the freeing of peasants in England helped drive the development of capitalism in the country, as it created a class of urban people who developed interests separate from those of the monarch and the aristocracy.[25] This causal mechanism does much to explain the English Civil War in 1640 and the empowerment of the English Parliament.

North found that the Bank of England was created in the seventeenth century due to the rise of a capitalist class and its unease with the sovereign powers of the monarch with respect to the extraction of resources. Under the English system, the king sold land, peerages, and monopolies to the wealthy. In addition, the monarchy often forcibly borrowed money from these wealthy individuals and repaid it irregularly and unfairly. The rising wealth of the industrial class and its growing unease with the powers of the monarch led to the Civil War (1640) and the Glorious Revolution (1688). During this period, the balance of power between the monarch and the wealthy industrial class shifted in favour of the wealthy. Parliament was accorded a central role in tax collection, and royal prerogatives were made subservient to common law. The crown could no longer legislate unilaterally. In exchange for a greater say in governance, Parliament agreed to put the monarch on sound financial footing. The Bank of England, thus, became the regulator of credit within the country. This bank needed Parliament's consent to lend money or purchase crown land for the monarchy. It could stop loan payments if the monarchy did not meet its obligation to pay interest. This arrangement succeeded in providing the British monarch with funds and enabled it to succeed in its imperial quest.[26] North subsequently identified a few causes of endogenous economic change in England that helped facilitate this new system—such as shifts in the relative prices of the factors of production (land, labour, and capital), cost of information, and technology.[27] All these variables could lead to internal processes that can bring about a change in the social balance of power and institutional change.

Leading contemporary historical intuitionalist accounts that stress conflicts between interest groups as the source of social change have identified different kinds of political processes that can engender a shift in institutions. For example, 'layering' involves the institution of new rules alongside the old ones, but allowing the new rules to grow differentially in relation to the old ones.[28] This book describes how the process of layering led to the consolidation of the office of the telecom regulator—the TRAI (in Chapter 4). The new rule of competition promotion competes with the old idea that telecommunications should be a government monopoly and has been firmly embedded in the institutions of government over time. Like conflicts of interest, ideational change within the policy elite can also be characterized as a tipping point in an evolutionary process. An alternative to the historical institutionalist view discussed above is the view that transformations are mediated by the gradual evolution of ideas, which inform elite interests and transform institutions and policies. Changes in ideas or beliefs, especially among technocrats and policymakers, could transform interests and bring the system to a tipping point. Under these conditions, an exogenous stimulus can produce far-reaching changes because policy puzzles have gradually undermined the old system. The relationship between changed beliefs and interests at a tipping point of a new system can inform us about the origins of new agendas that arise as from the formation of new interests.[29]

This view has appealed to game theorists who have realized the need to locate endogenous sources of change. Avner Grief calls these endogenous factors 'quasi parameters', which can either reinforce or undermine a system. For example, medieval Genoa's governing institution of the *podesta*, which was designed to maintain a balance of power among clans, was less enduring than Venice's *doge* based on the norm of collective security. As Grief described, a threat to any one clan in Venice posed a menace to every clan in the city. He found that inter-clan cooperation in Genoa was secure so long as there was an external threat. Yet, the balance of power resulting from inter-clan cooperation in Genoa collapsed much sooner than the collective security arrangement in Venice. According to Grief's argument, the norm or belief of collective security among Venice's elite was more stable than Genoa's balance of power as a means of securing inter-clan cooperation over time. The case of medieval Venice and Genoa invokes a tipping-point model of social transformation, where changes in endogenous 'quasi parameters' are more important than random events that superficially seem to have brought shifts in inter-clan cooperation.[30]

In another instrumental book, Douglass North, John Wallis, and Barry Weingast describe the rise of the West as a transition from a 'natural state' characterized by low levels of economic development to an 'open-access order', which is the hallmark of a developed world. Natural states manage violence through personal contacts, and there is a high correlation in these societies between the distribution of political and economic power among groups and these groups' ability to control violence. Open-access orders, on the other hand, limit violence through institutions, and a large number of impersonal corporate organizations compete for economic and political rents. Three fundamental conditions are essential for open-access orders: (a) the rule of law, (b) perpetually lived organizations, and (c) political control over the military.[31]

In this account of the West's rise, political systems have evolved from factional fights among the elite for privileges to the elite's granting rights to dominant groups in society because the elite feels secure with institutionalized rights. Over time, the rights of the elite became the rights of citizens. This story of the evolution of an open-access order in Great Britain seems intimately connected with the rise of the bourgeoisie. The ideational element in this story is the belief that the elite would be more secure with institutionally guaranteed rights rather than exclusive privileges.[32] The authors differentiate themselves from Acemoglu and Robinson's work on democratization by suggesting that democracy was much more a product of elite competition than of political pressures emanating from lower segments of society.[33]

Even though North, Wallis, and Weingast point to debates about the fear of factions in the early stages of evolution of an open-access order, it is not clear from their narrative how a change in beliefs among the elite produced a change in the perception that they would be more secure with rights than with exclusive privileges. The historical material in their book does not clarify whether the elite converted its privileges into rights because of economic interests or because some sections of the elite who believed in converting privileges into rights and prevailed politically.[34] It would have helped if North, Wallis, and Weingast's argument had they explicitly invoked an ideational tipping point for explaining the birth of an open-access order.

Strategic constructivism may hold the key to some puzzles posed by historical institutionalism, because the balance of social power may not explain many social phenomena if we did not consider how new ideas changed interests. Interest groups often strategically exploit available ideas to advance their interests. In his more recent work, Blyth has argued that the 1930s deflation in the West led to the rise of state intervention because the business class was confused about its interests. This confusion provided an opportunity for the state to assert itself. On the other hand, the US business class exploited the inflation of the 1970s to lobby the media and politicians for fiscal conservatism.[35] In a classic paper, Peter Hall demonstrated how the shift from Keynesian policies emphasizing government spending and intervention to monetarist policies deploying fiscal discipline and a greater role to private companies first occurred in Great Britain. The process began with incremental first-order alterations in routine decisions, such as adjustments to the country's interest rate. This was followed by second-order changes, involving experiments with new instruments that were deployed to control government spending. These first- and second-order changes were based on evaluations of past policies and were largely carried out by technocrats between 1976 and 1979. These initiatives reflected gradual changes that could only undermine the Keynesian system to a limited extent. Third-order change, on the other hand, involved then Prime Minister Margaret Thatcher's dramatic and risky political decisions after 1979. It was Thatcher's political power that enabled radical spending cuts, the downsizing of government, and an impetus to private-sector activity. In Hall's account, this change in policy paradigms resulted from a political and social process, which cannot be viewed as a strictly rational phenomenon. Hall finds that 'policy paradigms'—like the paradigms described by Thomas Kuhn in the history and philosophy of science—are distinctive and cannot be compared. A change in policy paradigm that was supported by politics, media, and think tanks in Britain was used to invoke the limits of rational technocratic assessment in producing large-scale economic change.[36]

The scholarship on endogenous changes leading to a tipping point discussed earlier in this chapter can help illuminate this institutional change in Great Britain during the late 1970s. Keynesianism was arguably facing a crisis in the mid-1970s, when industrial countries were searching for a way to deal with a grave economic situation characterized by low levels of economic growth and mounting inflation. These economic conditions prompted British officials who were insulated from social pressures to initiate limited experiments in policy, such as implementing monetarist ideas of expenditure control within a Keynesian institutional framework. In this interpretation, the dreary economic conditions of the 1970s, and the failures of these limited attempts at reform, undermined the Keynesian system to such an extent that Prime Minister Thatcher was able to introduce far-reaching changes in the institutions of economic policy. The arrival of Thatcher was the tipping point that produced change—change that was possible because inflation and low levels of growth had undermined the old system based on high levels of public spending. Even though the transformation of the economic order in Great Britain required political change and cannot be characterized as rational and endogenous change determined by technocrats, it had the mandate of the people who had suffered under the previous system implemented by Labour Party governments.[37]

The tipping-point model also helps explain India's path to globalization.[38] This book proposes a tipping-point model of economic change in India. The tipping point occurred when the exogenous shock of the balance of payment crisis in 1991 produced a paradigm shift, which was possible because of gradual endogenous processes that had prepared India for globalization and deregulation during the 1980s. New ideas arose within India's technocracy due to the failure of import substitution, the demonstration effect of the Soviet Union's decline, and the success of export-led growth in China, Japan, South Korea, and Southeast Asia. Gradual changes in policy arose in India due to low levels of productivity and an unsustainable fiscal crisis that characterized the country's import-substitution regime during the 1980s. The system underwent a paradigm shift in 1991 that built on the 1980s, as the technocracy leveraged the balance of payments crisis to deal with political opposition and produce far-reaching changes in economic governance. Indian economists and technocrats had pioneered ideas about deregulation and globalization, which have been discussed in the Introduction and in Chapter 3, and there were significant points of convergence between the IMF and India's technocrats. These technocrats' grasp over economic problems enabled the country to negotiate a structural adjustment programme with the IMF that was sympathetic to the concerns of a political economy within the framework of democratic rule.

For a number of reasons, this narrative of economic reform requires both an understanding of the balance of social forces within India and an understanding of Indian technocrats' economic ideas. First, India's capitalist-entrepreneurial class would acquiesce to the executive branch and the IMF during a financial crisis because they depended on foreign exchange for imports. Second, the consolidation of telecom regulations that engendered private sector competition—a development at the heart of much of India's economic change after 1991—was made possible by the gradual process of layering described above. It was not easy to deal with the DoT and its unions in the process of promoting competition, despite support for deregulation from the PMO and the Ministry of Finance. Moreover, in areas of the economy such as the power sector—which is characterized by the powerful farmers who refuse to pay for electricity—reforms have remained largely unsuccessful.

Table 1.1 summarizes four different paths to institutional change that have been discussed in the chapter. Quadrant one is characterized by slow-moving gradual processes of ideational change that culminate in institutional change. In this scenario, ideas evolve along a path and affect interests when old ideas cannot resolve contemporary social and economic problems. This is the earthquake model of social change, where the long-run causes of change are endogenous, ideational, slow-moving processes that make the system more susceptible to change at the time of an external shock.

TABLE 1.1 Paths to Institutional Change

	Ideas Shape Interests	Interests Change
Tipping Point	1. British deregulation (Hall, 1993); Open-access order (North, Wallis and Weingast 2009); Inter-clan cooperation (Grief 2006); India's globalization, Single European Market (Jabko 2006); Keynesianism and monetarism (Blyth 2006); Telecoms and airlines (Woll 2010).	2. British democracy (Moore 1966); State-making (Tilly 1992); Bank of England (North and Weingast 1989); Skill development in Germany (Thelen 2004)
Punctuated Equilibrium	3. Keynesianism (Blyth 2002); Indonesia 1966 (Liddle 1991); Singapore 1965 (Lee 2000).	4. International pressure and deregulation in the Third World (Stallings 1992; Haggard and Maxfield 1996a; Simmons and Elkins 2003); Post-war Keynesianism (Hirschman 1989)

Source: Author's own.

Various accounts of social and economic change discussed in this chapter support this interpretation. For instance, Hall's account explains why the crisis of Keynesianism gave birth to monetarism after it reached a tipping point when Thatcher became the Prime Minister of Britain.[39] North, Wallis, and Weingast describe the birth of the modern institutions of development as outgrowths of the belief that elite privileges should be converted into rights. Grief finds that while the belief supporting balance of power as the source of inter-clan cooperation undermined the Genoese system of the *podesta* in the long run, the Venetian doge survived because its norm of collective security was more resilient.[40]

The strategic constructivism interpretation can also be located in the model described in quadrant one of Table 1.1. According to strategic constructivism, interests do not determine outcomes, but they do play a role in determining which ideas are chosen. Jabko, for instance, tells us how interest groups strategically used the idea of the market to unify Europe—a phenomenon characterized as a 'quiet revolution'.[41] Blyth tells us that US industrialists gave the state substantial room for manoeuvre during the 1930s' depression because they were confused about their interests. During the inflation crisis of the 1970s, however, these industrialists were able to lobby for fiscal conservatism—a fact that led to promoting the idea of deregulation with hard budget constraints.[42] Woll tells us that the US and European telecommunications and airlines companies were uncertain about their interests during changes to the regulatory structure in the 1980s, but they were largely supportive of deregulation by the 1990s when they had learned more about the new policy environment.[43]

This book's interpretation of India's post-1991 economic reforms is located within the first quadrant of this schema, and comes closest to Hall's story of deregulation in Great Britain during the 1970s and 1980s. It makes the case that economic change in India was driven by policy puzzles that created a crisis for the import substitution industrialization paradigm of development. Import substitution generated low and moderate levels of growth, while demands for public expenditure in a thriving democracy had produced an unsustainable fiscal crisis. I argue that the balance of payments shock was a tipping point driven by internally driven changes in conviction among India's technocrats rather than largely by external pressure from the IMF.

The technocrats, who experienced and influenced the 1980s, won India's political battles at the time of the balance of payments crisis in

1991. Dramatic deregulation and globalization of industry was initiated almost immediately after this crisis, including the slow-moving process of dealing with the government's monopoly at the DoT (as discussed in Chapter 4). Yet, dealing with this department proved easier than dealing with the numerous and politically powerful farmers of AP, who resisted reform in India's power sector (as can been seen in Chapter 5).

The second quadrant of Table 1.1 includes the gradual processes of social and economic change, where new and powerful interests came into conflict with old ones as a result of economic processes, such as the development of capitalism. The difference in these cases of gradual change from the cases described in quadrant one is that quadrant two describes changes in the balance of social power rather than ideational changes. These accounts disregard the view that interests are mediated by ideas.

I have described influential accounts of social change in historical institutionalism that inhabits the intellectual space outlined in quadrant two. For example, Moore's account of the evolution of democracy in Great Britain depended on changes in the balance of power between the capitalist class and the aristocracy.[44] Tilly found that technological development and the rising expense of warfare created the need for the monarch to tax, provide social welfare, and create the citizen and the state. The need to tax citizens empowered them.[45] North and Weingast found that the birth of the Bank of England was associated with the rising power of the wealthy capitalist class in relation to the monarch.[46] Thelen (2004) demonstrated that the power of master artisans in industrializing Germany created a different basis for skill formation and comparative advantage than what existed in Great Britain or the US.[47]

If quadrants one and two deal with slow-moving processes, quadrants three and four describe changes that occur after a quick and impactful exogenous shock. The cases in these quadrants involve paths that invoke the punctuated equilibrium model of a meteoric impact when a sudden exogenous shock generates a new institutional path. The exogenous shock, often called a 'critical juncture', has a brief and quick effect on the changes it unleashes—changes that may take many years to unfold. In quadrant three, exogenous shocks like the Great Depression are said to result in extreme uncertainty that characterizes unsettled times, when policymakers are hungry for new causal explanations in order to deal with events about which there are no clear and tested explanations.

The appeal of new ideas can produce significant economic change at the time of an external shock. Blyth's account of the Great Depression shows that the appeal of new ideas shaped the policymakers' interests and drove the shifts to Keynesian and monetarist approaches at different historical junctures.[48] Likewise, the ideas that appealed to Lee Kuan Yew, in Singapore,[49] and Suharto, in Indonesia, at a critical juncture in the 1960s played a significant role in transforming those economies towards engagement with globalization.[50]

Quadrant four of Table 1.1 includes cases where an exogenous shock transformed the interests of elites involved with policymaking. For example, policy pressure from the IMF during balance of payments crises may have served as an exogenous shock that transformed developing countries' economic institutions by altering policymakers' interests. Policymakers' interests changed because there was no way to obtain the foreign exchange reserves essential for governing the economy without accepting resources from the IMF that carried stringent policy conditions.[51] Hirschman's account of the spread of Keynesianism after the Second World War adheres to this quadrant-four model, as it stresses the importance of the USA's mission to spread these ideas through its power to aid post-war reconstruction.[52] In these cases, it was the countries' need for foreign exchange—and the imposition of conditions by those who could offer aid at a critical juncture—that produced far-reaching changes. Changes did not occur because certain ideas about policy reform gained currency among a country's policymaking elite.

Economic Change in India

The cases in this book demonstrate that economic change in India after 1991 emerged because the country's technocratic elite and the political leadership had become disillusioned with import substitution, which had produced fiscally unsustainable growth. However, disillusionment with past policy could not, by itself, result in substantial policy change because powerful social forces were enmeshed in the ISI policy paradigm. Transformative change in 1991 occurred at the time of a severe balance of payments crisis and when the Soviet Union—India's trusted friend for more than four decades—had collapsed. At this critical juncture, India's policymakers viewed alignment with the globalizing international economic system to be superior to the continuation of an import-substituting regime, which had made India dependent on the IMF. Yet, India's policy elite did not advocate this change of a strategy during a similar balance of payment crisis in 1966.

This book provides a historically grounded account of economic processes and change in India through four structured, focused comparisons.[53] The 1966 financial crisis was not a tipping point for economic liberalization because the executive branch and the technocracy were not convinced about the merits of economic change and the industrial class opposed it. The balance of payments crisis of 1991, on the other hand, constituted a tipping point because the fiscal imbalance became hard to sustain within a closed economy. Moreover, the success of export-led growth in East and Southeast Asia—combined with the decline of the Soviet Union—reinforced the view that India needed new institutions for governing the economy. These ideas, which had evolved gradually beginning in the mid-1970s, generated a tipping point in the 1991 balance of payments crisis.

I have varied the independent variable, or causal factor—economic ideas and the extent of elite politics—in all the four historical cases discussed in this book.[54] India's large domestic market should have aided the country's strategy of autarkic industrialization. The comparison between 1966 and 1991 shows how changes in ideas and policies within the technocratic community backed by political will engender reforms in plural polities like India, where the state's capacity to deal with powerful social forces is quite limited. In polities characterized by such state-society relations, it becomes important to debate new ideas internally, even though the crisis can empower certain ideas over others, if the system has reached a tipping point. Limiting the cases to two severe balance of payments crisis episodes in India makes the cases amenable to a controlled comparison.

***

This chapter has explored various ways of thinking about economic change and located the Indian case as one characterized by the evolution of ideas and policies that reached a tipping point and produced a significant economic transformation after 1991. It also introduced the historical cases studies in this book and the rationale for deploying the tipping-point model of economic change for India. It further explored why certain areas of economic adjustment are more gradual than others in India.

This book combines a study of slow-moving processes[55] with structured focused comparisons to generate insights about economic change in India. I return to the cases discussed above in the next section of the book and explore them in greater depth.

Notes

1. For a similar view on institutions, see North, Douglass C. (1995: 17–26).
2. See Woll (2010: 137–54).
3. See Hall (1993).
4. See North and Weingast (1989).
5. See Gould and Eldridge (1977: 115–51).
6. Blyth (2002: 17–48) has deployed the sociological appeal of ideas in economic hard times to explain economic change in the West.
7. See Stallings (1992: 41–88).
8. See Varshney (2007: 158–63).
9. See David (1985: 332–7); Pierson (2000: 252–6).
10. See Moe (1994: 32–71); Offe (2006: 9–31); Pierson (2000: 257–62).
11. See Hall and Soskice 2001: 1–70. On the institutional stickiness of the welfare state in an era of globalization, see Garret (1998); Pierson (1996: 143–92); Swank (2002); Swank and Stienmo (2002: 642–55). Another classic case of institutional stickiness is land redistribution in India by legal change when powerful social actors oppose it on the ground. See Bannerjee and Iyer (2005); Frankel (2005: 94–112, 190–200); Kohli (2009: 226–52); Pai (2010); Rudolph and Rudolph (1987: 333–92).
12. See Bardhan (1984); Bhagwati (1993: 47–67).
13. See Acemoglu and Robinson (2012); Cappoccia and Kelemen (2007); Gould and Eldridge (1977: 115–51); Krasner (1984).
14. See Pierson (2004: 80).
15. See Gould and Eldridge (1977: 145–7).
16. See Hirschman (1989: 347–60).
17. See Haggard and Maxfield (1996a: 35–68); Simmons and Elkins (2003: 275–304); Stallings (1992: 41–88).
18. See Blyth (2002: 17–48, 2007: 761–77). It can be argued that Singapore's Prime Minister was similarly bowled by the idea of globalization after the country separated from Malaysia in 1965. For more information, see Haggard (1990: 100–14); Lee (2000: 47–88); Tan (2007: 855–8). Indonesia's President Suharto may have been similarly influenced by the Berkeley mafia in 1966 at the time of a balance of payments crisis. For more, see Chwieroth (2010: 496–527); Hill (2000: 65–6); Liddle (1991: 411–6); Mukherji (1999: 233–7).

19. For a few clear expositions of this important idea, see Cappoccia and Kelemen (2007: 351); Pierson (2004: 82–90).

20. See Goldstone (1991).

21. See Nicholas Taleb and Blyth (2001: 33–9).

22. See Grief and Laitin (2004: 633–52).

23. On the language policy that was unacceptable to the people in East Pakistan, see Rahman (1996: 79–102). On the relationship between economic exploitation and discontent in East Pakistan, see Misra (1972: 27–39).

24. See Tilly's (1992, 1985: 169–91).

25. See Moore (1966: 3–39).

26. See North and Weingast (1989: 803–32).

27. See North (1990). Another excellent piece of scholarship that exploits the idea of slow-moving processes that shift the social balance of power is Kathleen Thelen's *How Institutions Evolve: The Political Economy of Skills in Germany, Britain, the United States, and Japan* (2004).

28. For an example of layering, see Tsai (2006: 116–41). For the best account of layering and other processes, see Mahoney and Thelen (2010: 1–37); Streeck and Thelen (2005: 1–39).

29. Beland (2009: 701–18); Hall (2010: 204–23). For the classic account of how technocrats can bring about substantial changes in institutions, see Haas (1992: 1–35).

30. However, game theorists have not made much progress in pointing out *a priori* what these processes are. See Grief (2006: 158–86) and Grief and Laitin (2004: 633–52).

31. See North *et al.* (2009).

32. Ibid.

33. See Acemoglu and Robinson (2006).

34. For example, it is unclear from the narrative whether the distinction between economic assets in the secular realm and the king's command over them occurred because of beliefs that the monarch had held or due to the material interests of the capitalist class. The story of the evolution of the British Navy as an impersonal organization could also be interpreted to be the result of debt market, which professionalized the purchases of the British Navy. See North *et al.* (2009: 158–66, 181–7). North has also stressed on the importance of beliefs and learning in North's *Institutions, Institutional Change, and Economic Performance* (1990: 73–91) and his 2005 work *Understanding the Process of Economic Change* (2005: 1–8, 323–37). However, more work needs to be done to demonstrate how beliefs change.

35. Blyth (2006: 72–96). Other excellent applications of strategic constructivism include Jabko (2006); Woll (2010: 137–54).

36. See Hall (1993: 275–96).

37. For a similar view of Hall's article, see Blyth (2011). For a similar analytic narrative that describes a shift in Japan's economic regime, see Pempel (1998).

38. Taiwan also probably followed a similar path. For more information, see Amsden (1989: 107–68); Haggard (1990: 77–99).

39. See Hall (1993: 275–96); North et al. (2009).

40. See Grief (2006: 158–86); Grief and Laitin (2004: 633–52).

41. See Jabko (2006).

42. See Blyth (2006: 72–96).

43. See Woll (2010).

44. See Moore (1966: 3–39).

45. See Tilly (1992; 1985: 169–91).

46. See North and Weingast (1989: 803–32).

47. See Thelen (2004).

48. See Blyth (2002).

49. See Haggard (1990: 100–14); Lee (2000: 47–88).

50. See Chwieroth (2010: 496–527); Liddle (1991: 411–16); Mukherji (1999: 223–37).

51. See Haggard and Maxfield (1996a: 35–68); Stallings (1992: 41–88).

52. See Hirschman (1989: 347–60).

53. On structured, focused comparisons, see George and Bennett (2004: 67–72); Lijphardt (1971: 688); Mill (1987: 68–9); Snyder (1984: 105).

54. See King et al. (1994: 128–49).

55. On the importance of studying slow-moving processes for understanding social and economic change, see Pierson and Skocpol (2002: 693–721); Pierson (2004: 79–102); Thelen (2004). A large body of the literature in historical institutionalism is dedicated to this effort. Hall (2010: 205–23) recently talked about the need for a more encompassing view that takes both changes in ideas and social power seriously.

2 Globalization Aborted, 1966*

INDIA REVERSED ITS TRADE liberalization project within a year of devaluing the rupee in 1966. Chapter 1 suggested that exogenous shocks (such as wars and droughts) leading to balance of payments crises can engender a country's transition from import substitution industrialization towards export promotion.[1] Governments seek the conditional assistance of the IMF when they lack foreign exchange for even essential imports. Commercial creditors are not easily persuaded to lend to such risky customers. The classic dependence argument would suggest that a country's reliance on the IMF for precious currency during a foreign exchange crisis should empower the fund to dictate a policy of trade liberalization on the borrowers.[2] The Indian devaluation of 1966 challenges this view of economic transition. India bowed to external pressure in the immediate aftermath of this severe foreign exchange crisis, but its foray into liberalization was short-lived, and the country reverted to an ever-more stringent form of import substitution after 1969.

This chapter argues that the dominant economic ideas held by India's technocratic executive team during the 1966 balance of payments crisis mattered a great deal to how the country responded to external pressure. It analyses the political basis of an economic liberalization project that could not be sustained, and demonstrates that the economic ideas sustaining the institutions of import substitution and government control were quite entrenched in 1966. There was to going to be no flip-flop to the legacy of India's Second (1956–61) and Third Five-year Plans (1961–6), which emphasized state control over an Indian economy protected from

* This chapter has been adapted from Rahul Mukherji, 2000, 'India's Aborted Liberalization—1966', *Pacific Affairs*, vol. 73, no. 3, pp. 375–92.

the forces of globalization. The pressure from the US, World Bank, and IMF to promote exports, deregulate, and encourage private corporations was largely disregarded. India's executive-technocratic team deregulated the economy only briefly in June 1966 and reverted to the status quo within a few months.

India's decision to not sustain liberalization after the initial rupee devaluation in June 1966 constitutes a crucial decision sequence in India's trade policy. The country decided to forego growth opportunities provided by international trade that Japan, Singapore, Indonesia, Taiwan, and South Korea exploited so effectively in the 1960s. I contend that it is difficult to engineer economic transitions in developing countries as large and self-contained as India, purely on the basis of external pressure.[3]

The foreign exchange crisis of 1966 was unique in India's economic history. This was the one episode when the country faced a substantial foreign exchange shortfall when it was guided by an executive-technocratic team that largely favoured import substitution.[4] During the 1991 foreign exchange crisis, though, India was led by an executive team that believed in the fruits of globalization and deregulation, and this team initiated a fundamental transformation of India's industrial and trade policies. The crises of 1966 and 1991 provide suitable cases for comparison. In 1991, the liberal executive team, facing a balance of payments crisis, voted for globalization; in 1966, the foreign exchange crisis did not lead to sustained liberalization as India's executive branch was unwilling to conform to the donors' policy prescriptions.

This chapter examines India's 1966 balance of payments crisis and the importance of the executive branch's policy orientation on India's economic trajectory. Section one briefly describes the short-lived policy change in favour of trade liberalization in 1966. Section two analyses the causes behind the failure to sustain trade liberalization, describing the nature of the crisis for India and how international donors evaluated it. Prime Minister Indira Gandhi and the majority of the country's technocrats were not convinced of the merits of globalization and economic deregulation in 1966. The country's regime of import substitution was fairly well-entrenched at the time. Even though organized capital overtly supported the devaluation of the rupee, it was seeking protection and subsidies behind the scenes. The majority of the industrialists were involved with import-intensive import substitution. The devaluation of the rupee would hurt them by raising import prices.

FICCI, the country's most powerful industrial lobby, expressed public support for devaluation even as it secretly made a pitch for freer access to foreign exchange and cheaper imports. Both these factors interacted to produce a policy position that was averse to the donor agencies' emphasis on India allowing a greater role for the private sector and globalization in its economy. It did not help the situation when the US acted like a big brother trying to discipline India. The last section of this chapter draws conclusions about the relationship between India's executive-technocratic orientation and policy change during the 1960s balance of payments crisis.

Short-lived Liberalization

India's severe dependence on the IMF and the World Bank led to the country's temporary acquiescence to trade liberalization in 1966. India bowed briefly to foreign pressure to secure foreign exchange and food-grains such as wheat under the terms devised with the assent of the US. A number of significant policy changes were initiated. First, the value of the rupee was brought down from Rs 4.76 to the dollar to Rs 7.50. This devaluation was intended to promote trade, as Indian exports would become cheaper and imports more expensive. This strategy would expand India's exports while curbing the import propensity of its import substitution. Second, export subsidies in the form of the import-entitlement scheme and tax credits were abolished. The need for such assistance was to decrease, since devaluation would make Indian exports cheaper and more competitive on the global market.[5]

There was one exception to these changes in India's trade policy. India continued to charge export duties on traditional manufactures such as jute, tea, and raw cotton because India had a monopoly position as a supplier of these goods. The demand for these goods did not vary considerably with price. Therefore, these duties, by raising the price of exports, would bring the Indian exchequer additional foreign exchange.[6] Bhagwati and Srinivasan calculated the net devaluation after discounting for these policy changes: for exports it was 21.6 per cent and for imports it was 44.8 per cent.[7]

The policies of then Finance Minister Sachin Choudhury that were outlined in his aggressively pro-trade Budget speech on 6 June1966 were quickly reversed, beginning August 1966.[8] John D. Rockefeller reported to World Bank president George Woods in July 1967, 'The devaluation was a flop; India did not make the policy changes we expected.'[9] The Indian government replaced the pre-devaluation, import-entitlement scheme by another similar import-replenishment scheme; both these measures were a means of subsidizing exports.[10] In May 1967, the government reinstated a policy of subsidizing indigenous metals such as iron, steel, and tin plate at international prices, by refunding excise and import duties on direct inputs into exports.[11]

Trade was more stringently regulated after 1968. Import licences were made easily available to units that exported more than 10 per cent of their output. Collaboration with multinationals such as IBM or Coca-Cola were conditioned by export obligations. The Foreign Investment Board was also established in 1968 to scrutinize all investments with greater than 40 per cent equity participation. There were to be severe restrictions on foreign investment that was unaccompanied by technology transfers.[12] Bhagwati and Srinivasan note in their pioneering study of India's trade liberalization of 1966:

> By 1969–70, liberalization appeared to have been largely reversed. The import premium was back to 30–50 per cent on the average, export subsidies were reinstated and were up to high levels, industrial de-licensing amounted to little, especially because of continuing quantitative restrictions (QRs), automatic protection with QRs was still the order of the day, and the picture looked very similar to that which obtained during 1962–5.[13]

The Causes of Short-lived Liberalization

The 1966 foreign exchange crisis and the consequent dependence on international donors for financing India's development forced India to devalue the rupee. For then Prime Minister Indira Gandhi, financial need rather than a pro-trade orientation drove devaluation. There is substantial evidence to suggest that she was not a votary of devaluation, and her political supporters were opposed to it. Indian industry acquiesced to devaluation since it understood the need for foreign exchange to finance ISI. This foreign exchange could only be provided by donors who wanted to move India in a more export-friendly direction.

The Foreign Exchange Crisis

Wars and droughts placed a severe constraint on the financial resources available for India's fourth Five-year Plan. In the 1962 war between the two countries on the Himalayan border, India suffered a humiliating defeat at the hands of China and, emboldened by the Chinese success, Pakistan engaged India in fighting at the Rann of Kutch between April and June 1965, and had opened another front in Kashmir's Chamb sector by 1 July.[14] During that period of national emergency, the National Development Council granted sweeping authority to the then Prime Minister Lal Bahadur Shastri to 'reorient, alter, and amend the five-year plan as necessary, to meet the emergent situation and safeguard the country's security and long-term interests.'[15] Long-term five-year planning was abruptly disrupted and Shastri directed the Planning Commission to draft an annual plan for 1966–7 before the draft outline of the Fourth Five-year Plan.

In addition to these wars with China and Pakistan, India faced the failure of monsoon rains that was critical for a good crop. Poor harvests, severe droughts, and stagnant agricultural production ensued between 1960 and 1963. Grain production dropped by 17 per cent between 1964–5 and 1965–6. The wholesale price of foodgrain shot up by 14 per cent, and by November 1965, all buffer stocks of food had been exhausted.[16] India would have needed to pay USD 400 million for food imports at commercial prices.[17] Defence expenditures had also risen from 2 per cent of the GDP in 1960 to 4 per cent in 1964. Despite total net foreign aid of USD 1.3 billion in 1965–6 (2.4 per cent of the GDP), India's foreign exchange reserves of Rs 2 trillion would pay for only about two months of imports.[18] The need for food imports at reasonable prices and the foreign exchange for India's fourth Five-year Plan made India critically dependent on the US, World Bank, and IMF.

Suppliers were unwilling to oblige India when it most needed cheap foodgrain imports. Dismayed by India's war with Pakistan, the US terminated its four-year agreement for food aid to both India and Pakistan under the Public Law (PL) 480 programme in June 1965.[19] Subsequently, the Johnson administration implemented a policy of 'short tether', making stocks available for only a few months. Against India's estimated need of 8 million tonnes, the US released only 2 million tonnes between September and December 1965. The failure of seasonal monsoons in 1965 was followed by another such failure in 1966. In December 1966, US President Lyndon B. Johnson agreed to commit only half of the 1.8 million tonnes of PL 480 grains for the February and April shipments. Food aid was being used as a lever to coerce India to accept the US multinational Bechtel to set up fertilizer plants, and persuade India to embrace globalization and a private-sector orientation.[20]

Non-US donors were not willing to oblige India, either. France would only sell wheat on commercial terms; the Soviet Union was not prepared to listen to India's requests until December 1966; and Canada could only provide a limited amount of wheat, owing to problems at its West Coast grain terminals.[21] In 1967, India needed about 10 million tonnes of foodgrains, of which the US committed 3.6 million tonnes, the Soviet Union 200,000 tonnes, Canada 200,000 tonnes, and Australia 150,000 tonnes. President Johnson could take advantage of this vulnerability to nudge India in a market-friendly direction before supplying the 5.7 million tonnes of wheat that India still needed.[22]

India was, therefore, highly dependent on Western donors for foodgrain and foreign exchange on the eve of the devaluation episode in June 1966. India's resource position was fragile in 1965, with export earnings not likely to exceed Rs 51 trillion against import requirements of Rs 53 trillion. In addition, debt-servicing obligations would amount to Rs 13.5 trillion. India would be short by Rs 15.5 trillion even if no further developmental activity were undertaken. If the food and agriculture ministry's import requirement of Rs 11 trillion were added to this, India would need Rs 26.5 trillion in external assistance. The Planning Commission, on the other hand, asserted that the Fourth Five-year Plan could only be implemented if external assistance worth Rs 40 trillion were made available.[23]

The Donor Position

The early euphoria surrounding the promise of India's Second Five-year Plan (1956–61) began to erode gradually after the Aid India Consortium was set up in 1958 in the aftermath of India's first foreign exchange crisis in 1957.[24] As the sterling balances that India had built up largely during the Second World War dwindled, the country's planning became constrained by the availability of foreign exchange. Then World Bank president Eugene Black had asked 'The Three Wise Men' of the financial world—Herman Abs, the chairman of Deustche Bank in Frankfurt; Sir Oliver Franks, the chairman of Lloyds Bank in London; and Allan Sproul, a former chair of the Federal Reserve in New York—to review the economic conditions in India and Pakistan. They identified foreign exchange shortage, population growth, and lack of managerial talent as the three significant challenges faced by India. In their assessment, Pakistan's emphasis on the private sector and agriculture was preferable to India's reliance on state control and capital-intensive industrialization.[25]

John Lewis, an official of the United States Agency for International Development (USAID) who subsequently became a professor and dean of the Woodrow Wilson School at Princeton, held a rather more sympathetic view on the Indian strategy of development. He lamented that the US interest in India was dipping at the very moment when India needed foreign exchange and support to become self-sufficient. India's democracy, despite challenges of national integration, held promise as an exemplary political path to development. According to Lewis, India also deserved serious consideration because the Soviet Union was trying to woo India, and China had already embarked on a disruptive communist path. Poverty in neutral democratic countries like India was viewed as a challenge to democracy and the market in richer countries.[26]

The World Bank and donor community's concerns about Indian planning nevertheless grew with the passage of time. During the presidency of George Woods (1963–8), the World Bank was making the transition from being a commercial bank concerned primarily with project lending to an economic institution guiding the economic policies of its clients. Woods' tenure marked the beginning of the bank's policy of requiring recipients to make economic policy adjustments in return for development funds.[27] As part of this scheme, World Bank economists carefully analysed potential recipient countries before a provision of development funds was made. And these countries often needed to make policy reforms to oblige potential donors.

George Woods' presidency at the World Bank proved significant for India in 1966, as the bank played an important role in negotiating an aid package during the country's balance of payment crisis. Woods had previously interacted with the Indian government as a World Bank consultant, offering advice in the iron and steel sector and helping with the creation of the Industrial Credit and Investment Corporation of India (ICICI) in 1954. India was the country Woods felt he knew best, and transforming and modernizing India became his most serious concern.

In September 1964, Woods invited Bernard Bell to take a critical look at the Indian economy by evaluating the experience of the Third Five-year Plan (1961–6) in order to guide the fourth one.[28] The Bell Mission's frank, critical, and controversial 14-volume report reviewed India's Third Five-year Plan (1 October 1965). In volume one, Bell reported that although the overarching analysis of the Indian economy contained in its 35 single-spaced pages had drawn on the work in other volumes, they represented his views about what ailed the Indian economy rather than a consensus among the authors of the various sectoral reports. The report was critical of the Third Five-year Plan. It pointed to the problems of the Indian model of development and suggested ways of ameliorating them.[29] Bell insisted that even though advice on the exchange rate was normally within the purview of the IMF, any report on India's development strategy needed to deal with the exchange rate. Woods came around to this view despite some hesitation, especially after IMF Managing Director Pierre Paul Schweitzer supported it. In August 1964, Ben King, the World Bank's representative in India and a member of the Bell Mission, also prevailed upon Woods to consider the case for devaluing the rupee as part of the Bell Mission's recommendations.[30]

As part of an agreement between the World Bank and the Government of India, the Bell Mission's recommendations were kept confidential until 2010.[31] These recommendations, many of which appear sound with the benefit of hindsight, were quite controversial in 1965. The report noted India's low level of economic growth and negligible increase in per capita output during the Third Five-year Plan. Imports had grown to a considerable extent despite the policy of import substitution, but exports lagged far behind. Foreign aid was, thus, necessary to fill this gap. The increased requirement for foreign aid had also generated substantial debt-servicing obligations.[32]

These problems were further complicated by a couple of additional factors. First, India's population growth, at 2.4 per cent per annum, was eating up most of the country's additional economic growth. Second, there was a significant diversion of resources towards defence in the aftermath of the wars with China and Pakistan. Third, administrative delays in decision-making were posing serious challenges for the implementation of plans. Fourth, even though imports had surged in excess of exports, there was substantial underutilization of economic capacity in India—largely because of a shortfall in the importation of goods that could sustain the production process. Administrative processes in India and project appraisal by donors were excessively time-consuming. Finally, the report came down heavily on India's neglect of agricultural investment.[33] It claimed: 'Part of the danger we apprehend is in the past, simultaneous verbal ascription of "top" or "absolute" priority to agriculture and failure actually to provide the physical inputs and other conditions required for an adequate growth of agricultural output.'[34] Foreign exchange spent on food imports, especially on non-PL 480 rice imports, was consuming the resources that could be utilized for industrialization.[35]

The report suggested that overvaluation of the rupee and import controls were an inefficient way to deal with the foreign exchange constraint. The low price of imports under the prevailing exchange-rate regime ensured that there was high demand for imports and for the import licences that were supposed to curb this demand. Moreover, tax concessions to exporters on a case-by-case basis were also deemed inefficient. It was suggested that the regime should move away from such direct controls to indirect controls—such as a realistic exchange rate, which would increase the price of imports and render exports more competitive. For goods such as tea and jute, whose demand did not vary with price, it was suggested that a tax on exports could ensure that there was no foreign exchange loss owing to devaluation. The report opined that this strategy would alleviate the foreign exchange constraint, because imports would become more expensive and the country would make a push toward export promotion. This could reduce the trade gap between imports and exports. While imports of finished goods would be banned under this plan and imports used to manufacture non-essential goods be discouraged, the imports of goods that were considered essential for capacity utilization in industrial production would be freed from constraints.[36]

India needed to act on a number of fronts. The top four areas were (a) devaluation of the currency, but preserving export taxes on jute and tea; (b) removal of direct controls on the importation of intermediate goods necessary for industrial production; (c) population control; and (d) increased agricultural investment.[37] Additional areas that required policy action were: curbing defence spending; improving rural public goods such as roads, drainage, and irrigation; improving transportation; promoting greater competence in planning design and evaluation; granting greater autonomy to public-sector enterprises; improving the environment for foreign investment; abandoning import substitution; and reducing administrative inefficiencies. In return, the report proposed that the World Bank increase its level of aid to India during the Fourth Five-year Plan, with a higher non-project aid component in the total disbursement. Non-project aid would provide greater freedom for importing materials that were essential for capacity utilization in Indian industry.[38]

The Bell Mission concluded that India's import-substitution policy was inefficient. It was, therefore, necessary to transition towards enhancing the competitiveness of the country's exports. Such transitions constitute a paradigm change in policy. In India, the idea of import substitution and its institutions were quite entrenched in 1966. Domestic constituencies within the executive and technocratic community, as well as the larger political community, would oppose a move towards deregulation and globalization.

The Executive Branch's Economic Orientation

India's executive-technocratic team, led by Prime Minister Indira Gandhi after January 1966, was not convinced that donor agencies had benign intentions during the country's balance of payment crisis. The team's orientation toward the crisis was defined by their perception of the crisis. The Indian policy team held a largely positive view about the efficacy of import substitution enunciated in the Second and Third Five-year Plans,[39] as they began to embark on the fourth one. They needed to take into account the balance of power between domestically and internationally oriented producers at home and the pressures from abroad, as described earlier in this chapter. The orientation of India's executive branch leaders would define whether the policy team would exploit the 1966 crisis to engender change or merely orchestrate a temporary retreat so that old policies and institutions could endure in the long run.

The executive branch is likely to enjoy tremendous agenda-setting powers in times of a foreign exchange crisis. Consequently, this chapter does not focus attention on the divisions between the executive and the legislature. Foreign exchange crises often render a divided government less likely, because the executive's power to set the agenda and its ability to make side payments helps the executive in dealing with the legislature.[40] Moreover, in times of a severe foreign exchange crisis, when quick decision-making is of the essence, it is especially easy for the executive to craft a unified government. Indira Gandhi was able to obtain the majority of the votes in Parliament for the devaluation package in June 1966 despite widespread, publicly expressed opposition in the legislature.

Indira Gandhi was neither a convinced liberalizer nor an ideologically driven person in 1966. Her twin objectives in her early days as Prime Minister were to handle the foreign exchange crisis and consolidate power.[41] Gandhi ultimately tilted toward a radical version of import substitution due to the demands of her political base. She was popular with the young leftists in the Congress party and had friends in the Communist Party of India (CPI). These were the people who were vehemently opposed to the devaluation package.

Indira Gandhi became prime minister on 19 January 1966, after the death of Lal Bahadur Shastri on 11 January. She was a popular for two important reasons. First, she was relatively inexperienced and, therefore, the least threatening to senior party bosses. Second, she was perceived as being soft towards the left. She had supported activities organized by socialist forum groups in the late 1950s. She was very accessible to leaders of the leftist opposition parties and had enjoyed the friendship of Bhupesh Gupta and Mohan Kumaramangalam since her college days in London. Gupta and Kumaramangalam had subsequently joined the CPI.[42]

Gandhi's socialist image had helped her win the crucial support of Congress Party president Kumarasamy Kamraj, who was reputed to be committed to advancing socialist goals. Of the 63 politicians interviewed by Brecher, including 36 Congress members of Parliament, 30 ranked Congress president Kamraj first in his commitment to socialist goals, while 20 ranked Indira Gandhi first.[43] Apart from Kamraj's agreement with Gandhi on political goals, he was also satisfied that Gandhi's youth and inexperience meant she would pose less of a threat to his position as Congress party president. Kamraj's support was essential in helping Gandhi convert her political appeal into political power. In Parliament's vote to select the prime minister, Gandhi garnered 355 out of 526 votes and defeated veteran Congressman Morarji Desai.[44]

Gandhi was quite confused about economic policy in June 1966. Her speechwriter B.G. Verghese presents a detailed account of her mindset at that time. According to Verghese, Gandhi neither comprehended the intricacies of devaluation nor the politics of economic policy. She had to depend on her advisers, who explained that devaluation was necessary in order to import essential foodgrain, avert a famine, and secure finance for the Fourth Five-year Plan. Politically influential people, like Congress party president Kamraj and commerce minister Manubhai Shah, were kept in the dark about devaluation until 5 June. Even Sushital Bannerjee—a joint secretary to the prime minister and a key aide—was unaware of the policy shift. The executive technocratic team informed of the devaluation policy comprised Asoka Mehta (planning minister), C. Subramanium (agriculture minister), Sachin Choudhury (finance minister), Dinesh Singh (minister of state for foreign affairs), I.G. Patel (chief economic adviser, finance ministry), L.K. Jha (secretary to the prime minister), Pitamber Pant (Perspective Planning Division, Planning Commission), and economist K.N. Raj. Their most pressing concern at the time was to obtain wheat shipments on time to avert a famine.[45]

It is reported that Indira Gandhi, in a conversation with IMF managing director Pierre Paul Schweitzer, said: 'I don't know anything about economic matters. It was not a very good subject of mine at Oxford. But my technicians tell me that you're very concerned about this. I trust you. I trusted your uncle, who was one of the great men of our century. What should I do?'

Schweitzer replied, 'Well, I mean, it's up to you to decide. But I think you should devalue.'

Gandhi enquired, 'By how much?' (It was Rs 4.8 to a USD then.)

Schweitzer opined, 'Six would be good. Seven would be better. Seven and a half would be fantastic.'

Gandhi agreed, 'Okay, I'll do 7.5. Whatever you say.'[46]

The economists advising the government were largely against the donor-preferred policies of devaluation, trade liberalization, and adoption of an economic orientation that was friendlier to the private sector. A few documented examples show the mood within the Indian technocracy. Benjamin King arrived in India as the World Bank's representative in 1963. When Escott Reid—the head of the bank's South Asia and Middle East department—urged King to make a speech at one of the meetings of the Aid India Consortium, India's finance secretary L.K. Jha moved to stop this from happening. Jha, who was in office from 1960 to 1964, was considered a liberal technocrat and had won King's admiration even though they held different views.[47] But as the World Bank's Simon Aldewereld would later report, the bank and the Indian government had a difference of opinion regarding the role of the private sector in India's manufacturing industry. Even though the bank agreed to finance capacity expansion in private companies like the Indian Iron and Steel Company and the Tata Iron and Steel Company, the Indian government turned instead to bilateral donors like the Federal Republic of Germany, the Soviet Union, and the United Kingdom to fund public-sector steel plants.[48]

Senior advisers and ministers were not in favour of rupee devaluation and private sector promotion. The finance ministry's chief economic adviser I.G. Patel remarked in 1967 that India should never become so dependent on foreign aid again.[49] Asoka Mehta, the influential planning minister who was part of the team that negotiated the devaluation package, remained an ardent supporter of a state role in economic planning and industrialization. The secret Woods–Mehta agreement in April 1966 had expressed India's commitment to replacing import controls with tariffs, simplifying industrial licensing, and blocking new public sector investments, which were not as profitable as the private sector.[50] Despite this agreement, Mehta held the view that countries like India, which began industrializing at a late stage, needed state intervention rather than a free market. On the eve of the rupee devaluation, he assured Indians that aid was necessary for growth and that the economy's public-sector orientation would not be reversed as a result of US aid.[51]

Former finance minister T.T. Krishnamachari (August 1963–December 1965) was opposed to the devaluation. He had to be replaced by Sachindra Choudhury (December 1965–March 1967)—a pleasant, inexperienced politician, and an economics novice—to clear the way for devaluation. In his memoirs, I.G. Patel explained that Krishnamachari had to be replaced because of his incompatibility with the advice and demeanor of George Woods and US President Lyndon Johnson. The new finance minister Choudhury, on the other hand, was a personal friend of the governor of the Reserve Bank of India (RBI), P.C. Bhattacharya. This would make it easy for Bhattacharya to work with the new finance minister to implement policy changes.[52]

Two substantial Indian government reports from the 1960s lamented that industrial licensing had not produced its desired objectives and suggested intensification of industrial direction by the government. The first report called for more detailed planning to guide industrialization toward priority sectors through tax, credit, and pricing policies and a better appraisal of projects. The second report asserted that industrial licensing had led to the concentration of wealth in a few corporations rather than promoting equitable growth, and, therefore, proposed a monopolies commission. This report was the precursor of the Monopolies and Restrictive Trade Practices (MRTP) Act, 1969, which would curb the autonomy of the large private companies in India.[53]

Agriculture minister C. Subramanian was probably the one influential member of the executive team whose view was closer to the US position. He was keen to introduce price incentives and modern technology to the agricultural sector. His entry into the Planning Commission had helped to remove the commission's substantial opposition to agricultural reforms. Even though India quickly reversed its position on industrial policy, it used American advice and technology to usher in the green revolution in the late 1960s.[54]

Political Opposition

Indira Gandhi was learning to play the role of prime minister in 1966 and was particularly sensitive to the way in which members of Parliament reacted to the devaluation package. There was widespread opposition to devaluation among members of her ruling coalition. This persuaded her in an unambiguously pro-ISI direction for a variety of reasons. First, her supporters worried that she was becoming too independent. Second, Indian leaders who were committed to socialist goals were unhappy that market forces were being unleashed in an uncoordinated way. In addition, India's seemingly servile dependence on foreign aid was viewed with great distrust.

The secrecy with which Gandhi had to proceed in negotiations with the US government and the World Bank intensified the political opposition. She did not confide the matter with Congress party president Kamraj, who had received his advice from former finance minister T.T. Krishnamachari. Neither could Gandhi confide in Morarji Desai, with whom she had to compete to become prime minister in 1966; nor with commerce minister Manubhai Shah, whose empire based on export subsidy would be hurt by the devaluation. And with the devaluation package being a pro-market move, Gandhi could not rely on her old friends in the Left either. The result was widespread political discontent among her political supporters.[55]

Even senior Congress party members like Kamraj who had supported Gandhi for prime ministership quietly opposed devaluation. Kamraj's top aide R. Venkatraman characterized the situation as 'politically unwise and economically unsound'.[56] T.T. Krishnamachari (ex-finance minister), Manubhai Shah (commerce minister), and Morarji Desai all expressed their displeasure with the proposal. Shah is reported to have said that the devaluation had been India's biggest mistake since independence. He reinstated export subsidies by mid-August 1966.[57] Krishnamachari was not convinced of the Bell Report's recommendation to devalue the rupee, and he was forced to resign as finance minister in December 1965. Aid distribution was conditioned upon devaluation, and was, therefore, within the purview of his finance portfolio. As a sign of his opposition, Krishnamachari had delayed action on the Bell Report while he was finance minister.[58]

The political Left, represented by the CPI and the Communist Party of India–Marxist (CPM), took the most vocal position against the devaluation package. But criticism was not limited to these two parties. The more moderate socialists (Praja Socialist Party, or PSP, and the Samyukta Socialist Party, or SSP) and the right-wing nationalists (Jan Sangh, or JS) all opposed devaluation. They also expressed pessimism about the devaluation's ability to promote exports and about the possibility of curbing domestic inflation.

All of these parties agreed that India had bent to foreign pressure. Politicians from across the political spectrum complained about external pressure. Noted CPI parliamentarian Hiren Mukherjee articulated this view in Parliament in no uncertain terms:

> It should be common knowledge here that the decision to force India down to her knees had been made by the cloak and dagger aid givers of America long ago. The so called Bell Mission ... had reported at the end of 1964, but was for a while given a short shrift. Then the World Bank called in its ally, the IMF, which put the screw on when it got a chance to do so over the repayment of IMF standby credits ... Finally, a note was sent to members of the Congress Party which said: 'Action on devaluation could not be postponed as all further aid negotiations hinged on it'.[59]

Bhupesh Gupta (CPI) recounted the pressures faced by finance minister Krishnamachari before his resignation.[60] Noted parliamentarians with diverse ideological leanings such as R.M. Lohia (SSP), A.B. Vajpayee (JS), A.K. Gopalan (CPM), Banka B. Das (PSP), Frank Anthony (independent), and J.B. Kripalani (independent) all shared a similar view about the government's capitulating to foreign pressure.[61]

The view that there would be no significant trade benefits from devaluation was picked up within Parliament from the debate among intellectuals.[62] Mukherjee (CPI) reminded Parliament about the commerce ministry's report (1965–6), which had argued that devaluation would not benefit trade. Gupta (CPI) pointed out that only 18–20 per cent of India's exports required subsidies and would potentially benefit from devaluation. S.N. Dwivedi (PSP) and J.B. Kripalani (independent) raised the matter of the inelasticity of traditional exports. If the demand for India's exports was inelastic, the lower price of India's exports after devaluation would not increase the demand for these exports.

Third, there was near unanimity that inflation had been caused by rising import prices owing to devaluation.[63] The Congress party tried to counter these charges by suggesting that increased prices were due to seasonal variations and the continued impact of drought, but these arguments did not hold much water.

The reaction to devaluation among the free-enterprise Swatantra Party, which was the only pro-market opposition party with close links to the industrialists, ranged from ambivalence to support. Perhaps the most open support within the Swatantra Party came from M.R. Masani, who is reported to have said: 'If devaluation constituted a first step in a policy of economic realism in place of the doctrinaire policies pursued by the Congress Government, it would have some desirable results in boosting the export and promoting the inflow of foreign capital.'

Masani asserted—in no uncertain terms—that the predictions of Professor Bellikoth Raghunath Shenoy of Bombay University who was the most articulate critic of Indian planning, and veteran liberal statesman and freedom fighter C. Rajagopalachari had suddenly been realized on 6 June 1966. The government had been forced to take a course that he had predicted in Parliament on 22 March the same year. Among the other major spokespersons of the Swatantra Party, N. Ranga was ambivalent on this issue while N. Dandekar was sympathetic.[64]

Evidence of Political Necessity Driving the Rupee Devaluation

In her response to the 1966 balance of payments crisis, Prime Minister Gandhi was reacting to external pressure rather than implementing an indigenously generated policy based on the Indian technocratic community's firm beliefs. John Lewis, the director of USAID in 1966, mentions three instances that lend credibility to this view. Lewis had been more optimistic about India's prospects for economic development than the World Bank officials who favoured deregulation. First, Lewis was surprised that Pitambar Pant, a powerful technocrat within the Planning Commission, accepted not only the liberalization measures, but also the devaluation deal. Lewis writes:

[Pant] would have anticipated my surprise at finding the country's prototypical central planner in such a pro-market posture. Even though Pant is reported to have listened carefully to Jagdish Bhagwati's eloquent interventions in the internal debates, it is unlikely Pant took the stance he did because of the persuasiveness of his young neoclassicals. Rather, for him the main issue still was Plan scale; for the fourth plan to have the size he thought minimal would require major, indeed, increased, foreign assistance; and, as we have seen, in the autumn of 1965, with the replenishment of IDA (International Development Association), the country's second largest donor, in doubt, aid from the largest donor, the US, had been on hold since spring and doubly held up since the outbreak of Indo-Pakistani hostilities in September.[65]

Second, L.K. Jha, the secretary to the prime minister at the time of the crisis, provided confirming testimony to the pressure thesis 21 years later to Lewis. To quote Lewis once again:

When, in the course of a 1986 conversation, I asked him about the sources of the two great reform initiatives of the sixties, Jha was rather chauvinistic on the subject of agriculture; agricultural reform, he insisted, reflected mainly Indian ideas and initiatives. But when I asked about liberalization-cum-devaluation, he laughed merrily. 'Oh that', he said, 'that was what George Woods told us we had to do to get aid.'[66]

Indira Gandhi was ambivalent about the execution of the policy package just days before the devaluation was announced in Parliament. She approved the agreement between World Bank president George Woods and India's planning minister Asoka Mehta in May 1966. In early June, Gandhi called some Congress leaders for discussions, pretending that the matter was still up for debate. Congress party president Kamraj was outraged and insisted on a formal consultation with party leadership. At this stage, Gandhi wavered about the implementation of the devaluation package. It was on the insistence of the Indian ambassador to the US, B.K. Nehru, that the die had been cast as far as the aid-cum-devaluation deal was concerned that Gandhi decided to go ahead with devaluation.[67]

Capital's Acquiescence

Indian industry acquiesced to the devaluation package, even though a large segment of industry would feel the pinch. At FICCI, the foremost association representing Indian industry at that time, there was substantial divergence between the group's public statements and its internal expressions of concern. The small trading associations were also largely critical of the devaluation package. The tea producers and the Goa Mineral Ore Exporters' Association were two of devaluation's biggest supporters. The Associated Chambers of Commerce and Industry (ASSOCHAM), which represented foreign capital in India, chose to remain silent.

FICCI had developed close ties with leaders of India's struggle for independence and had often supported its concerns. Mohandas Gandhi, the pillar of strength within the Indian National Congress and the struggle for independence, had addressed the FICCI's Fourth Annual Convention on 7 April 1931. In that address, Gandhi sought to involve the commercial classes in the mainstream of the nationalist movement:

> I cannot forget the services rendered by the commercial classes, but I want you to go a step further. I want you to make the Congress your own and we would willingly surrender the reins to you. The work can be better done by you. But if you decide to assume the reins, you can only do so on one condition. You should regard yourselves as trustees and servants of the poor.[68]

Early FICCI presidents such as Sir Purshottamdas Thakurdas and G.D. Birla had turned down invitations from the British viceroy of India to sit on important consultative committees, and the federation opposed British rule in India.[69] It continued to work closely with the independent government of India after 1947 and positioned itself as the major industry association by 1966. FICCI had 170 members in 1965, including 49 chambers of commerce, 39 trade associations, and several other industry associations. In addition, FICCI's 366 associate members included representatives from banking, insurance, shipping, and manufacturing firms. It represented both industry and trade, and the federation acted as the mouthpiece for big business houses of India.[70]

FICCI's public reaction to the devaluation of 6 June was at odds with its real concerns. Even though Lakshmi Niwas Birla[71] made a radio broadcast favouring the devaluation, he doubted the efficacy of export duties that were designed to tax windfall profits. FICCI placed advertisements in newspapers supporting the devaluation.[72] Despite this public posture of support, the organization internally treated the devaluation as an admission of policy failure. Finance minister Sachin Choudhury made a private confession in an internal meeting that the devaluation was an extreme step that was absolutely necessary. The federation, in turn, sought freer imports of raw materials and machine parts, adjustments in export duties, and export assistance. Subsequently, Prime Minister Gandhi urged FICCI president Ramanbhai Amin to treat the devaluation episode as an established fact. She sought help to create a propitious political climate at a time when various forces were pulling the country in different directions.[73]

The devaluation had not reduced FICCI's appetite for export assistance. FICCI secretary-general G.L. Bansal urged commerce minister Manubhai Shah to consider the need for export assistance consequent upon devaluation. Bansal sent similar letters to Asoka Mehta (planning minister), I.G. Patel (economic advisor to the finance minister), S. Bhoothalingam (secretary in the finance ministry), and L.K. Jha (secretary to the prime minister). A number of proposals were suggested in these letters. First, Bansal urged easier access to foreign exchange and financing, preferably under generous rules provided under special schemes. Second, the federation sought easier access to raw materials and imports of intermediate goods. Third, Bansal urged that preference be given to exports of goods with lesser import content, such as processed foods and certain types of chemicals. Fourth, there was the matter of the scale and type of import entitlements; Bansal asked for greater leeway on both counts.[74]

The majority of the smaller industry associations were also opposed to the devaluation. B.D. Somani, president of the All India Manufacturers Organization, expressed concern about a spiralling of prices in projects with substantial import content and called for export incentives for non-traditional exports. The president of the All India Importers Association, R.C. Shah, asserted that devaluation won't solve the fundamental imbalance in India's imports, which were one-and-a-half times larger than its exports. Many of these imports were driven by defence and development needs and were, therefore, not easy to adjust with exports. K.K. Sheth, the president of the All India Exporter's Chamber, and J.H. Doshi, the president of the All India Association for Industries, both expressed scepticism about the possibility of an export surge due to the inelastic nature of global demand for most products. The president of the Cement Manufacturers' Association was worried that the withdrawal of export incentives and the imposition of heavy export duties would eliminate any of the export-friendly effects of devaluation. The vice-president of the Federation of Indian Mineral Industries worried that the inefficient State Trading Corporation would nullify the benefits of the devaluation.[75] This corporation was responsible for channelling exports in areas such as sugar, tanned hides, and silver.

Surprisingly, the representatives of foreign capital remained silent. ASSOCHAM, the business lobby representing multinational companies (MNCs), had been a strong proponent of economic liberalization. A volume discussing ASSOCHAM's history as a liberalizer did not mention the devaluation episode.[76] The organization's annual reports for 1966 and 1967 were also silent on the question of devaluation.[77] There is a view that ASSOCHAM's dismay was driven by the fact that MNC executives lost valuable salary as a result of the devaluation.[78]

The Indian Merchant's Chamber—an ASSOCHAM member with influence in the western region around Bombay (now Mumbai)—opposed the devaluation. P.A. Narielwala, a former president of the organization, criticized devaluation on the grounds that it would spur inflation and reduce the price of Indian exports abroad. The organization's vice-president R.C. Cooper asserted that the devaluation was a halfhearted measure. A judicious policy, he believed, would involve devaluation with export incentives. He also contested the idea that devaluation would bring import substitution to an early end by making imports dearer.[79]

Only two industry groups were overwhelmingly favourable towards devaluation. B.C. Ghosh, a leading tea planter, argued that devaluation would boost India's tea exports to the UK, the US, and Australia. According to Ghosh, the devaluation would neutralize the special advantages that tea-exporting countries such as Sri Lanka enjoyed due to better shipping facilities. The president of the Goa Mineral Ore Exporters Association opined that devaluation would boost mining exports and that about three-fourths of the extra earnings resulting from devaluation would go to the producer. This would inject life into the 400 idle iron ore mines in Goa.[80]

The majority of the Indian industrialists involved with import substitution were opposed to devaluation. But FICCI offered valuable public support to the ruling party and ASSOCHAM maintained a steady silence. The crisis caused industry to acquiesce to devaluation, despite its interests in perpetuating the pre-devaluation status quo. Opposing devaluation would be even more debilitating for Indian industry at the time of a foreign exchange crisis. Import substitution depended on foreign exchange to finance the imports of raw materials and intermediate capital goods. This would not be forthcoming from external donors if India did not devalue its currency.

***

The foreign exchange crisis of 1966 occurred at a time when Prime Minister Indira Gandhi and her executive team were not convinced of the benefits of devaluation. Gandhi had just become prime minister in 1966 with support from India's Left, both within and outside the Congress party. She was quick to understand the quid pro quo with donors of obtaining much-needed foreign exchange in return for the devaluation of the rupee. Yet, this substantial change in policy did not find support within the technocracy or the political class.

FICCI, an organization that represented the import-substituting Indian industry, made a variety of public announcements supporting the devaluation package even though the organization opposed it. ASSOCHAM, which represented foreign capital in India, was conspicuous by its silence. Yet FICCI, ASSOCHAM, and the overwhelming majority of industry organizations were concerned about the consequences of devaluation. The industry's support for liberalization through acquiescence was a short-run phenomenon inspired by the shortage of foreign exchange. It was driven by a desire to perpetuate import substitution in the long run rather than by an internal drive to seek international competitiveness.

The 1966 foreign exchange crisis, which happened at a time when India's executive branch favoured import substitution, produced a temporary retreat to trade liberalization. The momentum of trade liberalization could not be sustained after the crisis. This episode illustrates the inability of powerful foreign aid donors to pressure a country into adopting policy changes without technocrats in the country who believe in these policy changes. Had the dominant view within the Indian technocracy favoured export promotion, the policy team could have convinced the prime minister of the need for reform and made a virtue of necessity—which is what happened in India in 1991. But import substitution and state intervention were the dominant economic ideas in India in 1966, and the country's executive-technocratic team was focused on solving the problem of food scarcity and garnering resources for India's Fourth Five-year Plan. The executive branch needed to embrace global economic integration in order for this approach to develop a life of its own as a policy paradigm in India. The next chapter describes how this change in the executive branch began to occur and gradually reached a tipping point in 1991.

Notes

1. A typical ISI policy prescription is characterized by high tariffs, an overvalued exchange rate, and import licences. These measures are supposed to protect domestic producers from foreign competition at home. Export-oriented policies, on the other hand, define a situation where the effective exchange rate for exports is not significantly different from the effective exchange rate for imports. See Bhagwati (1986: 91–104).

2. For the concept of dependence, see Baldwin (1980: 471–506); Hirschman (1945/1980: 13–52); Waltz (1979: 18–37).

3. Haggard and Maxfield (1996b: 209–39); Nelson (1990); Stallings (1992).

4. The global oil price shocks of 1973 and 1979 did not pose a severe foreign exchange constraint for India, thanks to remittances pouring in from the Indians living abroad. See Ahluwalia (1986: 943); Mukherji (1999: 107–63).

5. See Choudhuri (1966), which is a text of the broadcast that created a furore in Parliament. Also see, Denoon (1986: 68–71).

6. See Choudhury (1968: 72–5).

7. See Bhagwati and Srinivasan (1975: 97).

8. See Choudhury (1968: 251–6).

9. See Denoon (1986: 72).

10. Under the import entitlement schemes, eligible exporters were allowed to keep a pre-specified part of the free on board (f.o.b.) value of their export earnings. Given the exchange-control regime prevalent at that time, these entitlements had a market premium, which could be construed as export subsidies.

11. It is easier to quantify net devaluation than the level of export assistance. Bhagwati and Srinivasan quote Frankenna's work that suggests that the cash subsidy for engineering goods and steel was 12.4 per cent and 8 per cent of the f.o.b. prices, respectively. See Bhagwati and Srinivasan (1980: 105–7).

12. See Kumar (1996: 378).

13. See Bhagwati and Srinivasan (1975: 17).

14. See Ganguly (2002: 31–50); Joshi and Little (1994: 74).

15. See Frankel (2005: 285).

16. Ibid.: 286.

17. See Paarlberg (1985: 146).

18. See Joshi and Little (1994: 73–4).

19. The PL 480 programme was very significant for India's food security. See Cullather (2007: 59–90).

20. See Frankel (2005: 285); Sagar (1966).

21. See Paarlberg (1985: 158–9).

22. See Bjorkman (1980: 232–3); Cullather (2010: 205–31); Paarlberg (1985: 146). Scepticism with Indian planning arose after 1963 after a period of substantial support for it between 1955 and 1962. See Mukherji (2010a: 301–22).

23. See Frankel (2005: 285–6).

24. See Kux (1992: 152, 188–9); Miurhead (2005: 1–22); Oliver (1995: 129).

25. See Oliver (1995: 129).

26. See Lewis (1964). The US embassy headed by Chester Bowles was more sympathetic toward India's developmental effort than the World Bank in the early 1960s. See the Oral History Program (1986a). In the early 1960s, Benjamin King was the World Bank's representative in India and a member of the Bell Mission. He retired as a director of the Development Economics Department of the Bank in 1981.

27. See Division of the Humanities and Social Sciences (1986: 5–17); Oliver (1995: 95–124); Oral History Program (1981: 3–6). Knapp was vice-president of operations and chairman of the loan committee for the World Bank and the International Development Association (IDA) between 1956 and 1962. He retired as senior vice-president and chairman of the loan committee for the World Bank and IDA in 1978. See Oral History Program (1986a: 11). Please was a part of the Bell Mission to India in 1964 and retired from the World Bank as senior adviser to the senior vice-president on structural adjustment.

28. See Oliver (1995: 127–34). Also see Bell (1965: i–iv) for the economic mission headed by him.

29. Ibid.

30. Oliver (1985: 133–4); Oral History Program (1986a), in which King raised the issue of exchange rates with Woods, before Bell's appointment as head of the economic mission.

31. The Indian government was very keen to keep the report secret. On the secrecy surrounding 1966, see Oral History Program (1986a: 23–4).

32. See Bell (1965: 1–4).

33. See Oral History Program (1986a: 4–12).

34. Ibid.: 11.

35. See Oral History Program (1986a: 9).

36. Ibid.: 13–20.

37. Ibid.: 34–5.

38. Ibid.: 35–6.

39. For a detailed analysis of the Third Five-year Plan, see Hanson (1966: 171–230).

40. See Milner (1997: 103–6, 109–12).

41. See Denoon (1986: 38). The author conducted interviews with P.N. Dhar and Arjun Sengupta on 29 July 1997, New Delhi; and with Jagdish Bhagwati on 14 November 1997, New York. Dhar was the principal secretary to the prime minister between 1973 and 1977; and Sengupta was special secretary to the prime minister between 1981 and 1984. One story of how dependent Gandhi was on the support of intellectuals was narrated to me by Bhagwati. She was perturbed when K.N. Raj, the influential vice-chancellor of Delhi University, expressed support for devaluation and then withdrew it. Bhagwati was a young economist in the pro-devaluation camp. He now holds a University Professorship at Columbia University, and is one of the world's most distinguished trade economists.

42. See Brecher (1961: 238–9); Frankel (2005: 288–92).

43. See Frankel (2005: 290).

44. Ibid.: 290–1.

45. See Patel (2003: 108–12); Verghese (2010: 87–93). The reading of a variety of sources shows that agriculture minister C. Subramaniam was probably the person whose view was closer to the US position. He was keen to initiate price incentive and technology to initiate the process of liberalization. See especially, Oliver (1985: 143).

46. See Oliver (1995: 141–2).

47. See Oral History Program (1986a: 18–22).

48. See Oliver (6 November 1985: 6–10). From 1952–63, Aldewereld served as director of projects. This position was divided between the then loan and economics departments. He retired as Vice-president of the World Bank in 1974.

49. See Denoon (1986: 72); Oliver (1995: 144). Patel claims that he was positive about devaluation in 1966 and that the technocrats could have convinced the political class about its appropriateness if the Bell Mission and the American government had not taken to pontificating on economic policy in an intrusive way. However, he also claims that the government was not prepared for it in 1966 and he acquiesced with the dominant view. See Patel (2003: 102–5).

50. See Denoon (1986: 75–6).

51. See Mehta (1973: 15–27); Special Correspondent (1966).

52. See Patel (2003: 102–8).

53. See Hazari (July 1969, 1985: 339–422). On Hazari's association with government and his contribution, see Hazari (1985: 1,967–8).

54. See Cullather (2010: 205–70); Oliver (1995: 143); Subramaniam (1966); Varshney (1998: 48–80).

55. Denoon 1986: 47–8); Indira Gandhi to Krishnamachari, June 8, 1965;T. T. Krishnamachari Papers (New Delhi: Nehru Memorial Museum and Library).

56. See Sundaram (1972: 1,883).

57. See Denoon (1986: 49).

58. Ibid.: 64–5.

59. See Lok Sabha Debates (1966: 1,653–4).

60. See Sundaram (1972: 1,889).

61. See Lok Sabha Debates (1966: 3,647–9); Sundaram (1972: 1,889–990).

62. See Sundaram (1972: 1,890–1).

63. Ibid.: 1,891.

64. For M.R. Masani's reaction, see Masani (1968: 222); Lok Sabha Debates (26 July 1966: 477–83). For the reactions of N. Ranga and N. Dandekar, see Sundaram (1972: 1,981).

65. See Lewis (1997: 135).

66. Ibid.: 136.

67. Ibid.: 141. Especially see fn 7 on p. 141.

68. See Gandhi (1977: 171).

69. See Kochanek (1974: 162–5).

70. Ibid.: 170–3; Kudaisya (2003: 296–353).

71. L.N. Birla was president of FICCI in 1967.

72. See Denoon (1986: 68)

73. See Venkatsubbiah (1977: 139).

74. See FICCI (1966: 51–5). This letter was dated 23 June 1966.

75. See Singhvi (1968: 224–8).

76. See ASSOCHAM (1995).

77. See ASSOCHAM (1966, 1967).

78. See Denoon (1986: 68).

79. See Singhvi (1968: 224–8).

80. Ibid.: 228.

3 The Path to Economic Globalization and Competitiveness, 1975–91

THIS CHAPTER DESCRIBES India's path of economic reform from the mid-1970s and explains why the severe balance of payments crisis in 1991 produced a remarkable transformation in economic policy and institutions in India.[1] The previous chapter noted how a similar crisis in 1966, by contrast, only forced policymakers to briefly retreat towards economic deregulation and export promotion. This retreat was overtaken by a phase of the most stringent regulation and autarkic development between 1969 and 1974. India did not buckle under foreign pressure in 1966. This chapter addresses the question: why was the response to the balance of payments crisis of 1991 considerably different from the one in 1966?

Many of the policy and institutional changes initiated after the 1991 crisis have earned India the recognition of an Asian tiger economy. The reasons for India's economic transformation lie in the interplay of ideas, interests, and crises. Pranab Bardhan's seminal work on India's political economy explains why economic dominant interest groups in India would obstruct the transformation to deregulation and trade. In this story, the Indian state, which enjoyed limited autonomy as a balancer of class forces, had increasingly begun to play to the tune of the dominant social coalition, which was comprised of industrialists, rich farmers, and professionals in the 1970s and early 1980s.[2]

How were the interests of these dominant groups preserved within the old system? First, privileged industrialists obtained licences and financing from the government for production in a market that enjoyed a high level of protection from foreign goods, as the government-controlled exports and imports. These and other privileges that the government could offer business-people preserved inefficient monopolies within India's substantial domestic market.[3] The companies with assured production and selling privileges were not eager to give up these luxuries for the uncertainties of greater domestic and international competition. Second, the populous rich and middle-class farmers who owned more than 2.5 acres of land became politically powerful during the Janata Party's government (1977–9) and continued to wield power throughout the 1980s. The Janata Party, which was the first non-Congress ruling party at the national level, enjoyed the support of backward caste (BC) groups who wielded agrarian power. Farmers obtained generous assured prices for foodgrain such as wheat, free electricity, and highly subsidized inputs.[4] These farmers would oppose any economic rationality that would promote public goods or target subsidies exclusively towards poor farmers in order to reduce wasteful government expenditure. Finally, the class of professionals in the bureaucracy earned their rents through regulatory powers over private companies. They controlled jobs in the public sector. Children of the professionals and the middle class enjoyed easy access to highly subsidized higher education in a country that had made anaemic progress in promoting literacy among the majority of people.[5]

This dominant coalition of protected industrialists, farmers, and middle-class professionals increased its demands on the state for more subsidies in the 1970s and 1980s. Bardhan and other scholars attributed India's slow pace of industrial and agricultural growth during this period to the rising subsidies to members of the dominant coalition. This had crowded out much-needed public investment.[6] The next section of this chapter suggests that social groups' demands for subsidies generated an unsustainable fiscal situation in India. The fiscal situation substantially contributed to the severe balance of payments crisis in 1991. Prime Minister Rajiv Gandhi accorded greater privileges to the business class during his tenure as prime minister (1984–9), whereas the United Front coalition that successfully challenged Gandhi's Congress party under the leadership of Prime Minister Vishwanath Pratap Singh (1989–90) sided with the farmers without undermining the momentum of industrial promotion and deregulation. Powerful social actors' demands kept growing, but the government did not have enough resources to meet these demands in the 1980s.

The third section of this chapter describes how India's economic transformation in 1991 posed a challenge to Bardhan's thesis about the stability of India's dominant political coalition. Powerful sections of the Indian business community did not support the devaluation of the rupee, tariff liberalization, or easier entry of foreign investment. Moreover, industrial de-licensing would take away the central government bureaucracy's power to grant licences to particular companies. The power of the farmer's lobby ensured that benefits such as fertilizer subsidies and free electricity could not easily be taken away from farmers, despite the grave fiscal situation. Moreover, the political clout of trade unions made it impossible to change labour laws. This chapter addresses the question: the considerable power of the dominant coalition notwithstanding, why did industrialists and professionals in India acquiesce to the shift from import substitution and stringent industrial regulation to riskier liberalization and deregulation?

This chapter suggests that institutional change required Indian industry to make substantial adjustments. This was as much a matter of ideas as it was a matter of politics. Technocrats favouring an engagement with the global economy took advantage of a balance of payments crisis to substantially alter the normative underpinnings of India's economic policies and institutions in the early 1990s. India gave up export pessimism and radically altered its view about the role of private enterprise, foreign capital, and trade in financing its economic development. Import-substituting industry acquiesced to the demands made by technocrats and multilateral agencies such as the IMF and World Bank for two reasons. First, these industrialists realized that they were dependent on finance from IMF and the World Bank for imports. Second, progressive and professional elements within the Indian industry supported the government's agenda of promoting competition, productivity, and India's globalization in a moment of crisis.

In explaining economic events in India leading up to the reforms of 1991, this chapter deploys a tipping-point model of economic change, where endogenous changes in ideas within the technocracy and among powerful politicians are quintessential factors. Ideational changes within the Indian technocracy were premised on the failure of import substitution and state intervention to deliver on their promises. Moreover, the international demonstration effect of the rise of Asia's tiger economies and the disintegration of the Soviet Union during this period also had an impact on India's course of action. The exogenous shock in this model— the balance of payments crisis of 1991—worked very differently from the crisis in 1966 because of the internal preparation for change that had occurred in India. This preparation helped the proponents of change take advantage of the country's dependence on IMF to deal with powerful industrial groups that were satisfied with the comfort of protectionism.

Changes in Economic Ideas and Policy Since the 1970s

The Indian state began to critically reassess its economic policies after 1975. Years of stringent economic regulation between 1969 and 1974 had not yielded the desired levels of economic growth or human development. Moreover, the situation resulting from unemployment, wage freezes, and political protests had incapacitated Prime Minister Indira Gandhi. She had to impose a state of national emergency (1975–7)—the only two years of authoritarian rule in India—after a high court in Allahabad ruled that she had been involved in electoral fraud. India's GDP had grown at the slow annual rate of less than 4 per cent since 1956.[7] The percentage of Indians living below the poverty line had not declined between 1947 and 1973. The state gradually began to consider export promotion and industrial deregulation as options after 1975.[8] This change of thinking is clearly reflected in various reports by the Indian government that have been described later in the chapter.

Critical evaluation of India's industrialization continued under the Janata Party regime (1977–9) and under Indira Gandhi's Congress party government (1980–4). As prime minister from 1984 to 1989, Rajiv Gandhi deregulated the economy substantially to favour private companies. The subsequent National Front government (December 1989–November 1990) respected elements of policy favouring the private business class, while also seeking to address the problems of the farming community. Aggressive promotion of trade and foreign investment would have to wait until July 1991, as discussed in the next section.

The Evolution of Economic Ideas in India

Government reports critical of India's economic policies from 1974 to 1985 outlined five key areas of concern. These concerns informed Prime Minister Rajiv Gandhi's economic reforms in 1985, and included: (a) management of publicly owned companies, (b) deregulation of domestic investment, (c) import liberalization, (d) export promotion, and (e) the need to attract foreign investment. The new economic ideas proposed in these reports made an impact on India's development policies in the 1980s.

Rajiv Gandhi had won a comfortable majority in Parliament in 1984 in the aftermath of his mother's assassination. He had served as an airline pilot with Indian Airlines before entering politics and was passionate about modernizing India. The budget of 1985, proposed in the immediate aftermath of his historic electoral victory, enjoyed a high degree of autonomy from the demands of some sections of the dominant coalition. It reflected the new mood within the government and among its policymakers. Political opposition to the economic processes that Rajiv Gandhi initiated can be viewed as a way that elements of the dominant coalition effectively fought back to retain India's status quo in the absence of a financial crisis.

We begin our discussion with the first of the five areas of economic policy that attracted the Indian government's critical attention in the 1980s—management of publicly owned companies. These largely inefficient publicly owned companies had come to enjoy the commanding heights of the Indian economy since the Second Five-year Plan (1956–61).[9] They had consumed substantial public resources, but had earned rather poor rates of return. The government, therefore, stressed the need to improve public enterprises' efficiency and productivity. The Industrial Policy Statement of July 1980, for example, noted that the Indians had lost faith in the public sector and that there was a need to develop management cadres.[10] The most serious criticism came from a committee chaired by Arjun Sengupta in September 1984. The committee noted both the phenomenal growth of public investment (with a turnover of Rs 467.77 billion, around USD 48.75 billion, in 1982–3) and the paltry net profit of Rs 322 million (USD 33.44 million) during the same year. It recommended that publicly owned firms gain autonomy from ministerial interference, and opined that the government should only remain involved with strategic policy decisions and not the day-to-day management of these companies. Financially viable publicly owned firms in sectors that were not the exclusive preserve of the government were encouraged to seek financing from sources outside the government's budget.[11] Over time, ideas about deregulation of public enterprises came to acquire policy salience. To give just one example, the industry ministry's Bureau of Industrial Costs and Prices suggested in the late

1980s that the steel sector, which had been dominated by public sector companies for decades, should deregulate the procurement of its inputs.[12]

Second, India's industrial controls were stifling growth. A substantial report submitted to the finance ministry under the chairmanship of Vadilal Dagli in 1979 made a detailed analysis of industrial controls and subsidies. It suggested the liberalization of industrial licensing, which was subject to the stipulations of the MRTP Act and the FERA Act.[13] The Industrial Policy Statement of 1980 made a similar suggestion.[14] Moreover, even some of the original architects of India's more protective industrial regulations policy, such as I.G. Patel, began to deplore them as antithetical for productivity by the 1980s.[15] It should be noted that while these government reports stressed the need for deregulation of domestic investment, they did not mention foreign direct investment.

In its section on subsidies, the Dagli Committee report also corroborated the hypothesis about the problematic consequences of the dominant political coalition's economic demands. Publicly owned companies were losing Rs 30 trillion (USD 3 billion) per year. In addition, 70 per cent of the government's subsidy burden went for food, fertilizers, and exports. The committee expressed a deep concern about the growing subsidy burden.[16] Despite this cautionary note, the long-term fiscal policy of 1985 depended to a large extent on augmented tax collection and an improvement in public sector performance. It was also opined that a reduction in the tax rates would aid the process of resource mobilization.[17]

Lakshmi Kant Jha, a pre-eminent Indian civil servant since the 1960s, was convinced that industrial and administrative controls were stifling India's growth potential. At one point in the 1980s, he told his junior colleague Montek Singh Ahluwalia that the Indian economy was one that was running 16 breaks on the momentum of economic growth. He was a firm votary of tax breaks. It was not enough to partially release a few breaks. Economic growth could be unleashed if a couple of breaks were released simultaneously.[18] This would have to wait until 1991.

Third, two influential government reports from committees chaired by P.C. Alexander (1978) and Abid Hussain (1984) stressed the need for easier access to imports, the promotion of exports, and more efficient import substitution. The reports also recommended licensing changes, discouraging licensing of capital goods, and of raw material imports for items not available in India. When tariffs were prohibitively high, they discouraged import licensing of certain items. The reports also stressed that government agencies should not conduct procurement of bulk imports. Instead, importers should make their own decisions.[19]

Fourth, these two committee reports emphasized the importance of foreign exchange availability, financial support, access to modern technology, and the promotion of competition to spur exports. The duty drawback scheme to compensate for domestic taxes for exporters, for example, was difficult to administer and it did not fully reimburse exporters for taxes they paid in India. Citing the government's control of two-thirds of India's foreign exchange, the report called for the deregulation of technology imports and industrial controls, as well as for import liberalization with appropriate safeguards. The reports commended the performance and marketing knowledge of Japan's External Trade Organization and Korea's Trade–Investment Promotion Agency, and called for the emulation of such organizations in India.[20]

A committee chaired by M. Narasimhan (1985) reiterated some of these issues in the influential report on financial controls it submitted to the Ministry of Finance. This report also stressed the need for foreign technology collaboration and foreign direct investment in order for India to access modern technology. It also suggested the need to shift away from quantitative import restrictions to tariffs. Indian Industries needed reduced tariffs in order to enhance their competitiveness.[21]

Each of these influential reports highlighted the need for prudent foreign exchange management to assist in export promotion. However, none of them made a strong case for drastic currency devaluation as a way of achieving aggressive export promotion. Nor was there any talk of amending FERA and inviting foreign capital into India. The government seemed convinced that the correct policy option was financing growth through export promotion and more efficient import substitution. It favoured the easing of barriers for domestic investment. While these measures pointed to the need for increasing productivity within India's closed economy, they did not constitute the aggressive strategy of export-led growth pursued by many East Asian countries.

Favouring Business and the Middle Class, 1985–9

What impact did these reports have on the industrial policies that Rajiv Gandhi initiated during his tenure as prime minister from 1985 to 1989?

Deregulation under Gandhi, which included the reduction of industrial controls and gradual import liberalization, benefited Indian business groups, but did not discipline them towards export promotion. It also seemed to substantially benefit one element of the dominant coalition, Indian businesses, without compromising the interests of another element of the coalition—the professional class.

Industrial deregulation favouring the domestic business class was quite significant. First, it became easier to increase industrial production beyond the country's licensed capacity. India had suffered from a regime where industrialists could not expand production without government permission. Second, the MRTP Act had stringently regulated the activities of firms with assets greater than Rs 200 million (USD 16 million). By raising the MRTP limit to Rs 1 billion (USD 80 million), about 50 per cent of India's large business houses were on longer subject to MRTP regulations.[22] Third, 32 industries and 82 pharmaceutical products were freed from industrial licensing requirements. Fourth, a major policy initiative deregulated the textiles industry, which could have become an export earner had India not opted for import substitution in the 1950s. Fifth, income and corporate taxes were reduced. Indirect taxation was to be the major plank for resource mobilization because direct taxes, as a proportion of total taxes, had not witnessed a substantial increase during the 1980s. Many of these taxes were raised from intermediate goods such as cement, steel, and rail freight, and could easily be passed on to the consumer. Sixth, a number of policies liberalized imports that were deemed necessary for export promotion and efficient domestic production. Despite all of these reforms, no special effort was made to invite foreign capital into India.[23]

Opposition to these policies was to be expected from rich farmers, who were a significant part of the dominant electoral coalition. They did not pay direct taxes and would be adversely affected by increased indirect taxation. Opposition even arose among the rank-and-file members of the Congress party, which described this approach to economic policy as elitist.[24] There is clear evidence to demonstrate that all of India's political parties, including the Congress, depended heavily on subsidies and loans at the village level.[25] Attempts to help business groups without addressing farmers' needs easily drew the ire of the farming community's politically powerful segments.

1990: Favouring Farmers and Business Groups

Before the 1991 balance of payments crisis, the dominant coalition's economic demands had made it impossible to promote India's private sector and exports aggressively. The underlying domestic conditions that led to the 1991 balance of payments crisis were already apparent by 1990. The country's fiscal deficit had shot up from 5.4 per cent of GDP between 1975–6 and 1979–80 to 10 per cent between 1985–6 and 1989–90.[26] This dramatic increase had three critical sources. The first was the rise in interest payments on loans owed to commercial banks that were financing India's economic growth in the 1980s. The second was the deployment of all manner of subsidies to please different political constituencies. The third was defence spending.[27] The fact that the Indian government had about two-and-a-half month's foreign exchange reserves to cover for imports before the Gulf War of 1990–1 had created a certain sense of complacency in dealing with economic conditions in the absence of a severe external shock.[28]

Vishwanath Pratap Singh was elected prime minister of the National Front coalition government on 2 December 1989, dethroning Rajiv Gandhi of the Congress. Singh (who served as prime minister till 10 November 1990) had become a nationally regarded politician as the Congress party's finance minister (1985–7) in the Rajiv Gandhi-led government.[29] The emergence of the National Front government in 1989 marked the year when India's economic policy turned to favour the farmer and the small-scale industrialist. The government continued a policy of gradual industrial deregulation, while responding more aggressively to the demands of the farmers.[30] This exacerbated a fiscal crisis that contributed substantially to the severe balance of payments crisis in 1991, which is described in the next section of this chapter.

Political parties favoured by prosperous farmers belonging to BC groups made electoral gains in 1989 when the economic situation demanded fiscal prudence. A major player in these gains was the anti-Congress coalition called the Janata Dal (JD), which contested elections in 1989 and comprised political splinter groups such as the Indian Congress (Socialist), two farmers' parties [Lok Dal (A) and Lok Dal (B)], and the Janata Party.[31] The JD's political appeal can be understood in terms by looking at its political base and the shift in economic thinking towards deregulation described earlier in this chapter. The National Front coalition government, of which the JD was a major component, was formed by farmers' leaders and socialists. Many of these political groups had come together under the ruling Janata Party in 1977 when the Congress party was first voted out of power in Parliament. The larger National Front coalition organized by Vishwanath Pratap Singh was a political front against the Congress party, and composed of lower-caste parties—Dravida Munnetra Kazhagam (DMK), Communist Party of India (CPI), Communist Party of India–Marxist (CPM), Janata Party, and Indian Congress (Socialist).[32] Many of the leaders of these parties represented the intermediate and 'other backward classes', who were socially situated somewhere between the upper castes (UCs) and the most marginalized untouchable castes known as the 'Dalits'. These 'other backward classes'—who made up 45–50 per cent of the Indian population—were largely middle-class and rich farmers in rural areas, and they demanded greater political influence in 1989.[33]

How did the backward caste-farmer coalition come to power in the elections of 1989?[34] The ruling Congress party won 39.5 per cent of votes and emerged as the single largest party in Parliament with 197 seats. JD had won 143 seats. It surpassed the Congress party and came to power by courting support from the Left (CPI and CPM) and the right-wing Hindu-nationalist Bharatiya Janata Party (BJP). This United Front coalition of opposing ideologies splintered less than a year later when the BJP withdrew its support.[35] The political uncertainties arising from electoral democracy in 1990 made one wonder whether democracy was good for stable economic governance in a poor developing country like India.

The new government's budget of March 1990 secured farming interests. Although finance minister Madhu Dandavate noted the problems of the fiscal deficit, inflation, and the precarious balance of payments situation, the JD expressed its solidarity with the farmers. Notably, the budget called for an agricultural policy resolution. Government loans owed to farmers until 2 October 1989 up to Rs 10,000 (USD 5,842) were waived. This action would add Rs 10 billion (USD 584.24 million) to government spending. In addition, Rs 40 billion (USD 2.34 billion) was allocated for fertilizer subsidies.[36] The government also increased the price support for foodgrain by USD 1.74 per quintal.[37] In his speeches, Prime Minister Singh stressed the importance of rural development and the need to promote agricultural processing industries.[38]

Meanwhile, gradual deregulation of industrial and trade policy continued. First, the investment limit in plant and machinery for industrial ventures classified as small-scale industry was raised from Rs 3.5 million to Rs 6 million (USD 204,000–350,000). Small-scale industries enjoyed much greater freedom than their large-scale counterparts, whose activities were stringently regulated under the MRTP Act. It was also decided to promote these industries in rural areas. Second, the process of industrial relicensing was further consolidated. Investors, for instance, would not need a licence for investments up to Rs 250 million (USD 14.61 million) in fixed assets in economically developed regions; the same privilege would be available for investments up to Rs 750 million (USD 43.82 million) in economically backward areas. All export-oriented units were de-licensed if their investment was Rs 750 million (USD 43.82 million) or less. Third, the export–import policy of 1990–3 made it easier for exporters to import goods and technology that were essential for exports. Fourth, even though the foreign equity limit was not raised from 40 per cent to 51 per cent, measures were taken to make foreign investment free of restrictions automatic within that limit.[39]

These policy changes combined a pro-farmer outlook with one that favoured the Indian business class. Economic thinking within the government was increasingly gravitating towards industrial deregulation and the promotion of competitiveness. Deregulation, however, was accompanied, in the short term, with fiscal profligacy—something that would not augur well for India's balance of payments situation.

Iraq's invasion of Kuwait in August 1990 and the consequent rise in oil prices hurt India's current account balance to the tune of 1 per cent of the GDP. India had weathered the first and second global oil price shocks of the 1970s with greater ease, even though the impact of oil prices on the country's current account was no less then than in 1990.[40] In 1990, when India's fiscal house was in disarray and government spending had gone beyond control, credit rating agencies began to discourage commercial banks from lending to India. In a vital report from October 1990, Moody's highlighted an increase in India's debt-service ratio, its dependence on commercial borrowing, the impact of the Gulf War, and the country's ballooning budget deficit as matters of grave concern. Moreover, India's political uncertainty and fragmented coalition government worried investors.[41] The deposits of non-resident Indians, which were USD 10 billion in October 1990, actually turned into a modest outflow of USD

300 million in 1991.[42] India's autarkic industrialization, which had become heavily dependent on foreign commercial bank loans and the savings of non-resident Indians, now faced a grave crisis.

This section has shown how economic thinking within the government had moved in a pro-liberal direction. It was well-known that public enterprises were inefficient; that investment deregulation needed to be accelerated; that import liberalization for import substitution was fundamentally different from import liberalization for export promotion; and that foreign investment and technology were both critical for India's development. Yet, politics had interfered with these reforms. The business class successfully lobbied for internal deregulation without accepting the discipline of global competitiveness. In addition, the business class and farmers convinced the government to grant them greater subsidies. How, then, did economically liberal ideas ultimately prevail in Indian politics, despite the opposition of the dominant coalition?

1991: A Severe Crisis and a Remarkable Transformation

The Political and Economic Crisis

Rajiv Gandhi's assassination by a Tamil militant on 21 May 1991 occurred at a rather inopportune moment. India, which was about to conduct national elections, desperately needed political stability to salvage its financial viability.[43] The IMF had loaned the country USD 1.8 billion in January 1991; India's reserves were still a paltry USD 1 billion in late May, barely enough to cover two weeks of imports.[44] The assassination of Gandhi delayed the prospect of quick election results and a stable government that would be able to implement politically challenging economic policy. India needed to boost its productivity and competitiveness, and enhance its trade and industrial policies. It also needed a budget that would curb the country's fiscal deficit. These measures were essential for convincing the international financial community of India's long-term creditworthiness. In late May and early June of 1991, the World Bank and IMF were testing India's resolve for economic reforms. Finance minister Yashwant Sinha of the minority JD government needed to sell 20 tonnes of gold to raise USD 400 million so that the government could avoid a default.[45]

In June 1991, the Congress party came to power and chose an experienced leader, P.V. Narasimha Rao, to be prime minister. Rao had been loyal to Prime Minister Indira Gandhi during the period of national emergency (1975–7)—India's only period of authoritarian rule in its post-independence history. He earlier held important ministerial portfolios, including home (1984), defence (1984–5), foreign affairs (1980–4), and human resources development (1985–9). A bitter struggle for power between senior Congress party leaders ensued after the assassination of Rajiv Gandhi. The Congress had fielded prime ministers from the Nehru–Gandhi family in the 1970s and the 1980s, and Rao was considered both a loyal Congressman and an intellectual who could steer India through an economic crisis of gigantic proportions.[46]

The crisis brought technocrats to the forefront of governing the Indian economy. Prime Minister Rao invited eminent economist Manmohan Singh to accept the finance portfolio. Singh had served as the chairman of India's University Grants Commission. Previously, he held key government positions, including governor of the RBI (1982–5), deputy chairman of the Planning Commission (1985–7), and finance secretary (1976–80). Singh's technocratic team would play a pivotal role in India's economic transformation, as detailed in the next section of this chapter.[47]

The balance of payments crisis enabled the government to act with great speed to secure its financial sovereignty. Singh accepted the finance portfolio on the condition that he be allowed to follow unpopular courses of action. He wrote a letter to the managing director of the IMF within 24 hours of assuming office. The Indian cabinet met to discuss the type of loan it should request from the IMF. India's scarcity of foreign exchange and need for IMF support meant that the government had only three–four weeks to initiate trade and industrial policies favouring India's private sector-driven economic globalization.[48] The IMF and the World Bank tested the willingness of India's political class to promote the private sector and trade, and to curb its fiscal deficit. These financial organizations would not agree to a bailout package before transformative industrial and trade policies were firmly in place.

The government needed to take immediate action. On 1 July and 3 July 1991, the government made two significant devaluations of the rupee—reducing its value by about 18 per cent—to increase the competitiveness of Indian exports.[49] The business class had generally opposed currency devaluation, which raises the price of imports and lowers the price of exports, because Indian business depended on imports for import substitution production and was not a significant exporter of goods and services.[50]

The enormity of the crisis and the pressure from the multilateral organizations was so intense that all of India's political parties, including the Hindu nationalist BJP, agreed to cut defence spending.[51] Moreover, on 18 July, India shipped 47 tonnes of gold to the Bank of England as collateral for a USD 400 million loan.[52] Serious negotiations with the IMF on an additional USD 2.3 billion loan would have to wait until the advent of new industrial and trade policies and a transformative budget.

India's crisis was further compounded by the collapse of the Soviet Union. Its preferential trade with the Soviet Union, which could have saved India some foreign exchange in the short term, had become unsustainable. India would need hard foreign currency to replace the imports from the former Soviet Union that were previously conducted through barter arrangements. India's exports to the Soviet Union declined from 16.1 per cent of its total exports in 1990 to 3.69 per cent of exports in 1995. The same figures for imports were 5.51 per cent and 3.23 per cent, respectively. India, therefore, needed to become more competitive and promote its trade with the United States (US), and the tiger and emerging economies of Asia.[53]

India's Political and Technocratic Team

India's political and technocratic team played the key role in transforming the country's economy when it was faced with a serious chance of a default in its balance of payments. Prime Minister Rao had a deep understanding of the Cold War and the dramatic changes that its end would entail. As minister for external affairs, Rao (1980–4) had been a participant in the movement of the non-aligned countries and the Group of 77 developing countries that sought to chart a development path not beholden to either of the two superpowers. One consequence of the Cold War was that it had made it impossible for India to engage politically and economically with countries that belonged to the Association of Southeast Asian Nations (ASEAN) because of those countries' close ties to the US. For instance, Rao did not attend ASEAN's 1980 annual meeting in Kuala Lumpur as minister of external affairs when India was invited to become a dialogue partner of ASEAN. Consequently, India could not secure dialogue partnership, despite its best efforts.[54] When the Cold War ended, India's foreign policy changed course as the country pursued an aggressive 'Look East' policy. It mended relations with ASEAN and secured dialogue partnership in 1995.[55]

Rao has described his situation in 1991 as being similar to the one faced by Jawaharlal Nehru when he became independent India's first prime minister in August 1947. During independence, India became free to chart its own development path, and Nehru had depended on such intellectuals as Prasanta Chandra Mahalanobis to help him draw up India's development plans.[56] The end of the Cold War and the country's economic crisis in 1991 had some parallels to 1947, as the situation required fundamental changes in India's approach to development and to engaging the rest of the world.[57] India was well-endowed with technocrats who understood both international best practices and India's own economic problems at this time.

It was in this context that Rao invited the eminent economist and experienced technocrat Manmohan Singh to become his finance minister.[58] Singh would be aided by an economic policy team that had accumulated a wealth of knowledge about the need for policy changes. This team had participated in producing substantial research about the need for policy and institutional change within the government, although prime ministers Rajiv Gandhi and Vishwanath Pratap Singh were only partially able to deregulate the economy during their tenures. Rao was not only convinced about economic reforms, his political support was essential for Manmohan Singh to execute his economic agenda.[59]India's reform team, though deeply engaged with Western institutions, had been looking at the Indian economy through Indian eyes ever since the government began to critically evaluate the country's economic performance in the mid-1970s.

How is one to understand Manmohan Singh's ideational framework as an economic agent of change? After all, he had presided over India's regime of trade and industrial controls in the 1970s and the 1980s. In a substantial interview in July 1991, Singh reacted to the assertion that he had been timid in previous decades and suggested that when people go to the archives, they would realize the truth about his personal views on economic policy that could not be implemented under the different political circumstances of the 1970s and 1980s. He pointed to the Sixth (1980–5) and Seventh Five-year Plans (1985–90) that suffered from grave implementation problems. He also highlighted a paper he had written for the Ministry of Finance titled 'What to Do with Victory', where he had made the case that all of India's industrial controls that had evolved in the name of socialism would stifle economic growth.[60]

Singh's classmate at Nuffield College (Oxford) and St Johns College (Cambridge), the eminent economist and Columbia University professor Jagdish N. Bhagwati, shared with me that a former Indian prime minister had said Singh provided unorthodox liberal economic policy advice in the late 1970s.[61] Singh is known to have fought for the autonomy of the RBI as its governor (1982–5), a fact that earned him the displeasure of Prime Minister Rajiv Gandhi. Serious journalists have reported that his views about India's trajectory in relation to developments in the rest of the world were affected by his stint as the secretary general of the South Commission (1987–90). These were the very years during which the Cold War was drawing to an end.[62]

It should be noted that Singh's doctoral dissertation at Oxford University in 1962, which was published by Clarendon Press in 1964, provided the first compelling and detailed empirical argument that India's needed to fund its imports by increasing its exports.[63] This was a period when most development economists in India and elsewhere were arguing that import substitution was essential for industrialization.[64] Singh had taken positions that were that were clearly critical of the dominant policy paradigm in a number of ways. He had contended that a rapid increase in exports would not be possible within an overvalued exchange rate regime. His fine-grained sectoral analysis of Indian exports led him to make some observations about the positive impact of devaluation. First, sectors such as cotton textiles would become more competitive after the devaluation. Second, in sectors such as tea and jute, where demand was not adequately responsive to price, an export duty could take care of the foreign exchange loss owing to a decline in export price due to devaluation. Moreover, the impact of devaluation on commodities such as jute and manganese ore would help counter the impact of subsidies being provided by exporters in other countries. Third, he argued that the impact of devaluation would not be inflationary and that it would push government-owned producers to become more concerned about wasting resources over inappropriate imports. Finally, he believed a sensible exchange rate with export duties would be easier to administer than a system based on export subsidies.[65]

Singh bemoaned the fact that India's economic policy dismissed trade promotion. Export incentives affected only 15 per cent of India's trade. Export controls had made it difficult for exporters to negotiate long-term contracts. Singh argued against conventional wisdom and asserted that India could successfully export both raw materials and finished products to markets in developed countries. Today, almost 50 years after Singh wrote this book, it reads like a clear statement of the strategy of export-led growth that propelled rapid economic growth in Asia.[66] Nobel laureate Amartya Sen has praised Singh's scholarly contribution by stating:

> While I must not fall for the implicit self-flattery of thinking that someone who saw something I could not see must be unbelievably perceptive, I have to acknowledge Manmohan's superior wisdom. The point, however, is not so much what Manmohan Singh did 'see,' but what he could definitively establish with impeccable empirical reasoning.[67]

Singh was a convinced liberalizer despite enjoying a successful career in the government during an era of economic controls and autarkic development. In the previous chapter, we noted that devaluation was opposed in 1966 by politicians, economists, and technocrats. In 1991, a convinced prime minister, finance minister, commerce minister, and their economic team did not waste any time to take advantage of the crisis to subject Indian businesses to the competitive pressures of the world market.[68]

A key member of the executive team was P. Chidambaram, who served as minister of state for commerce in the immediate aftermath of the foreign exchange crisis in 1991. He was one of the few qualified professionals in Prime Minister Rajiv Gandhi's team of ministers. Chidambaram had served as a deputy minister in the commerce ministry (1985) and subsequently as a minister of state in the Ministry of Personnel, Public Grievances, and Pensions (1986–9), and as minister of state for internal security within the larger Ministry of Home Affairs (1986–9). He was lawyer who held a master's degree in business administration from the Harvard Business School.[69] As somebody who believed in economic reforms, Chidambaram played a critical role in initiating export orientation and deregulation, even though he was not an economist.

Chidambaram's credentials as a reformer are evident from the columns he wrote for *The Indian Express* during the period when he did not hold a ministerial portfolio—between August 2002 and March 2004. These columns were concerned with the inadequacy of economic reforms during the period when the BJP ruled as the major party within the National Democratic Alliance (NDA) coalition. His policy positions in these columns demonstrate his zeal as a reformer when he was out of power. First, given India's growing foreign exchange reserves in the new millennium, Chidambaram favoured a swifter transition to the convertibility of the Indian rupee in the capital account. Freer convertibility, he argued, would boost India's exports. Second, he was concerned that the country's regulatory environment was not conducive for foreign investment, despite the foreign investment limit having been raised above the 51 per cent level in many sectors. Third, he worried that infrastructure sectors such as power and ports remained inefficient after a decade of economic reforms.[70]

Another noteworthy figure in the economic reform team was Chakravarthi Rangarajan, an eminent technocrat with a PhD from the University of Pennsylvania, who was promoted from the position of deputy governor to governor of RBI in 1992. He had earlier taught at the University of Pennsylvania and at the Indian Institute of Management (Ahmedabad) before embarking on a career in government. Rangarajan was a firm believer in devaluation and a market-driven exchange rate for promoting India's exports. He had argued in favour of increasing the trade orientation of India's economy in the 1980s.[71]

Montek Singh Ahluwalia was another key change agent. Before serving as commerce secretary in 1991, Ahluwalia had served in the finance ministry (1979–85) and the PMO (1985–90). He was a steadfast proponent of labour-intensive export promotion as opposed to capital-intensive import substitution since his days at the World Bank in the 1970s. He worked with a group of economists, led by Holis Chenery, which was quite averse to introducing unnecessary distortions to the market.[72] Working within the framework of 'redistribution with economic growth', this group had placed greater faith in the market mechanism than economists who belonged to another camp headed by Paul Streeten and subscribed to a development idea called the 'basic needs approach'.[73] Ahluwalia, who had been a Rhodes Scholar at Oxford with a brilliant publication record, was later a major force behind the economic reforms of 1991.[74]

Ahluwalia identified problems in the Indian economy at a conference organized by the Institute of Economic Growth in Delhi in 1990. He stressed the problem of overregulation at a time when the Soviet Union was itself undergoing substantial economic deregulation. First of all, India's looming balance of payments problems required the country to obtain foreign exchange by welcoming MNCs to invest in India. This would lead to technology upgrades and engender competition. Second, the MRTP Act was not serving the purpose of making the business environment more competitive for large business houses. Third, tariff protection was a major bottleneck for productivity. Ahluwalia argued, for example, that a 100–200 per cent tariff protection for synthetic fibres in a business environment inhabited by a few Indian companies did not augur well for improving efficiency. He believed that domestic and foreign investments with high levels of tariff protection would be extremely harmful for the Indian economy in the 1990s.[75]

Ahluwalia had authored a paper within the PMO in 1990 titled 'Towards Restructuring Industrial, Trade and Fiscal Policies', in response to Prime Minister Vishwanath Pratap Singh's fascination with the Malaysian growth story after a state visit to that country. In this paper, which became infamous because it was leaked to the press, Ahluwalia had drawn up a blueprint for reform. He had pointed to the need for a 20 per cent devaluation of the Indian rupee, a reduction in tariffs, closure of inefficient public sector units, easier entry of foreign direct investment, and the removal of excessive industrial regulations on large companies.[76]

The 1980s had generated a critical mass of reforming technocrats in India. Chapter 1 notes that Indian economists who lived in the US, such as Bhagwati and Srinivasan, had articulated the most powerful critique of overregulation. The interaction between Indian economists and technocrats occurred at a time when the Indian government had begun noting its policy failures in various reports that had appeared in the 1990s. The reformers had developed a sophisticated and home-grown reform agenda because they had confronted India's peculiar policy problems in a substantial way. They were able to engage the IMF and the World Bank and move towards a policy consensus in 1991. India's reforms would not have been successful had it not been for research on policy problems and limited experiments carried out in India before the balance of payments crisis of 1991.

Other key reformers included Shankar Acharya. He held a PhD in economics from Harvard and had served the World Bank between 1971 and 1982. Upon returning to India, Acharya had served as an economic adviser in the Ministry of Finance from 1985 to 1990. In 1991, he was the chief economic adviser in the finance ministry with the rank of a secretary. Rakesh Mohan held a PhD in economics from Princeton and had served the World Bank in the 1970s and the 1980s. He served as an economic adviser in the Ministry of Industry between 1988 and 1996. Two economic advisers in the Ministry of Finance, Jayanto Roy and Arvind Virmani, secured their PhDs from the University of California at Berkeley and Harvard University, respectively, and both had served the World Bank. Virmani had worked for the Indian government since 1987 and Roy since 1989. Raja Chelliah held a PhD in economics from the University of Pittsburgh and had served the IMF as the chief of its Fiscal Analysis Division (1969–75). He became the architect of tax reforms in India after 1991.[77]

Within India's technocracy, a new consensus was forming in favour of private sector promotion and greater trade orientation during the balance of payments crisis. People that deviated from that internal consensus—such as Deepak Nayyar, the chief economic adviser to the finance minister—quit their policy role. Others such as Bimal Jalan (of the Prime Minister's Economic Advisory Council) became quite supportive of the new agenda.[78] The crisis became an excellent opportunity to give new ideas a chance.

The Silent Revolution in July 1991

India's finance minister, commerce minister, and the RBI governor defended the two-step 18 per cent devaluation of the Indian rupee on 1 July and 3 July 1991. Such was the overwhelming support for this decision that this was one of the fastest files that moved from the Ministry of Commerce to the PMO via the Ministry of Finance.[79] First, finance minister Singh defended the devaluation by pointing to the devaluation experiences of China, Russia, South Korea, and the Southeast Asian countries. He argued that devaluation was essential for promoting India's export orientation.[80] In Parliament, he argued that the devaluation in 1991 would occur in an economic context that was substantially different from the one in 1966, which was when rupee devaluation had been accompanied with inflation. India's industrial structure was far more diversified now and the country's exports were rather price-sensitive.[81] Speed was of the essence for a determined technocracy in a moment of crisis; India's industrial lobby engaged with import substitution would have opposed a policy that would increase the price of imports under normal times.

Second, commerce minister Chidambaram defended the depreciation of the rupee as a move that would improve the competitiveness of India's exports. He believed that a market-driven exchange rate, rather than export subsidies, was essential for export promotion. He stressed that the government wanted importers to become exporters rather than producers whose goods could be characterized as a substitute for imports.[82] This became clearly evident in the shift from a regime of export subsidies to 'exim scrips', which allowed an exporter to import up to 30 per cent of the value of exports.

Third, Rangarajan supported the devaluation decision based on sound policy research. First, he pointed to the success stories of China and Indonesia from December 1980 to December 1989. Both these countries had depreciated their currencies to a greater extent than India and had also managed inflation in their respective countries with considerable ease. This was intended to answer critics in the industry and the government, who thought that devaluation and a rise in import prices would spur inflation. Second, devaluation—by reducing the price of imports—would reduce the need for any export subsidy. Third, India's annual exports had grown by 6.8 per cent between 1975–6 and 1978–9, a time when the rupee had depreciated by 20 per cent. Exports had stagnated, however, between 1979 and 1985, when the value of the rupee had appreciated. Rangarajan inferred from this data that India's exports responded quite favourably to price incentives. He noted an econometric study that suggested that a 1 per cent devaluation would lead to a 0.66 per cent rise in exports. Finally, technocrats defended devaluation on the grounds that it would encourage flows of private capital into India.

Rangarajan defended the two-step devaluation on the grounds that it was important to test the market before making a decision on the second devaluation. He asserted that devaluation was only one factor that improved the economy's competitiveness and that it would need to be complemented by other industrial policies. It was under Rangarajan's stewardship of the RBI that the rupee became fully convertible in the current account for trading purposes in 1994.[83]

India's national budget of 24 July 1991 articulated the philosophy of economic change in India. It clarified that India had merely two weeks of foreign exchange remaining and was faced with an unprecedented crisis aggravated by a rise in oil prices during the Gulf War. The roots of the crisis lay in unsustainable government expenditures and the low productivity of investment, especially in the public sector. Political uncertainty between 1989 and 1991, and the failure to produce a budget in March 1991 had eroded the faith of commercial banks and non-resident Indians who had a stake in the Indian economy.[84]

The fiscal deficit had surged from Rs 384.7 billion (USD 19.99 billion) in March 1991 to Rs 520 billion (USD 27.02 billion) in July. Non-planned government expenditures had produced an exponential increase in interest payment on debt, which was consuming about 38 per cent of government revenues. The major culprits in the area of non-planned expenditures were defence spending, export subsidies, and production subsidies on items such as fertilizers and sugar. Under the new budget, these expenditures were to be curbed, reliance on direct taxes increased, and tax collection improved. Citizens with unaccounted-for wealth were to be given a one-time (tax) amnesty if they made a deposit with the National Housing Bank by 30 November 1991.[85]

India's diverse industrial base was now exposed to the forces of global competition. Competition was designed to spur the process of capital accumulation. Prior to the 1990s in India, making larger profits had been associated negatively with greed. The country's new economic path would involve expanding the role of private companies and the market mechanism in industrial development. The country also encouraged foreign investment as a way to gain access to much-needed capital and technology during a moment of financial crisis. The devaluation of the rupee and tariff reduction was designed to enliven Indian industry's competitive instincts, and government-owned companies were to be made more efficient by disinvesting 20 per cent of their equity to private investors.[86]

Resources for industrial growth had to be raised by reforming the financial sector. India would deregulate its interest rate by providing a floor rate for banks. All restrictions on debenture interest rates were removed, and tax incentives were provided for equity-linked savings schemes such as mutual funds. Non-resident Indians were offered special investment incentives. An independent Securities and Exchange Board of India (SEBI) was quickly instituted to replace the Controller of Capital Issues.[87] SEBI has now become a relatively independent regulator that has played a significant role in reforming Indian stock markets, which have since attracted substantial funds from Indian and foreign investors.

India's trade protection was also reduced quite substantially. The finance minister reduced the country's peak tariff rate from 300 per cent to 150 per cent, a decision that could lead to a revenue loss of Rs 1.3

billion (USD 50.76 million).[88] Quantitative restrictions on most capital and intermediate goods were removed. Capital-goods imports would face lower tariffs. It was hoped that tariff reduction and cheaper access to capital and intermediate goods would reduce the impact currency devaluation had on the import prices of capital goods Indian producers needed. The weighted average of total nominal tariff came down from 81.4 per cent in 1991–2 to 60.6 per cent in 1992–3, and the process continued as reforms went forward.[89]

The significant reform effort that supported the philosophy behind the union budget was the Industrial Policy of 24 July 1991.[90] Both the budget and the policy were released on the same day. This revolutionary Industrial Policy overturned four important institutional legacies that had evolved since the 1950s. First, the Industries (Development and Regulation) Act, 1951, had initiated the process of industrial licensing. Industries needed governmental permission to set up commercial activity after 1951. The government, rather than commercial enterprises, took business decisions about which company will produce which goods and at which location. This kind of intervention had kept Tata Motors, the most successful Indian automobile company today, from manufacturing cars until 1991.[91] We have noted that only 30 industries and 82 pharmaceutical products were delicensed in 1985.[92] We have described earlier how technocrats had come to view licensing as an activity that served no purpose other than earning rents for politicians and bureaucrats. The 1991 document abolished licensing for all sectors, barring a few industries where permission would still be required for strategic, environmental, or social reasons. Granting entrepreneurs freer choice in their investment decisions would boost the productivity and competitiveness of Indian manufacturing.[93]

Second, the MRTP Act, which came into effect in 1970, had increased the industrial pre-approval requirement for an Indian company that was worth Rs 200 million (USD 7.81 million) or greater. We have noted that Rajiv Gandhi had increased this limit to Rs 1 billion (USD 39.04 million).[94] Regulations that required companies to secure approval for initiating business or expanding capacity had stifled growth and engendered unproductive expenditures. The policy of July 1991 stressed that while monopolistic propensities would have to be regulated, prior approval would no longer be necessary for initiating a commercial enterprise, expanding capacity, appointing directors, or merging large firms.[95] The demise of the MRTP Act meant that the government wanted to promote competitiveness by encouraging economies of scale.

Third, India's commercial environment was rather unfavourable for multinational companies. FERA in 1974 had reduced the maximum permissible foreign equity limit in an Indian firm to 40 per cent. The Act had curbed the powers of foreign companies in their Indian subsidiaries, which had led to the exit of such firms as Coca-Cola and IBM in the 1970s. Indian companies were comfortable with keeping foreign companies out from India and this Act could not be amended in the 1980s even after a gradual process of deregulation had been initiated. The policy document of 1991 changed the basic assumptions about dealing with foreign companies by stressing the need for a more dynamic interaction between Indian and foreign companies. Foreign investment was now supposed to bring capital, technology, marketing, and management expertise to India. The new policy allowed for automatic approvals up to 51 per cent foreign equity in a large number of industries, which would give foreign companies substantially greater powers in the operation of their Indian subsidiaries.[96] It was hoped that this new arrangement would lure more foreign companies to India.

Finally, the Indian public sector had ballooned since the 1950s, highlighting the low rates of return in government-owned companies. The finance minister reported in the budget speech that sick or bankrupt private enterprises had been taken over by the government to protect employment. These enterprises had contributed to a third of the public sector's losses. This legacy of public-sector dominance necessitated examining the portfolio of public enterprises, subjecting them to competition from private companies, and withdrawing government investments from commercially viable consumer goods and services. Instead of reserving vital sectors of the economy as the exclusive preserve of the public sector, the Indian government began focusing greater attention on promoting the private sector.[97]

Washington Consensus and Economic Reforms

To what extent did the Indian plan deviate from the 'Washington Consensus' on economic reforms? The Washington Consensus, as articulated by John Williamson in 1990, included: fiscal discipline; public expenditure that would facilitate high economic returns and improve income distribution; lower taxes with a broader base; interest rate liberalization; a competitive exchange rate; trade liberalization; privatization; deregulation of the economy for private companies; and ensuring property rights. This consensus arose when Ronald Reagan and Margaret Thatcher initiated deregulation in overregulated Western economies. This Washington Consensus provided the accumulated policy expertise that international financial organizations offered when Latin American countries, reeling under a debt crisis, asked for advice in 1989. Subsequently, Williamson acknowledged that privatization without regulation and financial liberalization in East Asia might not have been such a good idea.[98] In the introduction, we have discussed how Indian economists such as Bhagwati and Srinivasan, along with other economists such Annie Krueger and Gary Becker, had exposed the problems of overregulation.

India's interactions with IMF were characterized by cooperation and India's executive director Gopi K. Arora there did not fail to point out India's domestic imperatives. IMF's executive board cleared SDR (special drawing right)[99] 468.9 million on 12 September 1991 praising the budget and the Industrial Policy Resolution (24 July 1991) but requesting substantial fiscal discipline. Even though the meeting was marked with cooperation between the Indian government and IMF, Arora noted that fiscal restraint would need to be tempered with the imperatives of an open democratic society. Privatization of loss-making public sector enterprises was considered less prudent than subjecting public companies to competition from private companies.[100] Arora maintained this position when IMF approved SDR 1.56 billion on 31 October 1991 as part of its stand-by arrangement. This was despite the views of a large number of executive directors who opined that India's fiscal correction and monetary policy needed substantial further adjustment, in spite of the bold and credible measures taken by the government on 24 July 1991.[101]

The Indian technocratic team agreed with the paradigm of deregulation and globalization, but would not accept a bitter adjustment plan in a democratic political setting. Correspondences between Indian finance minister Manmohan Singh and World Bank President Lewis T. Preston in November 1991, at the time when the bank pledged a USD 500 million structural adjustment loan to the Indian government, shows the high level of understanding that existed between the multilateral organizations and India.[102] There was substantial cooperation among the World Bank, IMF, and the donor countries that became involved with resuscitating the Indian economy.[103] The bank was sympathetic regarding the industrial deregulation that India wanted to implement within a democratic framework. Both the bank and the government noted that India's previous industrial and trade policy changes had been crafted in the context of unsustainable macroeconomic expansion. The correspondence between Singh and Preston suggest the reasons why India's economic reforms have been hailed as home-grown rather than being externally imposed reforms.[104] The difference of opinion between the World Bank and IMF, on the one hand, and Indian technocrats, on the other, about initiating policies was easy to bridge because of shared understandings about the fundamental problems ailing the Indian economy.

Both parties understood the importance of fiscal correction,[105] but they also both deemed social spending to be important. The Indian government could convince the bank about the importance of social spending within a democratic polity.[106] Various issues raised in these documents point to the validity of such an assessment. First, both sides confirmed that India's public companies had been underperforming and that bankrupt private enterprises—which were taken over by the government—were not adding any value. Both these types of public companies were contributing significantly to India's fiscal deficit. As the government moved ahead with reforms, it set up a National Renewal Fund to ensure that the cost of economic adjustment did not fall directly on the workers.[107]

The government also formed an inter-ministerial group to reform laws governing labour relations, a move that could enhance productivity.[108] Despite these efforts, the power of organized labour in India's trade unions ensured that labour laws would not be changed. Consequently, the National Renewal Fund could only be used for workers who voluntarily decided to give up their job. The promise of disinvesting 20 per cent of public enterprises to private players was singularly unsuccessful. Public sector entities, like the telecom company Bharat Sanchar Nigam Limited (BSNL), became more efficient in response to private sector competition in a business environment that promoted competition rather than due to its sale to private players (as has been discussed in Chapter 4).[109]

The government made significant progress in a number of areas where technocrats exploited the crisis and dependence on the World Bank. First, the government and the bank were well-aligned on substantial changes in industrial policy.[110] Second, trade policy reforms were quite significant, even though their pace was slower than industrial policy reforms.[111] Third, the government initiated meaningful capital market reforms.[112] The minimum lending rates for banks, for instance, were increased while restrictions on interest rates for debentures were removed. A high-powered committee was established to review all aspects of the financial system. The government also pledged that the powers of the stock market regulator would be enhanced, and SEBI evolved as a successful regulator over the years. The mutual fund industry was to be opened to the private sector. The success of India's financial sector reforms has helped the country garner substantial resources for generating its economic growth.[113]

The 24 July 1991 budget and the finance minister's letter to the World Bank on the eve of a major structural adjustment loan on 11 November of the same year both stressed the importance of India making social expenditures to alleviate the transitional costs of adjustment. It was stressed that the government had succeeded in increasing the resources allocated for elementary education, rural drinking water supply, assistance for marginal farmers, and programmes for women, children, and other marginalized sections of the society.

Industrial Lobbying and Reforms

Industry acquiesced to the trade and industrial reforms of 1991 during a moment of crisis, when both the import-substituting and export-oriented industrial sectors were in need of foreign exchange for imports. The government could not have financed these imports from its resources. Despite differences within Indian industry with respect to the quality and extent of reform, it formally supported the reform programme.[114]

The most dramatic events in the organization of Indian business was the transformation of the Association of Indian Engineering Industry (AIEI) to the Confederation of Engineering Industry (CEI) in 1986, and the subsequent rechristening of this organization as the Confederation of Indian Industry (CII) in 1992. CEI became the most influential industry organization in 1991. When it was known as the AIEI, the organization had earned a name for representing the interests of the professionally driven Indian engineering industry. Its recommendations had made an impact on the Dagli Committee Report (1979) described earlier in the chapter.[115] AIEI trade fairs had showcased the achievements of the Indian engineering industry.

Prime Minister Rajiv Gandhi's special fondness for AIEI in the 1980s had spurred a cooperative relationship between business and government. Deregulation in the 1980s had stimulated economic growth. AIEI's consultations with the government had played a key role in charting this trajectory of liberalization. In 1984, AIEI requested the government to merge the Ministry of Industry with the Ministry of Commerce. It criticized curbs on large firms' production capacity and proposed a new industrial act. AIEI members, including the organization's chief executive Tarun Das, were part of Rajiv Gandhi's first visit to Moscow in May 1985, at a time when there was no precedent for the Indian prime minister to take a business delegation on a foreign trip.[116] CEI's president J.P. Chowdari articulated a policy roadmap in April 1990 that sought to abolish industrial licensing, simplify the process of investment clearance, invite foreign investments, and improve infrastructure provision to help promote competitiveness in the Indian industry.[117]

India's 1991 balance of payments crisis was important for galvanizing even a liberally oriented CEI to accept reforms. CEI welcomed the abolition of industrial licensing, a policy measure that would ease the process of investment for Indian companies. There were a number of aspects of the reform process, however, that raised concerns within the CEI. First, it worried about higher corporate taxation and the new method of calculating depreciation, which had been reduced from 33.3 per cent to 25 per cent. These measures would increase the costs of operation. Second, the rapidity of the 1991 reforms came as a pleasant surprise to some, but there were groups within CEI that were not comfortable with opening India to global competition so quickly. While liberalization of imports was considered important, many CEI members argued that the creation of national champions should have preceded import liberalization. Other members opposed the easier entry of foreign companies into India—a protest they articulated more clearly in 1993, once the crisis had passed. Third, CEI was of the view that the proposed reduction in import duty was not adequate to cover increased import costs of inputs, owing to devaluation. These policies could hurt the competitiveness of Indian industry.[118] Prime Minister Rao reportedly told a leading business leader within CEI—Jamshed J. Irani—that there was no alternative, and the Congress government had to make bold decisions as it was not expected to last long.[119]

The CEI's concerns became an important input in the reform process despite these differences of opinion, and it made considerable efforts to support and publicize the reforms. Key technocrats such as Montek S. Ahluwalia, Rakesh Mohan, and Arvind Virmani worked closely with the CII and especially with its chief executive, Tarun Das.[120] India's 1992 budget has been called the 'Tarun Das budget'.[121] The decision to promote globalization and competitiveness worked well for the Indian industry until 1997, when the Asian financial crisis created much scepticism among CII members about globalization. Detractors blamed the liberalizers for leading them down a road that was ridden with potholes.[122]

The influence of the Federation of Indian Chambers of Commerce and Industry (FICCI), which had been India's most influential industry organization since the late 1920s, had declined considerably by 1991. FICCI had represented the interests of large Indian industrialists who had become accustomed to negotiating with the regime of industrial controls. Industrial deregulation would hurt many of these industrialists, because regulations had insulated them from domestic and international competition.[123]

FICCI seemed more reluctant to embrace reforms, although all the peak industry organizations had acquiesced to reforms during this moment of severe crisis. FICCI president S.K. Birla argued for a reduction in taxes on imports, income, and indigenously produced goods. These measures were deemed essential for countering the impact of currency devaluation on India's imports. Birla was opposed to allowing 51 per cent foreign equity in Indian companies, because he believed it would render Indian companies second-class citizens within India.[124]

FICCI documents from January and March 1991 unambiguously show that the federation was opposed to devaluation or tariff reduction that would subject Indian industry to greater competition. FICCI demanded improved conditions for exporters in a number of ways. First, it called for the duty on capital goods not produced in India to be reduced. Second, the federation was unhappy with tying foreign exchange availability with export obligations. Third, it sought the simplification of administrative procedures governing productive activities and better access to infrastructure facilities such as ports, roads, electricity, and water. Finally, it desired greater inter-ministerial policy coordination and closer interaction between government and industry.[125] The federation, in other words, was arguing for internal rather than external liberalization. FICCI secretary general D.H. Pai Panandiker reported that industry was surprised when faced with a swift removal of industrial controls.[126]

The response of Indian industry to the 1991 balance of payments crisis shows why reforms of this magnitude could not have occurred in the 1980s, despite the birth of new policy ideas during that period. The 1991 crisis empowered India's political and technocratic elite, because the country had become dependent on the World Bank and IMF for sustaining its trade. Indian industry, which was largely dependent on import substitution, needed the IMF and World Bank to help finance its imports during a moment of severe financial crisis. India's industrialists could not thwart reforms because of their dependence on multilateral organizations for the sustenance of India's imports.[127]

The Parliament

How did India's political class handle economic reforms? Parliament concerned itself with the reasons why a vote on account rather than a budget was presented on 4 March 1991.[128] The minority government of Prime Minister Chandra Shekhar (Samajwadi Janata Party–Rashtriya) and finance minister Yashwant Sinha could have sent a strong signal to the international community that India would pursue necessary economic reforms even when its politics looked rather uncertain. Their minority government depended on outside support from the Congress party. Parliament debated whether the lack of a budget was due to the Congress party's opposition at a time when a budget was essential for the ruling party's survival. Former finance minister Madhu Dandavate argued that the budget could have been presented because it is constitutionally possible to have two budget documents within the same year, assuming that some other party would come to power shortly after presenting a budget that would be opposed by the Congress party. He argued that electoral reasons forced parties to oppose a harsh budget before upcoming elections.[129]

In his memoirs, Yashwant Sinha, who was the finance minister in 1991, has described his preparation of a comprehensive budget in March 1991, which had won the approval of senior economists and technocrats such as I.G. Patel and Arjun Sengupta. Sinha's version of events suggests that Rajiv Gandhi and his emissary, Pranab Mukherjee, who had held discussions with Sinha, were convinced that this would be a harsh budget before the elections. The Congress party would not support the budget within Parliament. Consequently, Prime Minister Chandra Shekhar dissuaded finance minister Sinha from presenting the budget on 4 March 1991, hoping that this would extend his party's reign.[130]

The historic economic reforms in India after the Congress party assumed power on 21 June 1991 stimulated heated debates within Parliament. On 19 July, members of the opposition inquired why the nation had not been informed before the devaluation earlier in the month. Finance Minister Singh argued that it was a calculated decision that was essential in a moment of crisis for a variety of reasons. First, he described how India's balance of payments had deteriorated, especially after 1989, owing to government excesses such as loan waivers for farmers. Second, the previous government of prime minister Chandra Shekhar had gone to the IMF, but did not implement corrective actions. Third, the 18 per cent devaluation would discourage non-resident Indians from taking their money out of India. Finally, the devaluation would boost India's exports and discourage unnecessary imports.

Some members of parliament (MPs) worried that the devaluation of 1991 would be a failure and produce food price inflation, as the 1966 devaluation had done. The devaluations of 1966 and 1991, argued Singh, were not comparable because India in 1991 possessed a diversified industrial base and did not depend on a foreign country for import of essential food-grains. Singh urged the House to be patient for another five days until 24 July, when he would articulate the relationship between devaluation and the overall new thinking on economic development in the context of the balance of payments crisis. He worried that there was a peculiar conspiracy between the Left and Right in India that wanted to stand in the way of India's globalization and economic growth.[131]

Congress party MPs, who had secured the largest number of seats in Parliament (244 out of 545), largely supported the July budget in the debates that ensued between 30 and 31 July 1991. Congress MPs who supported the budget during this period included K.V. Thomas, Sukh Ram, and E. Ahamed. They appreciated the fact that India had to promote competitiveness, curb its budget deficit, and make a critical examination of the public sector.[132] However, many Congress party MPs that supported the budget, such as Sukh Ram, opposed the reduction in fertilizer subsidy. They argued that a rise in procurement prices of foodgrain to level the impact of a reduction in fertilizer subsidy would disadvantage small and marginal farmers; these farmers only sold a small portion of their produce. A meeting of the Congress party's parliamentarians was organized to take a balanced view of a reduction in fertilizer subsidy.[133]

India's second most powerful party in 1991 was the right-wing Hindu nationalist BJP, which held 120 out of 545 seats in Parliament. The BJP was divided in its views about the radical changes in economic policy. Leaders such as L.K. Advani and Jaswant Singh lauded the changes in industrial policy and the freeing up of domestic investment from government controls, arguing that these reforms represented a clear and necessary break from the past.[134] The foremost leader of the BJP—Atal Behari Vajpayee—seemed more sceptical about the prospect of India's globalization. First, he urged the citizenry to voluntarily give up gold in return for 10-year bonds and the allotment of prime land available in the cities. Second, Vajpayee encouraged non-resident Indians to bring gold back to India. Vajpayee said 2,000 tonnes of gold could be raised in this manner, averting the need to approach IMF. Third, unearthing unaccounted wealth for resource mobilization was suggested. Fourth, Vajpayee opposed raising more taxes from ordinary citizens, smaller hotels and restaurants, and measures that would raise the price of fibre and yarn that would hurt small-scale textiles producers. Finally, he rejected the reduction in fertilizer subsidy proposed in the budget. His concerns seemed to reflect middle-class voters' interests.[135]

The non-Marxist parties with a socialist inclination—such as the JD, with its popular support among the farmers and 'other backward classes'—opposed the budget quite fiercely. With 59 parliamentary seats, these parties were the third most powerful bloc in Parliament after the Congress and the BJP.[136] Their immediate interests were rural. Over time, these parties wanted to gain a better foothold in the urban economy through the route of reserved spots in government jobs and educational institutions.

JD leaders such as Chandrajeet Yadav vehemently opposed the proposed economic reforms. They feared that the public sector, which had played a major role in the country's development, was now being undermined. They steadfastly opposed the fertilizer subsidy reduction. They also worried about conspicuous urban consumption and India's surrender to market-friendly multilateral organizations.[137]

Left parties such as the CPI and the CPM fiercely criticized the budget. With 49 seats, they were the fourth largest bloc in Parliament. They viewed the budget as a victory of the 'troika' of non-resident Indians, multinational corporations, and the private sector. For these parties, fiscal deficit control under IMF guidance was an austerity measure that meant hardship for the poor rather than the rich. They opposed a reduction in the size of the public sector and in fertilizer subsidies.[138] Their view, expressed in an alternative package they shared with the prime minister, was to improve revenue collection and reduce India's dependence on imports.[139]

On 14 September 1991, the Finance Bill passed unanimously in Parliament as major opposition parties abstained from voting for diverse and often antagonistic reasons. This sent a strong message to the IMF and the World Bank, and increased these organizations' confidence in the durability of the government. The BJP's reasons for walking out had more to do with the interests of the middle class, while the Left parties wished for greater austerity for the middle and upper classes and less dependence on the IMF and the World Bank. The JD, whose political base comprised rich farmers, worried that the philosophy of self-reliance that had originated in the struggle for India's independence was being abandoned. Had these three powerful political forces come together against the Congress government in 1991, the Finance Bill would not have passed.[140]

Reforms and Crisis Management

India's technocrats leveraged the balance of payments crisis to bring about structural changes that dramatically increased the country's reliance on private sector and trade. The challenge was to initiate these changes in the context of hard budget constraints. On 18 January 1991, the IMF's executive board approved SDR 551.925 million under the stand-by arrangement and another SDR 716.9 million under the Compensatory and Contingency Financing Facility owing to fluctuations in oil costs. Despite this approval, members of the executive board expressed concern on the fact that India needed more radical stabilization of its fiscal situation and structural adjustment than those suggested by the politically unstable government at that time.[141] This IMF funding did not produce the radical reforms in a climate of political uncertainty that the IMF had hoped for, since a full-fledged budget could not be tabled before the House in February 1991. In the next meeting on 27 February 1991, India remained committed to approaching the IMF for an upper credit tranche stand-by arrangement and to lowering India's fiscal deficit to 6.5 per cent of the GDP, even though a full-fledged budget needed to wait for the national elections in May 1991.[142]

The IMF rewarded what it viewed as India's positive pre-budget initiatives by granting the country a USD 225 million credit on 22 July, freeing India from the need to mortgage any more of its gold.[143] It provided this financial support on the understanding that India's rupee devaluation would be accompanied by transformative changes in industrial, trade, and fiscal policies on 24 July. IMF's executive board noted the rupee devaluation and changes in monetary policy, and agreed that there had been a transformation in the 'mindset' within the Indian goverment.[144]

The industrial policy and budget of 24 July 1991—that involved the devaluation of the rupee, industrial deregulation, and changes in trade policies earlier in the month—constituted a paradigm shift in India's economic orientation. Leading US papers such as *The New York Times* and *The Washington Post* praised the initiatives. Manmohan Singh gave interviews to major newspapers and signalled a clear shift that suggested India was willing to learn from Asian tiger economies' experience of export-led growth.[145] On 30 July, Reuters reported the prospect of a USD 250 million emergency loan and further long-term funding to the tune of USD 2 billion.[146]

Two weeks later, there were reports that India and the IMF had negotiated the provisional terms of a long-term loan that would be finalized by October. Another USD 300 million IMF loan was likely by the end of August.[147] In early September, it appeared that a USD 620 million emergency loan would materialize soon, with the possibility of USD 2 billion in long-term assistance.[148] The USD 620-million loan was approved on 12 September, signalling resolution of the immediate crisis.[149] This loan was approved at a meeting of the IMF's executive board which praised India's shift in policy paradigm.[150] On 20 September, just a few days after the vote on the budget, foreign donors made aid pledges of USD 6.7 billion, surpassing expectations. Significant pledges by Japan, Germany, Great Britain, France, the US, and Sweden sent a strong signal to the business community to promote commerce with India.[151] On 26 September, Standard and Poor's upgraded India's credit rating.[152] The IMF then approved a stand-by arrangement of SDR 1.65 billion on 31 October 1991.[153] This support of the IMF, donors and the credit rating agency brought the crisis under control. The meeting of the IMF executive board on 4 December 1992 praised India for the measures taken to bring the balance of payments crisis under control.[154]

Ideas, Interests, Crisis, and Reform

Indian technocrats' growing consensus since the 1970s around new ideas favouring industrial deregulation had to confront the country's dominant political coalition of industrialists, rich farmers, and professionals during the 1980s. Ideational change resulting from policy failures was essential for the paradigmatic institutional changes that altered the basic assumptions of Indian economic policy after 1991. Prime Minister Rajiv Gandhi and the technocrats had played an important role during the 1980s by ushering in gradual changes in economic policy. Moreover, large parts of Asia had witnessed rapid economic growth by placing greater faith in private enterprise and export-led growth. Meanwhile, the Soviet Union collapsed as it was unable to sustain its autarkic industrialization driven by inefficient public enterprises.

Indian technocrats, who had initiated the process of ideational change with their economic policy research in the 1980s, played a critical role during the balance of payments crisis of 1991. Many of them had earned their economics degrees from premier American and British universities and had both worked for the World Bank and Indian government for a considerable period of time. This chapter notes, for example, that finance minister Manmohan Singh had made a more convincing case for devaluation and export promotion in his dissertation at Oxford in the early 1960s than any Indian government report did during the 1980s. Similarly, Montek S. Ahluwalia had researched the relationship between growth and redistribution at the World Bank in the 1970s. He had accurately predicted the reform path in 1990, months before India embarked on a conditional relationship with the IMF.

This chapter shows that ideas favouring deregulation led to gradual policy changes in the 1980s that empowered India's business class. The period leading up to 1989 was one where the government increased private businessmen's privileges without subjecting them to the rigours of international competition. The period between 1989 and 1990 witnessed the emergence of a political coalition that continued gradual industrial deregulation within a closed economy and began to spend considerably greater resources on the powerful farming community. New ideas and the interests of the dominant coalition within Indian politics led to the expansion of farm subsidies, which was a recipe for uncontrolled fiscal expansion.

India was at a tipping point. A significant number of technocrats knew that deregulation and globalization was the way to go. But the country's dominant political coalition was blocking this reform initiative. When the fiscal crisis met with an exogenous shock due to oil price increases during the Gulf War, India's autarkic industrialization—which was dependent on imports, financing from Western commercial banks, and deposits from non-resident Indians—could no longer be sustained. Rating agencies declared India un-creditworthy, and India opted for conditional financing from the IMF when it had few other options.

India could either have used this opportunity in 1991 to bring about paradigmatic institutional changes or it could have beaten a temporary policy retreat, as had done during the 1966 crisis. India opted for the former because of the prime minister's and technocrats' determination to make virtue of necessity at a time when elements of the dominant coalition from the industrial and professional class would acquiesce to far-reaching institutional changes. Norms such as industrial deregulation displaced the idea that the public sector would dominate the economy within a policy framework where private companies needed to be regulated. Furthermore, India's devaluation and reduction in customs duties signalled the advent of a new economic orientation that would depend to a greater extent on export promotion. These were bold decisions based on a careful evaluation of past policy failures.

India's technocratic team used the country's dependence on the IMF to require the Indian industry to subject itself to the discipline of greater competition. The Indian industry needed foreign exchange, and there was no means by which it could obtain this indispensable resource from the government without an agreement with the IMF. Synergistic issue linkage among India's executive branch, industrial class, and the IMF ensured that options that had not been on the bargaining table during domestic budget struggles were now possible in a new situation that involved domestic and international actors.[155] This chapter has described how professional elements within the business class supported the government in this moment of crisis, despite internal differences about the efficacy of such policies. This chapter also suggests that while India's dominant political coalition was a major impediment to economic reforms, Indian industry adjusted to the pressures of international competition when a determined technocracy exploited a financial crisis to discipline it.

India's relationship with the IMF and World Bank reflected a mutual understanding where multilateral agencies did not require India to make adjustments that were not politically feasible. Two examples illustrate this point. First, India could not reduce subsidies on such items as fertilizers and power, because of rich farmers' political clout. Second, India's trade unions, which largely comprised a class of professionals and workers who earned a decent wage and made up about 8 per cent of the country's workforce, also prevailed over the adjustment programme. Notably, labour laws could not be reformed. The multilateral organizations understood that India was a poor country and a democracy, where a decline in public spending would have disastrous political consequences.

The Indian Parliament responded favourably to a home-grown strategy of economic adjustment. Even though the Hindu nationalist BJP desired more benefits for the middle class, the farmer-oriented JD raised its voice against the urban elite-oriented reforms guided by multilateral agencies; parties on the Left called for greater austerity rather than the rise of private capital and trade, and all these parties abstained from voting for the budget. This was perhaps possible because industry and the professional class had acquiesced to change, and the concerns of the rich farmers and organized labour had been reasonably respected in the budget.

While it is impossible to perform perfectly controlled experiments in social science, comparing the responses to India's balance of payments crises in 1966 and 1991 show the conditions under which institutional change was likely to become possible in India. In 1966, unlike in 1991, the country's technocrats were not convinced that export-led growth and industrial deregulation was the best path for India's development. The government's response to external pressure for industrial reform in 1966 was the exact opposite of the government's response to similar pressures in 1991. Not only did India eschew industrial deregulation and export-led growth during the first crisis in the 1960s—it embarked on an era of nationalization of private-sector assets and stringent controls on Indian industry between 1969 and 1971. Yet, a combination of new ideas and financial crises can produce institutional change in pluralistic polities like India, where social coalitions have to be confronted before an institutional change can happen.

This chapter demonstrates the power of the tipping-point model of economic change, where ideational changes within the technocracy were necessary for institutional change. Changes within India's executive–technocratic team produced gradual policy shifts in the 1980s, and prepared the country for substantial deregulation and globalization at the time of a balance of payments crisis in 1991. Politics also needed to change for certain ideas to take hold. Endogenous changes in India's political system enabled the country's economic policy team to engage constructively with the IMF, and the multilateral organizations responded in a manner that was appropriate for dealing with a democratic political system. In addition, the Indian government used its dependence on the IMF as a prod to discipline the Indian industry towards more market-oriented reforms. Consequently, an exogenous shock in 1991, building on slow-moving processes of endogenous change in the previous decade, produced India's paradigm shift in 1991.

Notes

1. Institutional change constitutes a change in principles or norms that undergird policies. A few seminal accounts of institutions and institutional change include Hall (1993: 275–96); North and Weingast (1989: 803–32); Ruggie (1983). For a detailed discussion, see Chapter 1.

2. See Bardhan (1984: 40–53). Other accounts that suggest that the Indian state was penetrated by powerful social actors, include Evans (1995); Herring (1999: 306–34); Kaviraj (1997: 45–87); Rudolph and Rudolph (1997: 177–86); Varshney (2007: 146–64); Weiner (1986: 596–610).

3. See Bardhan (1984: 40–5).

4. Ibid.: 44–51, 54–7. The backward caste groups are located between upper castes and the most oppressed scheduled castes in the Indian social spectrum. Even though some members of this social group are very poor and own very little land, a substantial number of them benefited from land reforms when tenant farmers were converted to owner cultivators. See Rudolph and Rudolph (1987: 333–92). The backward caste groups constitute 35–40 per cent of the Indian population. On the rise of backward caste groups and the Janata Party, see Jaffrelot (1988). The Conclusion chapter in this book elaborates the political power of the farmers in some detail.

5. See Jaffrelot (1988: 51–3, 57–9, 62–4).

6. See Jaffrelot (1988: 60–74); Joshi and Little (1994: 180–2); Mukherji (2007: 26–8).

7. See Kohli (2006: 1,254–8); Mukerji (2007: 49–53); Mukherji (2007: 125–6, 2009: 87–8); Nayar (2006: 1,886, 2006a: 10–3).

8. See Panagariya (2008: 129–56).

9. See Frankel (2005: 113–55); Hanson (1966: 123–70); Mukherji (2009: 83–6).

10. See Government of India (July 1980: 2–3).

11. See Sengupta (December 1984).

12. See Government of India (12 April 1995: 8–10).

13. MRTP, 1969, regulated the production, location, and variety of commercial decisions of all companies with assets greater than Rs 200 million, and FERA, 1973, had reduced the permissible foreign equity limit in Indian companies from 51 per cent to 40 per cent. Industrial licensing, or government permissions to initiate business, had begun in 1951 with the legislation of the Industrial Development and Regulation Act. See Dagli (May 1979: i–vii).

14. See Government of India (1980: 8).

15. See Dhar 1990; Patel (1987: 216–8). On the misuse of the MRTP Act by an insider within the central government, see Paranjpe (1986: 59–77).

16. See Dagli (1979: xvii–xix).

17. See Acharya (1988: 300–9); Government of India (1986: 60–4).

18. For details on his views, see Lakshmi Kant Jha (1986). I learned about this report from Kohli (1989: 308), and from a Personal interview with Montek Singh Ahluwalia, deputy chairman, Planning Commission, in New Delhi in May 2010.

19. See Alexander (1978: 1–4, 68–72); Hussain (1984: 81–3).

20. See Alexander (1978: 71–4); Hussain (1984: 84–95).

21. See Narasimhan (April 1985).

22. I am assuming a conversion rate of Rs 12.5 to a USD. See http://www.tradingeconomics.com/india/currency (accessed 12 January 2012).

23. See Denoon (1988: 51–2); Gwin and Veit (1985: 79–98); Kohli (1989: 1,251–74); Manor (1985: 30–44); Panagariya (2008: 80–93); Rubin (1985: 942–57); Tendulkar and Bhavani (2007: 58–71).

24. See Kohli (1991: 330–3).

25. See Chhibber (1995: 74–96); Mitra (1991: 390–413).

26. See Joshi and Little (1994: 226).

27. See Srinivasan (2011: 41–2); Mukherji (2007: 127–8).

28. See, for example, Prime Minister Vishwanath Pratap Singh's speech in Singh (1990: 6–7).

29. On the budget of 1985 under finance minister Singh, see Rubin (1985: 947–50).

30. Newspapers have reported that a Congress government may have approached the IMF and pursued fiscal discipline, an idea that was not pursued by the National Front government. See Housego (1990); Murthy (1990).

31. The Janata Party was an anti-Congress coalition that came to power in 1977. This was the first time the Congress party had lost the election at the central level. See Frankel (2005: 548–625).

32. See Butler, Lahiri, and Roy (1997: 149–53); Frankel (2005: 682–3).

33. On the electoral significance of the 'other backward classes', see Frankel (1997: 370–82); Rudolph and Rudolph (1987: 312–92); Varshney (2000: 8–10); Jaffrelot (2000: 8–108).

34. On the rise of this pro-farmer coalition, see Gupta (1998: 33–105); Jaffrelot (2000: 86–108); Varshney (1998: 81–145).

35. See Butler, Lahiri, and Roy (1997: 153–4).

36. See Hazarika (1990); Mishra (1,256–8).

37. See Sharma (1990).

38. See Singh (1990).

39. See Panagariya (2008: 99–100, 455–9); Tarrant (1990).

40. See Joshi and Little (1994: 114, 149, 189); Mukherji (2007: 128–9).

41. See Bhaduri and Nayyar (1996: 29); Clark and Lakshmi (2003: 288–9); Joshi and Little (1994: 67).

42. See Bhaduri and Nayyar (1996: 29); Joshi and Little (1994: 67).

43. On the consequences of Rajiv Gandhi's assassination, see Housego (1991); Miller (1991).

44. See Bhaduri and Nayyar (1996: 28–9).

45. See Sinha (2007: 22–4).

46. See the website of Prime Minister's Office, http://pmindia.nic.in/pm_rao.htm, for a detailed curriculum vitae of P.V. Narasimha Rao (accessed 13 April 2011).

47. For a detailed curriculum vitae of Prime Minister Manmohan Singh, who was the finance minister in 1991, see http://pmindia.nic.in/pm_manmohan.htm (accessed 13 April 2011).

48. See Bhattacharya (1991). Montek Singh Ahluwalia, the deputy chairman of the Planning Commission was the commerce secretary at that time, also confirmed this view (author interview, New Delhi, 5 January 2005).

49. See *The Economic Times* Editorial (1991a); Seshan (1991); Tarrant (1991). This was among the fastest decisions that were ever taken within the Government of India, according Montek S. Ahluwalia (author interview, 5 January 2005, New Delhi).

50. It is not surprising that India's trade to GDP ratio, which is a good measure of India's globalization, remained constant at 13 per cent between 1980 and 1990. The author gathered this data from *The World Development Indicators*, which is a database of The World Bank. Date of access 15 April 2011.

51. See Naqvi (1991).

52. See Bhaduri and Nayyar (1996: 29).

53. See Aggarwal and Mukherji (2008: 225–6).

54. See Kaul (2005: 43–88); Sridharan (1996: 33–162).

55. See Mukherji (2008: 171–6); Tan and Mun (January 2009: 25–41).

56. On the contribution of Prasanta Chandra Mahalanobis to Indian planning, see Byres (1998: 41–50); Kudaisya (2009: 960–8).

57. On the impact of the Cold War on India's foreign policy, see Ganguly and Mukherji (2011: 18–59); Srinivasan (2011: 43–6).

58. I am grateful to the late Prime Minister P.V. Narashimha Rao for these insights (author interview, New Delhi, February 2001). See Katyal (1991). I am grateful to Montek S. Ahluwalia, India's commerce secretary in 1991, for elaborating on the significance and conviction of P.V. Narasimha Rao in 1991 (author interview, 5 January 2005, New Delhi).

59. See Bhattacharya (2011). Several senior technocrats have also shared the depth of Rao's conviction and his support for reforms.

60. I am grateful to Manmohan Singh for sharing his personal insights with me (author interview, New Delhi, 8 August 1997). See also, Thakurta (1991: 34–7).

61. I am grateful to Jagdish Bhagwati for sharing his views about Manmohan Singh (author interview, New Delhi, 14 November 1997). See also, Bhagwati (1998: 23–4, 35–6).

62. See Rajghatta (1992: 9–10). The South Commission had been established to examine whether economic cooperation among developing countries would constitute the optimal pathway for development.

63. Dr Manmohan Singh enjoyed a stellar academic record. He stood first in the Intermediate, BA (Honours), and MA examinations in Punjab University, and secured an economics tripos from Cambridge with first class honours. For details, see the website of the Prime Minister's Office http://pmindia.nic.in/meet.htm (accessed 13 April 2011).

64. See Bhagwati (2007: 36–9); Cullather (2007: 73–8).

65. His doctoral dissertation was published by Clarendon Press. See Singh (1964: v–vii, 323–6).

66. See Singh (1964: 337–51).

67. See Sen (1998: 81).

68. Some who argued that Singh had enjoyed an excellent career in government during the height of import-substituting industrialization in India could, therefore, not be convinced about the radical changes in policy that he was about to implement. His college mate at Nuffield College (Oxford) and St Johns College (Cambridge), the eminent economist and University professor Bhagwati, explained to me how he had always had a mind of his own on policy matters. Prime Minister Moraji Desai had shared with professor Bhagwati in the last 1970s, that Manmohan Singh had a mind of his own (author interview, New York, 14 November 1997).

69. A slightly dated curriculum vitae of the current home minister is available on the Ministry of Finance website, http://financeminister.gov.in/fm_profile.html (accessed 6 December 2013).

70. See Chidambaram (2007: 33–46, 51–8).

71. Chakravarthi Rangarajan serves as the chairman of the Prime Minister's Economic Advisory Council and his profile is available on the council's website, http://eac.gov.in/aboutus/chpro.htm (accessed 6 December 2013). For his views during the 1980s, see Rangarajan (1981: 17–61, 1987: 702–5, 2010: 100–16).

72. See Ahluwalia (1974: 73–88).

73. See Streeten et al. (1981).

74. Ahluwalia is the deputy chairman of the Planning Commission. A list of his publications is available on the commission's website, http://planningcommission.nic.in/aboutus/history/msapro.htm (accessed 20 April 2011). Also see Acharya and Mohan (2010: 1–5).

75. See Khusro et al. (1990: 87–104).

76. See Shastri (1997: 43–44).

77. For a quick and ready reference to the backgrounds of these different individuals, see Sengupta (2009: 208–10). I have also benefited from personal interviews with Rakesh Mohan (Mumbai, 3 January 2005), Shankar Acharya (New Delhi, 5 January 2006), and Arvind Virmani (New Delhi, 9 January 2006).

78. I am grateful to senior technocrats for this insight. Also see, Baru (1991).

79. I am grateful to a key player in 1991 for this insight.

80. See Thakurta (1991: 35).

81. Lok Sabha Debates (1991a: 1–10).

82. See Thakurta (1991a: 54–5); and (1991: 12–16).

83. See Rangarajan (1991: 905–9, 2010: 100–8).

84. See Lok Sabha Debates (1991b: 271–5).

85. Ibid.: 283–7.

86. Ibid.: 275–7.

87. Ibid.: 278–1.

88. Ibid.: 315.

89. See Tendulkar and Bhavani (2007: 116–25).

90. See Government of India (1991: 1–20).

91. On the Industries (Development and Regulation) Act, 1951, and the subsequent Industrial Policy Resolution (1956), which imposed controls on Indian industry, see Frankel (2005: 94, 129–39); Kudaisya (2003: 304–18); Panagariya (2008: 31–41).

92. See Panagariya (2008: 81–5).

93. See Government of India (1991: 7–8).

94. See Panagariya (2008: 83).

95. See Government of India (1991: 14–15).

96. Ibid.: 9–11.

97. Ibid.: 11–14. A comprehensive statement on the challenge of economic reforms can be found in Singh (1996).

98. For a discussion on the Washington Consensus, see Srinivasan (2000: 265–70); Williamson (2000: 251–64).

99. SDR stands for special drawing right, which represents the claim to currency held by IMF member countries for which they can be exchanged. It is defined as a weighted basket of four major currencies: US dollar, British pound, Japanese yen, and the euro.

100. See IMF (1991c: 12, 30).

101. See IMF (1991d: 54–6).

102. See World Bank (1991). This document was accessed from the Parliament library in New Delhi, which is open to Indian citizens. Finance minister Manmohan Singh's letter of development policy (11 November 1991) is an annex within the same document. This is an important document because it reflects how far the government had moved in the direction desired by the IMF and the World Bank after the policy changes that were initiated in July 1991.

103. See World Bank (1991: 38-39). The document clearly suggests that the World Bank and IMF worked closely to create a stabilization and structural adjustment package for India.

104. Indian policymakers such as Montek S. Ahluwalia (author interview, New Delhi, 5 January 2005) and Rakesh Mohan (author interview, Mumbai, 3 January 2005) have stressed the importance of country ownership of the Indian programme. Ahluwalia also served as director of IMF's Independent Evaluation Office between 2001 and 2004. On country ownership of the IMF programmes, see Khan and Sharma (2003: 227–48). On the country ownership of another India-IMF programme, see Choudhry et al. (2004: 59–81).

105. See World Bank (1991: 5–6, 47–8).

106. Ibid.: 22–3, 58.

107. Ibid.: 20–3, 54–5.

108. Ibid.: 60.

109. On BSNL's improved efficiency as a result of competition from the private sector, see Mukherji (2006: 57–94).

110. See World Bank (1991: 1–20).

111. Ibid.: 11–7, 50–2, 61–3.

112. For an account of political opposition to these reforms, see Echeverri-Gent (2010: 328–59).

113. See Echeverri-Gent (2010: 17–20, 55–6, 64–5). To get a sense of the significant gradual home-grown reforms in the governance of India's stock market many years after the involvement of the IMF had ended, see Echeverri-Gent (2010: 329–58), and also see the chapter on telecommunications in this book.

114. This was shared separately by Dhruv Sawhney, president of the CEI in 1991 (telephone interview, Singapore, 10 February 2010), and D.H. Pai

Panandiker, secretary general of the Federation of the Indian Chambers of Commerce and Industry (FICCI) in 1991 (author interview, New Delhi, 2 June 2009).

115. See Dagli (1979a).

116. See Kantha and Ray (2006: 139–56); Kochanek (2007: 424–7); Pederson (2000: 268–71); Sinha (2005: 1–27). I am grateful to Tarun Das, chief mentor of CII and its Secretary General in 1991, for sharing his views (author interview, New Delhi, 2 June 2009). I also benefited from the views of Dhruv Sawhney, president of CEI at the time of the balance of payments crisis in 1991 (telephone interview, Singapore, 10 February 2010).

117. See Chowdari (1990).

118. On CEI's issues with policy change, see *The Hindu* Editorial (1991b).

119. See Kantha and Ray (2006: 172).

120. Ibid.: 173–5. The importance of the reform process was publicized a few years later in a report—CII (1994). I also benefited from interviews with Das (author Interview, New Delhi, 3 June 2009) and Ahluwalia (author interview, New Delhi, 5 January 2005).

121. See Kochanek (1974: 424–5).

122. Interview with Tarun Das (author interview, New Delhi, 2 June 2009).

123. See Kochanek (1995–6: 529–50).

124. See Bajpai (1991); *The Hindu* Editorial (1991, 1991c).

125. See FICCI (1991: 338–51).

126. See Krishnan (1991); Varam (1991). I am grateful to Panandiker, secretary general of FICCI in 1991, for these insights (author interview, New Delhi, 2 June 2009).

127. All the industry associations formally supported the reform programme, according to Dhruv Sawhney, president of CEI in 1991 (telephonic interview, Singapore, 10 February 2010). For the view that Indian industry was not the author of the economic reforms programme, see Chibber and Usmani (2013: 208–10).

128. A vote on account is Parliament's vote on the resources that an interim government is likely to draw from the consolidated fund of India before an impending election. The budget, on the other hand, is a statement of the financial position of an administration for a definite period of time, based on estimates of expenditures during the period and proposals for financing them. A full budget thus spells out both the manner in which the money is to be spent and how it is to be raised.

129. See *Lok Sabha Debates* (1991: 831–5). The Congress party's opposition to the budget mattered a great deal because the government was a minority coalition, which needed the support of the Congress from outside to get a budget passed and remain in power.

130. See Sinha (2007: 1–24).

131. See *Lok Sabha Debates* (1991a: 1–10).

132. See *Lok Sabha Debates* (1991c: 285–305, 264–71, 303–10).

133. See *Lok Sabha Debates* (1991c: 266); Naqvi (1991a); Naqvi (1991); Sharma (1991); *The Hindu* Editorial (1991d).

134. See *The Economic Times* Editorial (1991b).

135. See *The Times of India* Editorial (1991).

136. On the political rise of the 'other backward castes' in India, see Jaffrelot (2000: 86–108).

137. See *Lok Sabha Debates* (1991c: 288–305).

138. On the combined opposition of political parties to the fertilizer subsidy, see Naqvi (1991b).

139. See Dasgupta (1991); *The Economic Times* Editorial (1991); *The Hindu* Editorial (1991a).

140. See Khosla (1991); Kumbhkarni (1991).

141. See International Monetary Fund (1991).

142. See International Monetary Fund (1991a).

143. See Reuters News (1991).

144. See International Monetary Fund (1991b).

145. See Chellaney (1991); Hazarika (1991).

146. See Reuters News (1991a).

147. See Reuters News (1991b).

148. See Reuters News (1991c).

149. See Reuters News (1991d).

150. See International Monetary Fund (1991c).

151. See Reuters News (1991e).

152. See Agence-France Press (1991).

153. See International Monetary Fund (1991d) .

154. See International Monetary Fund (1992: 3–54).

155. See Putnam (1988: 427–60).

4 Institutional Change and Competitiveness*
The Boom in Telecommunications

H ow DID THE INSTITUTIONAL FRAMEWORK governing the delivery of telecommunications services in India become transformed within the country's pluralistic political setting?[1] Institutions of economic governance represent a set of formal rules based on principles of governance that provide incentives for certain kinds of behaviour and disincentives for other kinds of behaviour. These rules are backed by third-party monitoring and enforcement mechanisms. For example, one principle of economic governance embedded in institutional rules could suggest that government monopoly is optimal for efficient service delivery in telecommunications. Another technocratic view could provide a compelling logic for promoting regulated competition among a few players.[2] If institutions represent an industry's rules of the game, rules have certain principles embedded in them, then a movement from rules based on government monopoly to ones that promote competition would constitute institutional change.

This chapter addresses key issues in institutional change, such as how evolutionary change travelling along a certain institutional path becomes redirected towards a new path. For example, rules

* This chapter has been adapted from Rahul Mukherji, 2009, 'Interests, Wireless Technology and Institutional Change: From Government Monopoly to Regulated Competition in Indian Telecommunications', *Journal of Asian Studies*, vol. 68, no. 2, pp. 491–517.

facilitating further government sector expansion or enhanced economic liberalization constitute movements along the same path, but a shift from government monopoly to regulated competition involving private players represents a movement in the direction of a new institutional path.[3] Other key questions include: How are new ideas embedded within certain parts of the state, ideas that ultimately succeed in changing the status quo? Are these changes in ideas driven by a rational assessment of material conditions—such as economic crises and technological change that make it difficult to sustain the old ideas[4]—or by the powerful appeal of the new ideas themselves?[5] Are changes in material conditions, which could affect a change in an institutional path, the result of exogenous shocks or an accumulation of endogenous processes, or both?[6]

This chapter argues that new policy ideas in the 1980s, economic crises, and technological developments led to the evolution of new interests in India, interests that are central to understanding the institutional change that facilitated the birth and consolidation of India's telecommunications regulator. India's fiscal crisis, which stemmed from the country's 1991 balance of payments shock and the Gulf War-driven oil price shock, was the major reason that influential parts of the government located within the PMO and the Ministry of Finance decided to promote private investment in telecommunications services, in spite of the displeasure of the DoT.[7] This process was aided by technological developments in the relatively less capital-intensive area of GSM cellular telephony,[8] which helped undermine the power of DoT. Despite political and commercial interests favouring change, new ideas were embedded within amended laws through an evolutionary and intensely conflict-ridden process. It was not easy to undermine the DoT's monopoly over the telecommunications service provision in India.

Institutional change involving the birth and empowerment of India's telecom regulator resembled a process that is aptly called 'layering'. As discussed in Chapter 1, layering connotes the mechanism of adding new elements to an existing institution whose status changes gradually over time. Layering facilitates institutional change through differential growth of the new institution, which is set up on the edges of the old one. A subordinate institution could rise to prominence as powerful actors defect to the new institution, undermining certain institutional aspects of the old one. In India, while the policy role of the DoT within the communications ministry remained intact, the need for a level-playing field for private service providers required the development of an independent regulator, which would protect private players from government predation. DoT—which was simultaneously a policymaker, a regulator, and a service provider—had a strong incentive to rig the rules of the game in favour of government-owned telecommunications companies. Inter-bureaucratic struggles ensued, aided by inputs from private telecom companies, which led to the birth and consolidation of the Telecom Regulatory Authority of India (TRAI) and the Telecom Dispute Settlement Appellate Tribunal (TSDAT). This ensured that DoT would have to give up its regulatory powers over time, a process that contributed to a private sector-aided telecommunications revolution in India. This story resembles another account of layering, when opponents of the public pension system in the United States (US) orchestrated the expansion of individual privatized retirement accounts.[9]

The story of crises and institutional evolution is a never-ending one. This chapter ends with the most recent crisis in Indian telecommunications, which was driven by the controversial decisions of the former minister of communications and information technology, A. Raja. The government is still seized with the scam that enveloped the issuance of 2G cellular licences in January 2008, and Prime Minister Manmohan Singh reiterated the need for initiating legislation granting regulators greater independence and accountability during his 2011 Independence Day dspeech.

Despite several investment crises in India, the results of the country's institutional transformation to private investment have been quite remarkable. Indian telecommunications companies are now among the most efficient telecommunications service providers in the world. The number of staff required to service 1,000 direct exchange lines in India came down from more than 70 in 1990 to just five in 2003. Cell phone connections increased from 13 million subscriptions to 35 million subscriptions between 2002 and 2004. India's New Telecom Policy of 1999 set the goal of achieving a teledensity target of seven telephone lines per 100 people by 2005, and that target was reached ahead of schedule in 2003.[10] India was consistently adding more than 11 million new wireless subscribers per month between June 2010 and June 2011, and the sector expanded by 34 per cent during the course of that 12-month period. There were 886 million telephone connections in India at the end of June

2011, with an overall teledensity of about 74 connections per 100 people. The rate of growth of rural connections surpassed the rate for urban areas during this period.[11] The average revenue per Indian GSM cell phone user for a unit of calling time was less than that of a Chinese user, even though Indian users spend more time talking. The Indian mobile industry, which was the main growth sector in Indian telecommunications, had become more efficient than its Chinese counterpart.[12]

Key elements of the story of regulatory evolution in India, described in the subsequent sections of this chapter, are worth noting. First, the political costs associated with institutional change were significant. Second, endogenous ideational changes driven by the 1991 balance of payments crisis as well as the exogenous price shock driven by the Gulf War created interests within the PMO and Ministry of Finance that opposed the DoT's propensity to retain its monopoly. Over time, the private sector acquired a substantial voice in the country. Third, the evolution of GSM cellular technology aided private players because they had bet on this sector expanding, whereas the government had initially ignored it. Moreover, GSM technology was less capital-intensive and required fewer government permissions compared with the laying of telephone lines across the length and breadth of India. Last, but not least, institutional change favouring regulation enhanced the relative power of private actors. Institutions stabilize power relations, and institutional change brings about changes in power relations.

This chapter will trace the historical process that facilitated regulation and private investment in Indian telecommunications. Tracing a historical process has advantages over analysing snapshots of history. As suggested in Chapter 1, slow-moving processes such as fiscal constraints and technological change make an impact that can only be captured in an incremental way until they reach a tipping point. They create interests that become empowered over a period of time.[13] Change can become more abrupt when it reaches a threshold or tipping point. An exogenous shock is likely to have a greater impact on change when the system reaches a tipping point. In this story, one needs to explain how interests are born and over time and become substantially empowered to transact institutional change. The Indian case of telecom de-monopolization resembles a mechanism described above as layering, which involves creating a new institution—in this case, a regulator—along the edges of an old one and allowing it to grow differentially.

New Ideas about Telecommunications
and Development in the 1980s

The arrival of new developmental ideas arising out of policy puzzles, highlighted in Chapters 1 and 3, was critical for the transformation in Indian telecommunications. The government reformed its view about telecommunications services in the 1980s from one that considered it a service for the elite to one that visualized telecommunication's central role in economic development. This section describes how prime ministers Indira Gandhi (1980–4) and Rajiv Gandhi (1984–9) sought to reform telecom services in India. These reforms were stalled, however, when the DoT pushed back against proposals by the PMO. These early attempts at reform laid the foundations for the subsequent success in India's telecom sector after the balance of payments shock in 1991.

In the early 1980s, Indira Gandhi's government began to question the role accorded to telecommunications in India's development. The Department of Electronics, which reported to the PMO, urged the Ministry of Posts and Telegraphs to accord a higher priority to telecommunications and directed the ministry to use advanced switch technology and user equipment, which was considered elitist at that time. A committee headed by H.C. Sarin emphasized the need to give telecommunications greater prominence in relation to postal services. The Sarin Committee recommended the establishment of two departments within the same ministry—one that would be dedicated to postal services and another that would deal with telecommunications. A separate department dedicated to telecommunications would enable the sector to receive greater attention. In addition, Indian Telephone Industries Limited, a government-owned company that manufactured telephone equipment under the supervision of the Ministry of Industries, was moved to the Ministry of Posts and Telegraphs.[14]

The executive branch's new views were consolidated and implemented under the premiership of Rajiv Gandhi (1984–9).[15] A number of policy decisions highlighted the government's resolve to harness telecommunications for engendering efficiency. First, the Centre for Development of Telematics (C-DOT), which enjoyed substantial autonomy from the Ministry of Communications, was established in August 1984 soon after Rajiv Gandhi became prime minister. Under the leadership of Sam Pitroda, the centre manufactured the celebrated

Rural Automatic Exchange Switches (RAX), which competed with the best telecom switches produced in India and abroad. These switches were licensed to private companies for production. This constituted the private sector's first-ever entry into Indian telecommunications. C-DOT switches continue to serve more than 50 per cent of the fixed-line telecom infrastructure in India. The ministry resented that C-DOT research surpassed the research in the ministry's own Telecommunications Research Centre.[16]

Second, the Ministry of Posts and Telegraphs was divided into two departments—DoT and the Department of Posts—in 1985.[17] The government planned to more than double its investment in telecommunications between the Fifth Five-year Plan (1980–5) and the Sixth Five-year Plan (1985–90).[18] Both these measures were in accordance with the Sarin Committee's recommendations.

Third, corporate entities were created out of government departments and given autonomy to pursue profit and efficiency with less political interference. A largely government-owned corporate entity, the Mahanagar Telephone Nigam Limited (MTNL), was created in 1986 to serve the metropolitan areas of Delhi and Mumbai. Rajiv Gandhi had wanted commercially oriented telecom operations for more Indian cities, but had to settle for opening Delhi and Mumbai to competition, due to strong opposition from DoT employees. The creation of MTNL, although still largely owned by the government, constituted a separation between the telecom policymaker (DoT) and the service provider (MTNL, which enjoyed greater autonomy from the government). As a service provider, the MTNL was driven by considerations of profitability. Similarly, another government-owned autonomous corporate entity— the Videsh Sanchar Nigam Limited (VSNL)—was created out of a government department (Overseas Communications Service) in 1986 to serve the international long-distance sector.[19]

DoT workers, who served the entire country outside of the metropolitan areas of Delhi and Mumbai, vehemently opposed the corporatization of MTNL. These 380,000 DoT employees also opposed the granting of a performance bonus of Rs 100 (USD 3.90) to 70,000 MTNL employees in 1990. The DoT urged Prime Minister Chandra Shekhar to merge MTNL with DoT so as to remove any discrimination between the performance and rewards of the two companies. This was the state of the telecom sector on the eve of the balance of payments crisis in

1991. The PMO had understood the centrality of the telecommunications services for India's development, but DoT, which desired to retain its absolute command over policymaking and service provision, fiercely resisted the PMO's efforts in this regard.[20]

Initiating Competition: The National Telecom Policy (1994)

This section will demonstrate the conflict over telecommunications between the PMO and the Ministry of Finance on the one hand, and the DoT on the other.[21] Faced with an unsustainable fiscal crisis from the mid-1980s onward, the PMO and the Ministry of Finance wanted to promote private investment in telecommunications services. India's fiscal deficit shot up from 5.4 per cent of gross domestic product (GDP) between 1975 and 1980 to 10 per cent of GDP between 1985 and 1990. In the previous chapter, we discussed how India's internal fiscal crisis contributed to the balance of payments crisis of 1991. During that year, the country was exposed to an exogenous shock caused by the Gulf War. It was of no greater importance than the oil shocks of 1973 and 1979, but since India's fiscal situation was more precarious in the 1990s, it contributed substantially to the country's balance of payments crisis.[22]

The PMO and the finance ministry, therefore, wanted the Indian government to withdraw from commercially viable sectors after 1991. Between the onset of the balance of payments crisis in 1991 and the articulation of the National Telecom Policy (NTP) in 1994, the Indian government was only able to promote private initiative in areas that the DoT thought were not commercially viable. Moreover, the DoT did not permit the establishment of an independent telecom regulator during this period. The DoT was the policymaker, regulator, and service provider all in one, which loaded the regulatory game strongly in favour of government monopoly.

The previous section demonstrated how the PMO under Rajiv Gandhi (October 1984–December 1989) had played a crucial role in shifting policy attention to telecommunications in the 1980s, but it could neither privatize the government's business nor corporatize substantial portions of it.[23] Faced with the prospect of an impending balance of payments crisis, the PMO, under the premiership of Chandra Shekhar (November 1990–June 1991), set up a high-level committee on the reorganization of the telecom department. The committee was also charged with responding to the DoT's demand that it be merged with MTNL. The chairman of this committee—M.B. Athreya, a PhD in business from the Harvard Business School—had previously served as a professor at the Indian Institute of Management in Calcutta (Kolkata). The Athreya Committee submitted its report in March 1991, a couple of months before India went to the International Monetary Fund because of its desperate balance of payments crisis in June. The committee formulated a plan for the entry of private Indian corporations into the telecommunications business. These recommendations—which had the support of the PMO and finance ministry under prime ministers Chandra Shekhar and Narasimha Rao (June 1991–May 1996)—were fiercely opposed by the DoT.[24]

The Athreya Committee stressed the need to separate the policymaking, regulatory, and field-oriented roles in telecommunications. The government as policymaker and regulator could easily privilege government-owned service providers over private players.[25] Second, the committee suggested that value-added telecommunications services such as cellular telephony be opened up to competition first, followed by basic services such as local, domestic long-distance, and international long-distance services, in that order. Athreya also provided a blueprint for the privatization of government assets.[26]

The DoT, under the leadership of its minister Sukh Ram and secretary H.P. Wagle, fiercely opposed the Athreya Committee's recommendations. The department was aided by the provisions of the Indian Telegraph Act of 1885, which granted the DoT enormous powers. During this conflict, the DoT successfully opposed interference from all outside organizations, including the World Bank. The DoT's only concession was its acquiescence to the idea of allowing private investment in value-added services such as electronic and voice mail, data, audio and video text messages, videoconferencing, radio paging, and cellular mobile services.[27] The DoT failed to predict the commercial potential of cellular mobile telephony at this time.

In the absence of an independent telecom regulator, DoT began the process of licensing telecommunications services to private players, even though it was aware of the consequences of such an institutional design. Quite apart from the Athreya recommendations, the DoT commissioned the ICICI to recommend a design for the institution of the Indian regulator in 1993. The study's findings would not be implemented before the first cellular licences were awarded in 1995.[28] DoT was unwilling to give up absolute licensing powers under the Indian Telegraph Act.

Given the slow progress made by DoT, the PMO acted swiftly after secretary Wagle retired from the department. N. Vittal, a secretary in the Department of Electronics directly under the Prime Minister, was appointed DoT secretary in 1993, since the PMO wanted Vittal to reform DoT from within. This was a landmark appointment, because the DoT and the Department of Electronics had adversarial relations in the past, and the DoT's top brass had resisted Vittal's appointment. Minister of communications Sukh Ram opposed the blueprint of the new telecom policy that Vittal prepared after wide-ranging consultations. Ram ultimately acquiesced to a new telecom policy under pressure from Prime Minister Narasimha Rao, on the eve of Rao's visit to the US in December 1993.

The result was India's NTP of 1994, which permitted private investment in basic telecom services. This was a minor concession because basic services in the government sector were cross-subsidized by domestic and international long-distance services. This privilege would not be available to private players. Second, the NTP did not mention the need for a regulator, which had been a part of the Athreya Committee recommendations in March 1991, as well as the ICICI study of January 1994. Third, DoT resisted the corporatization of its telecom service provision functions. Vittal was transferred from his position as telecom secretary in less than a year, so the inspiration behind the 1994 NTP would not be present at the time of its implementation.[29]

This section has demonstrated the conflict between the PMO and DoT in the aftermath of the balance of payments crisis of 1991. Empowered by the Indian Telegraph Act of 1885, DoT seemed to be winning the game of trying to retain its monopoly powers, aided by a colonial-era law. The next section of this chapter will describe how the idea of privatization, which did not fit into India's existing legal framework, gained currency and resulted in telecom sector changes.

The Birth of a Regulator

This section will demonstrate that the NTP's vision for private investment in 1994 did not fit India's existing institutional design, in which DoT played the combined role of policymaker, regulator, and service provider. DoT's absolute powers under the Indian Telegraph Act of 1885 meant that private telecom investors had only tenuous property rights. The Supreme Court pointed out the irreconcilability of the new institutional idea of trying to promoting private investment in the absence of a regulator. On account of the DoT's tremendous political and legal powers, the Indian government ultimately created a regulator—TRAI— with limited powers to check DoT's predatory propensities. The main area of concern for private investors was the commercial viability of GSM cellular mobile technology in urban areas, where almost all of the India's private telecom investment had occurred.

DoT made extensive use of its powers under the Indian Telegraph Act to secure advantages for government-owned service providers. First, opening up basic services for private investment before liberalizing long-distance service put private players at a disadvantage, because DoT had used domestic and international long-distance services to subsidize its local operations. This opportunity for cross-subsidizing local calls would not be available to private players.

Second, DoT defined bidding rules in a manner that gave the greatest weight in awarding the bid (72 per cent) to the size of a bid rather than the operational capability of the bidder. This provided a perverse incentive to make unreasonably large bids in order to obtain licences. The bidding system was essentially a tax on private service providers that DoT did not have to pay.[30] The higher the size of the bid, the easier it would be for DoT to compete with the private operator. The bidding rules had the desired effect, as the early stages of the bidding process witnessed unreasonable financial pledges for securing licences. According to a reliable estimate, cellular operators bid Rs 200 billion (USD 5.04 billion) over 20 years, or Rs 20 billion (USD 503.5 million) a year. Considering DoT's waiting list of 2.5 million clients in 1998, one could reasonably assume a market of at least 2.5 million cell phone users in India in the mid-1990s. If mobile operators were working for a market of 2.5 million clients, this would amount to an annual licence fee per client of Rs 8,000 (USD 201.41), whereas DoT was charging Rs 3,600 (USD 92) per client, and the cellular operators were allowed to charge only Rs 1,872 (USD 47.13). Private operators were being lured into an unreasonable business model by DoT, creating all the conditions for an investment crisis.[31]

Third, DoT made use of its exclusive licensing powers to diverge from the terms of the bidding process. DoT awarded no cellular licence in nine service areas because it considered the bids to be too small, even though the criterion of a minimum reserve price was not mentioned at the time of bidding. As a result, there were no takers in eight of the nine circles for which a minimum reserve price had been announced.

Fourth, DoT tried to destroy the GSM cellular business by setting high interconnection rates for cellular service providers. Because DoT constituted almost India's entire telecommunications network at this time, cellular service providers needed to connect more often with DoT's network than DoT did with other cellular operators' networks. This was a source of network power for DoT. Cellular service providers were also dismayed by DoT's administrative order of September 1996, which advised that cellular operators would be charged on a 'receiving party pays' basis. For calls originating in the DoT network and received by a cellular subscriber, the receiving party using a cell phone paid Rs 1.4 (4 cents) per minute. The cellular provider, on the other hand, could not charge DoT for calls that originated in its cellular network and that were received in the DoT network. Predatory pricing of interconnection was DoT's way of making it difficult for private cellular providers to survive in the telecommunications market.[32]

Finally, political patronage increased the uncertainty associated with the cellular bidding process. The most scandalous case was that of Himachal Futuristic Corporation Limited, which bid Rs 8.5 billion (USD 236.97 million) for cell phone licences in nine telecom circles when it had annual revenue of just Rs 2 billion (USD 55.76 million). After the bidding process was completed, the Tender Evaluation Committee decided to place a cap of three circles for all companies, but allowed Himachal to choose its three circles rather than awarding the company the three circles in which it had made the highest bids. Moreover, rather than reward the six remaining licences according to the ranking of the bids, fresh bids were invited in January 1996. The privileged treatment of Himachal led to charges of corruption against communications minister Sukh Ram. This case was brought to court, where DoT escaped penalty by virtue of a clause that stated that DoT held the right to restrict a company to a certain number of service areas. Sukh Ram had to resign as communications minister in August 1996 after the Central Bureau of Investigation caught him on corruption charges not directly related to the licensing process. Parliament debated the corruption issue for two weeks in December 1996.[33]

Faced with an investment crisis and courts pointing the finger at DoT's predation, Prime Minister Narasimha Rao's Congress government submitted an ordinance establishing TRAI on 27 January 1996. On 2 February, justice A.M. Ahmadi of the Supreme Court affirmed the constitutionality of the 1994 NTP.[34] Thereafter, in the case of Delhi Science Forum vs the Union of India (1996), the Supreme Court ruled that a telecommunications regulator was necessary to create an even-playing field for private investors. The court ruled that India's existing legal framework was inconsistent with the spirit of the NTP of 1994:

> The existence of a Telecom Regulatory Authority with appropriate powers is essential for introduction of plurality in the Telecom Sector. The National Telecom Policy is a historic departure from the practice followed during the past century. Since the private sector will have to contribute more to the development of the network than DoT/MTNL in the next few years, the role of an independent Telecom Regulatory Authority with appropriate powers is essential for introduction of plurality in the Telecom Sector.[35]

The regulator became essential because there was no institution charged with securing the property rights of private investors. Parliament was rocked with debates over the propriety of the tendering and licensing process. The Rajya Sabha (Upper House) blocked the TRAI Bill after it was passed by the Lok Sabha (Lower House). The Bill passed by the Lok Sabha in 1995 would have brought the regulator directly under the director general of telegraphs. In that case, the regulator would have no independence from DoT. TRAI was born with the help of a presidential ordinance issued in 1996, which lapsed after six months. The President was able to extend TRAI's existence three times through ordinances, but Parliament would ultimately need to act. Somnath Chatterjee, head of Parliament's Standing Committee on Telecommunications, played a constructive role,[36] and Parliament finally passed the TRAI Bill in February 1997.

Even though the TRAI Act (1997) established a regulator, the regulator was vested with few powers to check DoT's predatory propensities. First, TRAI could resolve disputes between service providers, but not between the licensor (DoT) and a service provider. In other words, it had jurisdiction over DoT as a service provider but not as a licensor. Second, TRAI did not have the power to issue or cancel licences—the Indian Telegraph Act gave this exclusive right to DoT.

This was a serious disability for TRAI, as other regulators—such as the Federal Communications Commission in the US and the Oftel (now the Ofcom) in the United Kingdom—were vested with licensing powers.[37]

Even though this new institution lacked teeth, TRAI was endowed with able technocratic leadership. Its first chairman, justice S.S. Sodhi, was a former chief justice of the Punjab High Court. Ambassador B.K. Zutshi, the first vice-chair, had been India's chief negotiator to the World Trade Organization. Ambassador Zutshi provided the much-needed technocratic expertise given his experience as a senior public servant and negotiator for India. The regulators were respected for their integrity and enjoyed the trust of investors.[38]

This section has highlighted problems that arose from the mismatch between regulatory ideas promoting private investment and India's existing legal structure, which was designed to empower the state monopoly. Private investment needed an independent regulator, and a regulator was established after the Supreme Court clearly highlighted this problem. Political will within the PMO and Parliament was important. However, TRAI was born with an infirm mandate, which would require further regulatory evolution. This evolution involved a process of institutional layering—allowing a new institution to develop on the edges of an old one and then to grow differentially. In addition, advances in GSM cellular mobile technology kept investor interest alive despite the monopoly that upheld DoT's predatory powers.

Regulatory Consolidation (1997–2000)

This section further describes the process of layering—that is, allowing nascent institutions to grow differentially as a way of promoting institutional change. The Indian telecom regulator (TRAI) had an infirm mandate and lacked the powers required to secure private investors' property rights. At this critical juncture the PMO, under Atal Bihari Vajpayee (March 1998–May 2004), with the support of the Ministry of Finance and the private sector, creatively devised institutional mechanisms that secured property rights and empowered the regulatory system. The institution of the regulator was consolidated, and a new TDSAT was established as a special court of law for telecommunications-related cases.

DoT realized the commercial potential of the GSM cellular business after the bidding process ended in 1996. Most of the private investment in Indian telecommunications was in this sector. In November 1997, MTNL—the government-owned service provider in the metropolitan areas of Bombay (Mumbai) and Delhi—announced its intention to enter the cellular service market after raising SD 358.74 million from global depository receipts. MTNL was looking for tie-ups with one of 20 global companies, which could take up 49 per cent of its stake.

The COAI, representing the cellular mobile operators, was opposed to this decision. It argued that MTNL was working like a corporation, therefore, it was inappropriate to treat it the same as the government. MTNL should pay a licence fee to even the playing field with private investors, the association argued. Private telecom operators Bharti Cellular and Sterling Cellular challenged DoT's decision to allow MTNL into the market without seeking TRAI's recommendation.

TRAI ruled in favour of private cellular operators. Its two-member bench argued that even though DoT was the licensing authority, it was necessary for DoT to request TRAI's recommendation before allowing MTNL to enter the cellular services market. The regulator was concerned that DoT was using its licensing powers to reduce the commercial value of the cellular licences that had been offered to private players in 1996. The cellular licence, after all, was a property right that was granted to some operators after a bidding process.[39]

This regulatory confusion was resolved by the Delhi High Court in response to an appeal DoT made after receiving TRAI's unfavourable judgement.[40] Justice Usha Mehra of the Delhi High Court read the letter of the law and found it tough to reconcile TRAI's actions with its mandate. She argued: 'For the reasons stated above, it can safely be concluded that the Authority fell in error in concluding that the power of the Government to grant or amend the license is subject to the recommendations of the TRAI or that these recommendations are mandatory in nature.'[41]

Granting licensing power to TRAI, the court argued, would make DoT's power under the Indian Telegraph Act redundant. Consequently, TRAI's role was limited to advising the Indian government about the need for new service providers and directions to service providers. TRAI did not have the power to take up disputes between DoT and private service providers.[42] On appeal, the division bench of the Delhi High Court upheld the decision, rendering TRAI's role with respect to the licensing process redundant.

This decision would hurt private telecom investors that had gambled on the GSM mobile sector. They were affected by the saga of unreasonable bids resulting from peculiar licensing conditions, described earlier in this chapter. Moreover, these private investors in the telecom sector had borrowed heavily from government financial institutions such as ICICI. It was in the interests of the government-owned financial institutions to ensure the profitability of the telecommunications sector. DoT commissioned two independent financial assessments of the sector. One was commissioned from ICICI (in April 1998) and another from the government's Bureau of Industrial Costs and Prices (BICP, in November 1998). The ICICI study found that Indian telecom companies were not operating below world standards in terms of their earnings before interest, depreciation, and amortization. The looming industrial sickness was attributable in large measure to the substantial licence fee commitments described previously.[43] These unreasonable commitments would lead investors to conclude that telecom liberalization had failed in India. The BICP study concurred with the ICICI study and also stressed on the substantial costs of starting business operations in India's telecommunications sector.[44] Thus, MTNL's entry into the market without paying a licence fee would further aggravate the financial plight of the cellular industry.

This crisis was met with determined leadership. The PMO became deeply interested in modernizing telecommunications and promoting India's information technology exports when Atal Bihari Vajpayee assumed office for the second time (March 1998–May 2004). The PMO developed a model of inter-ministerial coordination through the formation of the National Task Force on Information Technology. The task force, which was formed in March 1998 soon after Vajpayee assumed office,[45] paved the way for ending DoT's monopoly over India's long-distance carrier, VSNL, and over Internet service provision.[46]

In addition to the PMO's resolve, the Delhi High Court judgement in the TRAI case created an unprecedented unanimity among investors. The COAI, the Association of Basic Telecom Operators, FICCI, and CII all worked overtime to change the regulatory regime. The Central Vigilance Commissioner, N. Vittal, who had been the author of the NTP of 1994 as telecom secretary, wrote a memo to FICCI, in which he advised the industry that the PMO and the Ministry of Finance would support the institutional changes that they desired. CII's National Committee on

Communications stressed the need for DoT to consider TRAI's views before granting licences and before settling licensor-licensee disputes. It also argued that the regulator should be able to deliver interim relief in a situation of dire financial stress.[47]

The PMO's resolve, aided by support within the industry, yielded the high-powered Group on Telecommunications (GoT) in early 1999. The committee was modelled after the National IT Task Force and worked with remarkable speed. The deputy chairman of the Planning Commission and foreign minister Jaswant Singh chaired the group. It also included other senior representatives from the PMO, Planning Commission, finance ministry, law ministry, DoT, the National Informatics Centre, the National Institute of Advanced Studies (Bangalore), and the Department of Space. GoT signalled an inclination within the PMO to give a voice to the pro-competition elements within the government after giving due consideration to DoT's concerns.[48]

It is to GoT's credit that the blueprint for the NTP was ready within a couple of months—by March 1999. The 1999 NTP was implemented despite the displeasure of communications minister Jagmohan Malhotra, who was extremely averse to the bailout package. Under these circumstances, the minister had to resign and the prime minister took direct charge of the Ministry of Communications. Important opposition leaders supported the new initiative. Congress party leader Pranab Mukherjee, CPI's Somnath Chatterjee, and the Samajwadi Party's former communications minister B.P. Verma all supported the new regime. Chatterjee asserted that this move was essential to ensure that private companies would not get swept away by the government's predatory behaviour in this sector.[49]

The Group of Ministers on Telecommunications was set up in November–December 1999. This inter-ministerial group, which had Prime Minister Vajpayee's blessing, implemented the provisions of the NTP of 1999 with remarkable speed. The TRAI Act was amended, and a TDSAT was set up in 2000. The Department of Telecom Services within DoT was corporatized into Bharat Sanchar Nigam Limited (BSNL) in 2000. In the past, DoT had been both the policymaker and the service provider. Now, DoT's entire service function was separated from the ministry with the creation of this new government-owned corporate entity—BSNL. India's long-distance carrier VSNL was also privatized, with a majority of the shares being sold to the Tata group of industries in 2002.[50]

The March 1999 NTP shifted the balance of power in favour of TRAI. The problem of unreasonable bids was acknowledged, and the new licence regime was changed to one that included a reduced licensing fee plus a revenue-sharing commitment. Private operators were bailed out of financial hardship through a migration package that cost the government USD 857 million.[51] Private investors were happy with GoT's results.[52]

India's telecommunications regulatory institutions were allowed to grow. First, DoT would now need to consult TRAI on the number and timing of new licences; the TRAI Act was amended in 2000 to allow for this provision. Second, DoT was allowed to become the third operator in all service areas. Third, DoT's view that TRAI could not adjudicate disputes between the licensor and service providers was respected, but a new institution, TDSAT, was created in January 2000 to deal with these issues. It could as also deal with conflicts among service providers. A retired Indian Supreme Court judge justice D.P. Wadhwa was at the helm of this new telecom court, which was to function at the level of a high court. The only court of appeal higher than the TDSAT would be the Supreme Court.[53]

This section of the chapter, like the previous one, has demonstrated that a glaring mismatch between regulatory design and intention could not be sustained. The telecom regulator had to grow with respect to DoT, if the property rights of private investors were to be secured and a financial crisis averted. The Supreme Court identified this mismatch. The PMO, aided with private sector support, played a critical role in adjusting the regulatory system by empowering TRAI and creating TDSAT. Layering, as an approach to institutional evolution, involved not only the differential growth of TRAI, but also the establishment of a specialized court, TDSAT. The process of layering ensured that institutional change remained an incremental process in which new institutions evolved slowly and differentially with respect to old institutions without undermining existing institutions in a radical manner.

Regulatory Performance: Averting the WLL Crisis

The legal developments described in the two previous sections of this chapter did not necessarily check DoT's propensity to impose its will on India's telecom regulator. Now that the TRAI had legal standing, it needed independent-minded personnel manning the regulatory institution. This became apparent when DoT engineered a potential crisis for the GSM cellular industry when it convinced TRAI to introduce a new technology licence with a lower financial commitment, benefiting one major business house and hurting the interests of cellular operators in the GSM mobile sector. A crisis was averted when Reliance Infocomm was penalized after a change in the regulatory leadership. Measures taken by TRAI, under the chairmanship of Pradeep Baijal, facilitated the telecommunications revolution in India by unleashing the forces of competition.

The 1999 NTP allowed the use of Qualcomm's code division multiple access (CDMA) technology with a 'wireless in local loop with limited mobility' (WLLM) facility in January 2001.[54] The CDMA technology was a rival to the GSM technology and Indian companies sought to harness its potential in India. The WLLM facility was introduced as a fixed rather than a cellular service, with a lower licence fee commitment than cellular services,[55] but with expensive rural service obligations. It was justified on the grounds that a combination of limited mobility and expensive rural obligations would secure the commercial prospects of the competing GSM cellular players and promote rural teledensity. Moreover, the GSM cellular players had been aided by the migration package in 1999. The notable beneficiary of the WLLM policy was Reliance Infocomm (with licences in 17 circles). A WLLM controversy emerged, however, when it was established that Reliance Infocomm was in violation of its licensing conditions.

Period 1: DoT Averse to Introducing WLLM as a Fixed Service (March 1999–August 2000)

There is evidence to suggest that DoT was, on balance, averse to the idea of allowing India to adopt CDMA/WLL technology until August 2000. The 1999 NTP maintained a clear distinction between fixed services and cellular services, but allowed the use of WLL with limited mobility for fixed providers. DoT was aware of the problems that could arise if fixed-licence holders were permitted to use the limited roaming facility. It appears that both DoT and the cellular providers had a similar interpretation of the NTP until August 2000. This interpretation suggested that wireless technology could be allowed as a fixed service because it was cheaper to install. But this wireless service would not, under existing rules, be permitted for mobile phone use.

A number of DoT decisions lend weight to this interpretation. In August 1998, DoT rejected a Bharati Telenet's proposed commercial code on the grounds that mentioned it would use WLL services with limited mobility. Tata Teleservices' commercial code was approved in January 1999 after clearly stating that it would not be allowed to use mobile handsets. In a letter dated 17 September 1999, DoT responded to TRAI's letters dated 9 June 1999 and 27 August 1999, and clarified that fixed providers were not allowed mobile services under their licence agreements. In March 2000, Shyam Telelink's commercial code, which involved wireless handsets without mobility, was approved by DoT. Similarly, in August 2000, Essar Comvision's commercial code for operations in Punjab was approved on the condition that WLL technology could be permitted only without the use of mobile handsets. While DoT resisted WLL with mobility, India's fixed-service providers interpreted the 1999 NTP as favouring the use of WLL with limited mobility. In late August 1999, MTNL sought TRAI's approval for its Cellular Mobile Telephone Services using CDMA technology under its cell phone licence. The CDMA technology, as we noted earlier, is also the standard for the WLL technology with limited mobility. TRAI rejected this suggestion on the grounds that cellular service providers could only use the mandated GSM technology.

DoT began to change its mind about allowing CDMA technology for cellular mobile telephony in September 1999. It made licences for cellular operators technology-neutral, which meant that both GSM and CDMA technologies could be used for cellular operations. MTNL then informed TRAI that technological neutrality allowed it to use CDMA technology for cellular services. On 17 September 2000, DoT clarified that fixed providers could not provide mobile services, as mentioned earlier. Evidence suggests that DoT was averse to the use of WLL technology with limited mobility for fixed providers until August 2000. Efforts by MTNL to use CDMA technology either as a WLLM-fixed service or as a technology for its cellular operations were largely unsuccessful. Competitive bidding for fixed providers was announced with a nominal entry fee, and no mention of WLLM, in August 2000.

Period 2: Introducing WLLM (September 2000–January 2001)

The haste with which WLLM was introduced in India—between September 2000 and January 2001—was quite remarkable. DoT was the guiding force behind the introduction of WLLM services by fixed providers. Support for these moves came from industry organizations that represented the interests of the fixed-service providers—including the Association of Basic Telecom Operators, the Associated Chambers of Commerce and Industry, and the Confederation of Indian Industry. The COAI, representing the cellular mobile industry, opposed the introduction of WLLM without much success.

On 3 October 2000, a senior DoT official prepared a detailed policy note permitting the use of WLLM. DoT justified this move on the grounds that WLLM would help the faster rollout of telecommunications services and help bridge the rural-urban divide. On 10 October, DoT requested that TRAI reconsider WLLM and related issues, such as the scope of service area, the basis of assigning frequency, and the amount of entry fee.

TRAI was surprised by this turnaround in DoT's view and requested fresh consultations, as WLLM had not been a part of its earlier considerations. In a letter to Shyamal Ghosh, India's telecom secretary, TRAI chairman M.S. Verma expressed concern that there might not be adequate safeguards to ensure that WLLM would remain a service within the short-distance charging area, as defined by DoT. He was worried that it would be difficult to maintain the distinction between WLLM and cellular services.[56]

How could the TRAI chairman allow the institution to furnish recommendations for WLLM in January 2001 when he was not convinced about the propriety of this move in October 2000?[57] TRAI had failed to take an independent position on the WLLM issue. This was a very different situation from the one that prevailed when TRAI, under justice S.S. Sodhi, had opposed MTNL's entry into the cellular business. In 1998, TRAI did not have advisory powers, but was able to take a position independent of DoT. Verma's TRAI, on the other hand, had been endowed with advisory powers in 2000, but it had failed to express its independent opinion.

TRAI conducted hasty consultations without seeking participation from the cellular industry, which was the aggrieved party in this case. On 11 November 2000, within a month of DoT's request to TRAI, the regulator issued a consultation paper. On 8 January 2001, TRAI recommended that fixed providers be allowed to offer limited mobility services under restricted conditions. It recommended that roaming services, the use of mobile switching centres, and several value-added services would not be allowed for fixed providers. These would be the exclusive preserve of cellular operators. Empowered by the regulator's recommendations, DoT issued orders that gave fixed operators the right to offer WLLM on 25 January 2001.[58]

Adjudicating Conflicts of Interest between Fixed and GSM Cellular Operators

GSM cellular operators appealed to the legal system against the provision of WLLM, which had seriously affected their profitability. The COAI appealed to the TDSAT on 22 January 2001. TDSAT gave a judgement in favour of fixed operators in March 2002. COAI then appealed to the Supreme Court. The Supreme Court bench, headed by chief justice G.B. Pattanaik, maintained that TDSAT had not offered an opinion on the issues on which its opinion had been sought. TRAI needed to express an opinion on whether WLLM was a new service according to the NTP of 1999, whether WLLM was within existing policy or constituted a policy change, and whether conditions TRAI had attached to its recommendations dated 1 August 2001 had been satisfied. The case was sent back to TDSAT.[59]

TSDAT's majority opinion, delivered by two former government servants, R.U.S. Prasad and P.R. Dasgupta, upheld the DoT's position—which sought to secure the rights of WLLM operators. They argued that WLLM had always been a part of existing policy, as the NTP of 1999 allowed it. Second, they stressed that policy needed to keep pace with technology in order to uphold public interest. Wireless technology was essential for faster rollout obligations and for serving rural areas. Third, they maintained that it would be possible to respect the distinction between cellular services and fixed services with WLLM. Fourth, the court ruled that cellular operators had benefited from migration to a revenue-share regime. Therefore, they need not be averse to a policy change that would be favourable to fixed operators.[60]

In his minority opinion, justice D.P. Wadhwa, the chairman of TDSAT, argued against the introduction of the WLLM service. He held that a realistic interpretation of the 1999 NTP could not be taken to mean that WLLM was available to fixed operators free of cost. The NTP had treated fixed operators as being separate from cellular operators. Second, he was worried that extraneous considerations benefiting a sector or a business house were involved in this decision. Third, he found that the notion of a rural service dividend was only a pretext. Tata Teleservices, for instance, had provided only 1,314 of the 9,635 village public telephones that it had promised. Reliance Infocomm had installed only 502 of the 8,635 telephones it committed to provide. Fourth, the short-distance charging area was a notional concept without an objective geographic delimitation criterion and, therefore, would be impossible to monitor. Finally, justice Wadhwa opined that there had been no sudden march of technology that necessitated hasty radical changes in the approach of DoT and the regulator, between September 1999 and January 2001.[61]

The cellular operators went back to the Supreme Court in October 2003 after receiving the unfavourable majority opinion from TDSAT in August, and then withdrew the case from the Supreme Court in January 2004. According to one view, the cellular operators withdrew the case because the government had acknowledged and corrected the mistakes of the previous policy. Further aggression on the part of the COAI could result in policy changes that could adversely affect the cellular providers.[62]

Resolving the WLLM Crisis

TRAI's Recommendations on Unified Licensing were a salutary move.[63] These recommendations—which came under the new TRAI chairman, Pradip Baijal—led to an out-of-court settlement that satisfied the cellular operators. They increased competition in the sector and sowed the seeds for India's telecommunications revolution. Reliance Infocomm was penalized for not adhering to TRAI's guidelines, as it was using WLLM as a roaming facility and did not respect the distinction between cellular operations and WLLM operations. It was also using mobile switching centres,[64] which make it difficult to restrict mobility, as desired by the WLLM methodology.

Under chairman Baijal, TRAI called for unified licences, given the impossibility of maintaining the distinction between WLLM and cellular services. Consultations in September 2003 led to a cellular-versus-WLLM provider conflict, with the latter desiring a unified licence and the former opposing it. TRAI argued that WLLM had introduced competition, which had doubled the subscriber base between March and September 2003. Such growth rates would help India catch up with China's mobile explosion. Therefore, the TRAI proposed that unified licensing should include all services covering all areas and using any technology within six months. The fixed WLLM providers that wanted to migrate to a unified licence would pay the difference between the entry fee paid by the last cellular operator in a service area and the entry fee paid for a fixed WLLM licence.[65]

TRAI recommended that Reliance Infocomm should pay Rs 10.96 billion (USD 241 million) for migration to a unified licence (combining cellular and fixed features) and Rs 4.85 billion (USD 107 million) as penalty for previously using its WLLM licence like a cellular licence. The cellular operators withdrew their case from the Supreme Court, even though many cellular players believed that Reliance should have been punished with a heavier penalty.[66]

The resolution of the WLLM crisis demonstrated that the people who run institutions are as important as the principles that the institutions seek to uphold. The independence displayed by Justice S.S. Sodhi—the first regulator—was not protected by the legal mandate of TRAI at that time. Despite TRAI's enhanced regulatory powers under the chairmanship of M.S. Verma and a separate dispute settlement mechanism, DoT's view prevailed, even though TRAI and the TSDAT chair knew the WLLM policy would adversely affect GSM cellular operators. The resolution of the WLLM crisis occurred under Pradeep Baijal, whose legal mandate as chair of TRAI was no different from that of M.S. Verma. There is reason to believe that his effectiveness, however, was enhanced by the presence of communications minister Arun Shourie, who played a positive role in the matter. Shourie had taken over from Pramod Mahajan when the crisis had peaked. This resolution boosted investor confidence, laid the foundations of India's telecom revolution, and regulated competition was born. The telecom regulator now needed to shift its attention from government predation to curbing the private sector's monopolistic propensities.

Another Grave Crisis: The 2G Scam in 2008

The Comptroller and Auditor General (CAG) of India blew the whistle on the infamous 2G scam in 2008, signalling the birth of another significant crisis that could hurt investor sentiment. The report suggested that the 122 telecom licences that involved parting with 2G spectrum hurt the exchequer to the tune of Rs 650–680 trillion USD 14–14.7 billion), depending on how one calculated the loss.[67] The minister of communications and information technology A. Raja, who was then put behind bars before being let out on bail after 15 months, made the crucial licensing decisions in this case, disregarding TRAI, the Ministry of Law and Justice, and the prime minister. He convinced a reluctant finance ministry of his view on the pricing of spectrum, which allowed licences to be granted to companies that should have been disqualified in the first place. Not only was the licence fee of Rs 16.5 trillion (USD 350.5 million) well below the market rate, fictitious companies sold the majority of the shares to foreign companies to reap the gains that should have accrued to the government exchequer. There were allegations that the favoured company in terms of spectrum allocation, Swan Telecom, was a front for Reliance Telecom. Rationing a scarce resource such as spectrum below market price created enormous opportunities for rent-seeking.

How did this scam occur despite India's regulatory consolidation described above? Communications and IT minister Raja used TRAI's recommendations of 28 August 2007 to support his agenda. First, Raja accepted the recommendation that there should be no cap on the number of 2G service providers, given the need for competition to drive down prices.[68] However, this recommendation was not followed to the T. Second, TRAI opined that the spectrum charges for 800 MHz, 900 MHz, and 1,800 MHz[69]—which had been distributed earlier—should not be changed to ensure a level-playing field with those who had previously acquired spectrum at a reasonable cost.[70] TRAI was aware of the fact that reductions in licensing fees had promoted competition in the past as it had reduced the barriers for the entry of smaller players. In all other cases, spectrum was considered a scarce resource that had to be de-linked from the price of the licence. TRAI recommended the establishment of a multidisciplinary committee to determine how the price of spectrum should be determined through an appropriate auction.[71]

The principle of allowing no cap on the number of service providers was to be implemented on a first come, first served basis.[72] Those who applied for a licence first would also be the first to obtain a licence. This was consistent with the principle followed by the government when communications minister Arun Shourie resolved the WLL crisis in 2001 (as has been described in the previous section).[73] Past practice was used as the basis of the subsequent actions, even though there was no TRAI guideline supporting this principle.

Yet, the principle of no cap on the number of licences was violated in the issuance of the 2G licences. On 24 September 2007, India's communications minister announced that applications made until 1 October 2007 would be accepted on a first come, first served basis. This was a way of putting a cap on licences when 167 applications were already pending review. The sudden imposition of a 1 October deadline led to 408 additional applications within the next eight days. These developments showed that spectrum was a scarce resource that was in substantial demand. The government then went a step further, and stopped accepting applications on 25 September rather than the 1 October deadline.[74]

The main issue for DoT seemed to be the availability of spectrum for such a large number of applications. The policy of no cap was clearly not working at a time when spectrum was a scarce commodity. In addition, the principle of first come, first served was violated in the crudest possible way. The last application deadline was retroactively moved to 25 September 2007 through a press release on 10 January 2011. On the same day, another press release directed all the companies that had submitted their applications to DoT before 25 September to send their representatives immediately to collect the department's response by 3.30p.m. DoT issued a total of 121 letters, and 78 of the 121 2G applicants complied with the terms and conditions on 10 January. All the applications that had accumulated over the years were resolved on the same day, making a mockery of the first come, first served principle. Thirteen of the applicants were ready with demand drafts drawn prior to 10 January, implying that they knew about the changes in policy even before they had been announced through the 10 January press release. The first come, first served principle based on the date of application was conveniently changed to assign priority to those who complied with the conditions of the letter of intent first.[75]

The awarding of 2G licences defied the rules of the game. Many of the companies who received licences should have been disqualified for a variety of reasons. First, 13 of the 122 successful applicants did not have the required amount of share capital at the application deadline. Eight companies of the Unitech group, for example, had been incorporated in August–September 2007 with an authorized share capital of Rs 500,000 each. These companies passed special resolutions on 20 September 2007 in extraordinary general meetings of the respective companies to increase authorized share capital. They deposited the requisite government taxes (stamp duties) for increase in authorized share capital on 3 October, which was well past the 25 September deadline. Allianz Infratech Private Limited claimed Rs 100 million in share capital in their application dated 5 September, but it was later found that the actual figure was Rs 500,000. Other companies who should have been debarred for similar behaviour included Datacom Solutions Private Limited, S Tel Private Limited, Shipping Stop Dot Com (India) Private Limited, Swan Telecom Private Limited (now Etisalat DB Telecom Private Limited), and Datacom Solutions Private Limited (now Videocon Telecommunications Limited). CAG noted that 85 of the 122 licence applicants suppressed facts and submitted fictitious documents in order to access spectrum.[76]

Swan Telecom enjoyed a rather privileged status among applicants. First, Reliance Telecom's 10.71 per cent equity stake in Swan Telecom was not within the permissible limit, because Reliance was operating in all the areas being served by Swan. Rather than refer the complicated matter of equity shares to either the Ministry of Corporate Affairs or the Ministry of Finance for judgement, Swan Telecom was allowed to submit a revised stakeholding pattern in December 2007, seven months after the company's initial application. Various sources point to the possibility that Swan may have been a front company for Reliance. CAG found that the email address of Swan's corporate office to be hari.nair@relianceada.com. In addition, the corporate office of Tiger Traders Private Limited, which was a substantial investor in Swan, was located at the Reliance Energy Centre in Santa Cruz, Mumbai.[77]

Swan also received special favours from BSNL—the corporatized government-owned cellular service provider. BSNL signed a memorandum of understanding with Swan on 13 October 2008, which allowed it to use BSNL's infrastructure for its roaming operations—a privilege that had not been granted to any operator in the past. When the Public Accounts Committee charged with investigating the 2G scam queried this issue, Swan justified its course of action by pointing to the charges it paid for using BSNL's infrastructure. The case was touted as a non-exclusive agreement that was being tried out with Swan. This arrangement continued after Swan had been taken over by another company, Etisalat DB.[78]

Rent-seeking propensities involved with selling licences below market price were exposed when the two major beneficiaries of the licensing process, Swan and Unitech, sold substantial equity to foreign partners. First, Swan mopped up Rs 32.1 billion (USD 701.3 million) by selling 44.73 per cent of its equity to Etisalat International India Limited, a Dubai-based firm. Swan Telecom, which was incorporated in July 2007, was previously known as Swan Capital Private Limited and owned by Anil Ambani. It was sold to two real estate entrepreneurs, Shahid Balwa and Vinod Goenka, who were imprisoned along with former communications minister A. Raja. Second, Unitech sold 67.25 per cent of its shares to Telenor Asia, a subsidiary of one of Norway's largest companies, for Rs 61.2 billion (USD 1.3 billion). It is this sale that led CAG to determine that the loss to the exchequer from selling licences below market value could be in the range of USD 14 billion. Moreover, another company, S Tel Limited, had voluntarily offered a much higher price for the licences—a fact that increases the plausibility of CAG's assessment of a USD 14 billion loss for the exchequer.[79]

How could communications minister A. Raja escape the scrutiny of the prime minister and other relevant ministries such as law and justice, and finance? In a letter dated 2 November 2011, the prime minister had expressed concern about the paucity of spectrum in India and the consequent need for discovering its price beyond the one set in 2001.[80] The communications minister sought to assuage the concerns of the prime minister by arguing that TRAI and the Telecom Commission did not share his assessment of the problem. Moreover, the communications minister asserted that 60–65 MHz of spectrum was available for distribution in the 900 MHz and 1,800 MHz bands.[81] The communications minister misled the prime minister by hiding the fact that the matter of spectrum pricing had only been considered by internal members of the Telecom Commission and not by its external members. They included the senior civil servants dealing with finance, information technology, the Planning Commission, and industrial policy and promotion. No meeting of the entire Telecom Commission had been called on this important issue.[82] Moreover, the Telecom Commission within DoT had sought in-depth analysis of the issue before recommending further action. India's communications minister dismissed this concern about spectrum pricing in 2007 in a file that is now a public document.[83]

Was Prime Minister Manmohan Singh unconvinced about the manner in which spectrum had been disbursed? Some critics who held that the PMO wanted to distance itself from the spectrum scandal point to a file noting of the private secretary to the prime minister on 23 January 2011: Does not want formal communication and wants PMO to be at 'arm's length'.[84]

There is a view that the prime minister should have been more proactive in dealing with communications minister A. Raja's excesses. Prime Minister Singh, who belongs to the Congress party and heads the United Progressive Alliance (UPA) coalition in Parliament, has publicly acknowledged the imperatives of coalition politics on television, and coalition politics could have played a role in this crisis. Raja went to prison on 2 February 2011, not long after his party the Dravida Munnetra Kazhagam (DMK) lost elections in Tamil Nadu. Was the Congress party worried that putting Raja in jail might prompt the DMK to withdraw from the UPA coalition and create substantial problems for retaining a majority in Parliament?

The deputy chairman of the Planning Commission, Montek Singh Ahluwalia, has defended Prime Minister Singh. In an interview with Karan Thapar on 7 August 2011, Ahluwalia argued that the prime minister in a cabinet form of government cannot micromanage the affairs of every ministry. Ahluwalia said that the prime minister was satisfied that TRAI's recommendations were adhered to in this case and that the Ministry of Communications and Information Technology and the Ministry of Finance were ironing out their differences through dialogue. The PMO wanted to remain at 'arm's length', Ahluwalia said, because it was a matter between two ministries. It did not, therefore, formally wish to interfere in the matter. Public opinion remains divided on how the prime minister should have dealt with this 2G licensing issue.

Like the prime minister, India's finance minister P. Chidambaram acquiesced to the decision after raising concerns about selling spectrum below market value. The PMO and the Ministry of Finance had desired spectrum to be a part of the issues to be discussed by the Group of Ministers in 2006.[85] The finance secretary had also conveyed the need for a sound spectrum policy in June 2007.[86] The ministry further raised concerns about the wisdom of using a price discovered in 2001 again in November 2007.[87] The internal finance member within DOT's Telecom Commission also supported this view during the same month.[88] DoT, on the other hand, justified its position by pointing to a cabinet decision of October 2003, where DoT was granted the power to set the licensing fee in consultation with TRAI.[89]

The finance minister remained unconvinced about this approach. In a letter to the prime minister on 15 January 2008—immediately after many of the licences had been issued—he reiterated that spectrum is a scarce resource that should be auctioned, and that the past should be treated as a closed chapter.[90] In this respect, the minister took a position that clearly deviated from the TRAI and the minister of communication's position.

Why did the finance minister finally acquiesce to the view of the DoT, despite his scepticism with respect to the manner in which spectrum was sought to be auctioned by the communications minister? DoT had been cautioned by the Ministry of Law and Justice when it had sought the opinion of India's solicitor general about dealing with the rush of applications after setting 1 October 2007 as the deadline for 2G licence applications.[91] The Ministry of Law and Justice had argued that the matter could not be settled by the solicitor general alone and needed the intervention of an Empowered Group of Ministers. In cases where a difference of opinion exists between two ministers, as happened between telecoms and finance in this case, the matter is vetted under the authority of the cabinet, a collective of senior ministers of the Government of India.[92] DoT resisted the view of the Ministry of Law and Justice by reiterating that no policy advice had been sought and that there was no need for a Group of Ministers, but this was a difficult position to sustain.[93] It was clear from the discussion that DoT had deviated from both the policy of no restrictions on the number of players as well as the policy accommodating applicants on a first come, first served basis.

In addition to giving away 2G licences below market value, DoT also used TRAI's August 2008 recommendations to convert licences for the use of CDMA technology into dual technology licences that could use either the GSM or the CDMA technology. The most significant beneficiary of this process was Reliance Communications Limited, which received licences for 20 service areas for Rs 16.45 billion (USD 365.5 million). Industry insiders suggest that this was a big benefit at a time when operators wanted to shift from CDMA technology to GSM. One senior retired civil servant, who will remain anonymous, said this new GSM licensing arrangement was the principal reason why Reliance sold Swan Telecom to Shahid Balwa and Vinod Goenka. The ability to use GSM technology in areas where Reliance already had approval for CDMA operations—and the attendant reasonably priced spectrum that came with it—quite satisfied Reliance's appetite for spectrum. After this decision, there was no need for Reliance to own Swan. CAG has detailed the haste with which the licences were given to Reliance Communications, Shyam Telelink, and HFCL Infotel on 18 October 2007, a day before DoT's 19 October press release announcing the policy. This significant decision was made without taking the cabinet into confidence.[94]

How will the government respond to the regulatory mess after putting Raja, the key players in Swan Telecom, and other associates behind bars? A number of cellular companies have failed to meet rollout obligations despite obtaining 2G licences at bargain prices. Granting cheap licences to companies should have ensured swifter rollout of telecom services, but that has not happened. TRAI has argued that the licences of 69 such companies should be cancelled. DoT, under communications minister Kapil Sibal, on the other hand, has a different interpretation of such obligations. It wanted only eight licences to be cancelled.[95] Prime Minister Singh has gone one step further to suggest that the government will initiate legislation that will make the regulators overseeing economic governance more independent and accountable.

India's regulatory environment needs greater inter-ministerial coordination and stronger enforcement as infrastructure sectors such as telecommunications become a hotbed of corruption. A minister without firm regulatory oversight can turn out be a wanton maximizer of rents. If the past is any guide, the political and the business class' rent-seeking propensities will lead to more problems such as the WLL crisis and the 2G scam if India does not close regulatory loopholes. The hope is that these crises, emerging from Indian telecom's rent-seeking environment and weak protection of property rights, will inspire regulatory reform. There is reason to expect that India's telecom sector—which continues to be one of the most efficient in the world, despite this crisis—will embark on a reform path similar to the one that India followed after its balance of payments crises in 1991. There is a strong case for establishing a more powerful and accountable Indian telecom regulator with licensing powers. In addition, it may help if regulators endowed with technocratic ability—rather those who have worked in top positions in the very ministries that they are supposed to regulate—are selected for top-level positions.

Conclusion: Ideas, Interests, and Institutional Change

The evolution of India's telecommunications regulator and dispute-settlement mechanisms lends support to theories of institutional change premised on the emergence of new ideas and interests. The process of change in India's telecom sector was aided by the presence of a legal system that was quick to point out the mismatch between regulatory institutions and intentions. It was essential that certain ideas began to take root in India in the 1980s, such as separating service providers from the policymakers and welcoming private investment. There could be no private investment without secure private property rights enforced by third parties.

India's process of regulatory evolution was driven by a diversity of interests located primarily within the PMO, Ministry of Finance, DoT, and private sector lobbies. DoT, empowered by the Indian Telegraph Act of 1885, had tremendous legal powers to protect its monopoly and thwart competition. Curbing DoT's monopoly powers involved a process of evolutionary change. Certain ideas that had evolved since the 1980s reached a tipping point in 1991, when a balance of payments shock enabled the government to initiate private sector participation in mobile telephony. Thereafter, a series of internal crises of investment engendered a process of regulatory reform best described as 'layering'. This process involved establishing a new regulatory institution along the edges of an existing one and then allowing it to grow differentially. The story began in the 1980s, when the idea of engendering efficiency in telecommunications by curbing the powers of the Ministry of Posts and Telegraphs had taken root. The process began when the government created DoT and then undermined its monopoly by establishing C-DOT and MTNL in the 1980s. The private sector was also invited to participate in the manufacture of telecom equipment.

The 1991 balance of payments crisis enabled the PMO to initiate private sector participation in mobile telephony, despite opposition from DoT. But without the presence of an effective telecom regulator, private sector participation created a messy business environment. DoT was able to continue its predatory and rent-seeking behaviour because the function of governing the private sector was established within DoT itself.

The litigious environment that ensued as a consequence of this arrangement was not conducive to attracting private investment, and it forced the Indian government to create a new telecom regulator, TRAI, alongside the existing regulator within DoT. The process of layering produced further institutional differentiation. TRAI was born with an infirm mandate in 1997, a time when investors could not secure property rights through privatization without a regulator. It was further empowered in 2000 with the establishment of a new dispute settlement mechanism, as investors still had concerns about the lack of appropriate legal powers to curb DoT's monopolistic propensities in the Indian telecom sector. In the 2G case, the regulator (TRAI), the prime minister, the finance minister, and the minister of law and justice failed to check the rent-seeking propensities of a communications minister, despite being very well aware of the pitfalls of his actions. Even though the 2G scam has not checked the rapid growth of telecommunications in India, owing to the country's substantial promotion of competition in the past, it has the potential to dampen investor sentiment in the future.

The regulatory evolution discussed in this essay involved changes in policy ideas that emerged from the Indian government's attempts to address policy puzzles and resolve conflicts of interest between 1980 and 2011. It was not driven by the powerful and sudden appeal of a new idea in a time of economic crisis. The PMO became convinced of the importance of telecommunications in India's development in the 1980s. It expended substantial political capital to reduce the monopoly powers of the Ministry of Posts and Telegraphs and enhance private sector participation, policies that were challenged by the DoT.

The telecom sector reached a tipping point during the 1991 balance of payments crisis, but the sector had already been preparing for deregulation. The PMO and the Ministry of Finance increased their resolve to promote private investment in commercially viable telecom sectors after the balance of payments shock. The deterioration in India's fiscal health heightened the need to promote efficiency and reduce government involvement in areas of the economy where the private sector could play a significant role. These efforts were resisted by DoT, which wanted to preserve its monopoly. Regulatory evolution, therefore, involved resolving conflicts between the PMO and Ministry of Finance on the one hand, and DoT on the other. As the private sector evolved, its involvement with government financial institutions and fierce lobbying made an impact on the Ministry of Finance, PMO, and DoT. The process involved political costs, including the resignation of communications ministers Sukh Ram, Jagmohan, and Raja. During times of financial crisis in the telecommunications sector, the PMO often took direct charge of DoT. The political investment in setting up a regulatory institution was, therefore, quite formidable.

Regulatory evolution was necessary, but not sufficient, for securing property rights in India's telecom sector. An empowered regulator and specialized court was not able to secure the property rights of the GSM cellular operators during the WLLM crisis in 2001. But the same institution, under another regulator and minister, not only resolved the crisis but also sowed the seeds of the telecom revolution in India around 2003. Even though TRAI (the more recently established telecom regulator) was not party to the 2G scam, it could have been more proactive in checking the communication minster's rent-seeking propensities. Could TRAI have been more circumspect about recommending no cap on the number of companies allowed to bid for telecom licences, the sale of spectrum at 2001 prices, and the dual technology licence? Could it have nudged India's executive branch toward an inter-ministerial approach so that decisions would be made in consultation by a group of ministers? This raises the issue of the independence of the regulator with respect to the minister of communications and information technology. This chapter supports Prime Minster Manmohan Singh's view that regulatory evolution should be directed towards the creation of more independent and accountable regulation, with less discretion with the political class and bureaucracy. India's executive branch could provide clearer guidelines on licensing issues, which the regulator should interpret and execute.

Three significant lessons can be gleaned from the WLLM crisis and the 2G scam. First, an empowered TRAI needed people who could express themselves freely with respect to DoT. Second, in addition to taming the government's predatory propensities, TRAI needed to curb the monopolistic propensities of the private sector. And three, coalition politics and political funding in India have thwarted authorities from checking the corruption that could debilitate competition in the sector. If an independent Election Commission is central to free and fair elections, it seems plausible that establishing independent and accountable regulators may be critical for curbing rent-seeking propensities among India's politicians and civil servants. Moreover, it was an independent institution, CAG, that blew the whistle on the 2G scam. It is worth considering whether TRAI should have greater say in the licensing process and clearer objectives, as telecom regulators in Great Britain and the US have.

The impact of slow-moving processes such as fiscal crises and technological development on the evolution of interests and institutions in India is captured by studying evolving processes rather than by analysing snapshots of history. Private sector participation began in 1992, but TRAI was born in 1997. It was further empowered and a special court was set up in 2000. The process of regulatory evolution involved increasing the coherence between policy intention—the promotion of private investment by securing property rights—and the design of the regulatory institution. That process of evolution is an ongoing one, as institutions constantly come face-to-face with new challenges. Each crisis of investment in India's telecommunications sector necessitated regulatory empowerment. After regulatory powers were consolidated in 2000, a crisis was averted by TRAI, and the seeds of India's telecommunications boom were sown after 2003. The 2G scam of 2008 is likely to produce similar regulatory reform in the telecom sector. And despite these regulatory challenges, India remains among the most rapidly burgeoning telecom markets in the world.

Notes

1. There is a dearth of historically informed theoretical accounts of institutional change in India. This chapter suggests a mechanism for institutional change in India and situates the argument in the context of debates about institutional change in Western plural settings. See Kapur and Mehta (2005) for a comprehensive account of Indian institutions that fail to address the major debates on institutional change.

2. For different types of accounts of new principles being embedded within institutional rules in stories of institutional change, see Blyth (2002); Hall (1993: 275–96); North and Weingast (1989: 803–32); Ruggie (1983: 195–232).

3. For an account of why institutional change is incremental and occurs largely along a certain path, see North (1990: 95–6, 1995: 17–26); Pierson (2000: 253–7, 2004: 17–53).

4. See North (1990: 73–91); North and Weingast (1989: 803–32).

5. See Blyth (2002).

6. See Campbell (2004: 183–6).

7. See Mukherji (2007: 117–45).

8. GSM stands for Groupe Spécial Mobile, or as it is currently known—Global System for Mobile communications. The GSM technology competes with code division multiple access (CDMA) technology in various markets around the globe. GSM is the European standard, which has gained worldwide acceptance, whereas CDMA was developed in the United States.

9. Other mechanisms of institutional change include displacement, which involves the rise to prominence of new institutions at the cost of old ones; drift, which involves the deliberate neglect of certain institutional forms; conversion, which involves the deployment of old institutions to new purposes; and exhaustion, which involves the gradual withering away of an institution. See Hacker (2005: 40–82); Schickler (2001); Streeck and Thelen (2005: 1–39).

10. See Department of Telecommunications (2005: 97–102).

11. See Telecom Regulatory Authority of India (2011a).

12. See Telecom Regulatory Authority of India (2006: 5–7).

13. On the reasons why slow-moving processes such as technology and demography require a dynamic analysis, see Pierson (2004: 79–102); Pierson and Skocpol (2002: 703–4).

14. See McDowell (1997: 127–35); Singh (1999: 141–3).

15. On economic policy change under Rajiv Gandhi, see Kohli (1989: 305–28); Patel (1987: 209–31); Rubin (1985: 942–57); Shastri (1997: 32–42).

16. See Athreya (1996: 11–7); Petrazzini (1996: 40–1); Singh (1999: 141–63).

17. See Desai (2006: 43).

18. See Planning Commission (2001: 32–3).

19. See Mukherji (2006: 64–5); Planning Commission (2001: 44).

20. See Athreya (1996: 16–7; author interview, New Delhi, 8 May 2004).

21. The Ministry of Communications was divided into two separate departments, the DoT and the Department of Posts, in 1986. This was to ensure that telecom development would not receive less priority than postal services. The Department of Electronics, which had worked directly under the PMO since the early 1970s, was in favour of modernizing telecommunications. In 1998, the Department of Electronics was renamed the Ministry of Information Technology, and in 2001, a Ministry of Communications and Information Technology was created by merging the Ministry of Communications with the Ministry of Information Technology.

22. See Bhaduri and Nayyar (1996: 19–53); Joshi and Little (1994: 294–312); Mukherji (2007: 126–9).

23. Corporatization in India is a way of giving government-owned companies autonomy from their parent ministries so that they can be run as corporations. See Desai (2006: 43–5); Mukherji (2004: 280–1); Petrazzini (1996: 40–1); Saha (2004: 3,917–21).

24. The views expressed on Athreya in this section benefited from a personal interview with Athreya in New Delhi on 8 May 2004.

25. At this time, there were two government-owned service providers. The DoT serviced the entire country except the metropolitan areas of Delhi and Mumbai (then Bombay), which were serviced by the government-owned corporation MTNL.

26. See Athreya (1996: 16–21).

27. See Desai (2003: 45–71).

28. See Desai (2003: 51).

29. These views expressed here benefited from personal interviews with Vittal (Chennai, 6 September 2004) and Athreya (New Delhi, 18 August 2004). See Vittal (2004: 5–15).

30. See Bureau of Industrial Costs and Prices (1998)

31. See Desai (2003: 47–8).

32. See Desai (2003: 48).

33. On the licensing process and its implications, see Athreya (1996: 20–1); Desai (2003: 78); Dokeniya (1999: 111–22); Gupta (2002: 1,668–75); Petrazzini (1996: 49–50); Sinha (1996: 32–5).

34. See Swaminathan (1997: 422–3).

35. See Supreme Court of India (2006: Paragraph 25).

36. See Dokeniya (1999: 122–3); Gupta (2002: 1,679–90); Singh (1999: 180–1), with the author interviewed T.H. Chowdary on 7 September 2004, Hyderabad. Chowdary was the founding managing director of India's long-distance carrier, VSNL. He heads the Centre for Telecom Management and Studies in Hyderabad.

37. On TRAI's mandate, see Chowdary (2000: 428–39); Dokeniya (1999: 123–5).

38. This assessment is based on interviews with the former chairman of TRAI, Pradeep Baijal (New Delhi, 18 August 2004), and with various industry players, including T.V. Ramachandran, director general of the Cellular Operators Association of India, and S.C. Khanna, secretary general of the Association of Basic Telecom Operators of India (New Delhi, September–December 2004). I also interviewed justice Sodhi and ambassador Zutshi (New Delhi, 28 September 2004).

39. See Desai (2003: 52–3).

40. On the TRAI–DoT conflict regarding TRAI's licensing powers, see Gupta (2002: 1,670). See also, Economist Intelligence Unit (1998).

41. See Delhi High Court (1998: 51).

42. Ibid.: 40–51.

43. See ICICI (1998).

44. See Bureau of Industrial Costs and Prices (1998).

45. See National Taskforce on Information Technology and Software Development (1998: chapter VII).

46. Personal interview with Prime Minister Vajpayee's political associate and telecommunications adviser Sudheendra Kulkarni at the BJP office (New Delhi, 18 October 2004).

47. I am grateful to T.V. Ramachandran for sharing the documents mentioned here. I benefited from personal interviews with S.C. Khanna and Arun Seth, managing director of British Telecom, India and South Asian Association for Regional Cooperation (New Delhi, October 2004).

48. On the composition of GoT, see Economist Intelligence Unit (1999). Also see, National Taskforce on Information Technology and Software Development (1998).

49. On the politics and economics of the shift to revenue sharing, see Economist Intelligence Unit (1999b, 1999c).

50. My views on inter-ministerial coordination are based on a discussion with Sudheendra Kulkarni at the BJP office (New Delhi, 18 October 2004). Montek Ahluwalia, who was a member of GoT, expressed the view that GoT worked very well (author interview, IMF office in Washington, DC, 17 May 2004).

51. See Gupta (2002: 1,670). This figure was confirmed independently in a conversation with T.V. Ramachandran in January 2005.

52. This view is based on discussions in New Delhi in October 2004, with Virat Bhatia (AT&T), Arun Seth, T.V. Ramachandran, and S.C. Khanna.

53. On the gains to TRAI and DoT from the 1999 NTP, see Gupta (2002: 1,671). See Economist Intelligence Unit (1999a). The NTP of 1999 can be accessed on the Web at http://www.trai.gov.in/TelecomPolicy_ntp99.asp (accessed 15 May 2011). For an excellent account of regulatory institutions in India, see Raghavan (2007: 167–223).

54. Cellular service providers in India had used the European GSM technology since 1994. The CDMA technology was not permitted at that time.

55. In addition to lower licence fees, WLLM operators enjoyed a favourable interconnect regime and did not pay spectrum charges. These advantages over the GSM providers, plus the fact that they would compete with cellular players within the short-distance charging area—where most of the cellular business lay—led to charges of unfairness by cellular operators.

56. The letters between Verma and Ghosh were published by Gupta (2004). T.V. Ramachandran made available much of the other material regarding correspondences that is used in this section.

57. See Telecom Regulatory Authority of India (2001).

58. See Bajpai and Hans (2005: 16–25).

59. See Supreme Court of India (2002).

60. See TDSAT, B (2003a).

61. See TDSAT, A (2003). The Wadhwa judgement is an exhaustive one, covering the substantial history of the WLL saga. It was a good way for me to

double-check the validity of the correspondences between TRAI and DoT that I had received from T.V. Ramachandran.

62. T.V. Ramachandran held the view that the cellular operators needed to reach a compromise.

63. See Telecom Regulatory Authority of India (2003).

64. See Telecom Regulatory Authority of India (2001).

65. See Telecom Regulatory Authority of India (2003).

66. Ibid.: 23–4.

67. See Comptroller and Auditor General of India (2010: 51–6). There are also higher estimates depending on how one assesses the loss.

68. See Telecom Regulatory Authority of India (2007: 16, 25–6).

69. This would not work if a company sought spectrum beyond 10 MHz in the 800 MHz, 900 MHz and 1,800 MHz bands. In that case a special charge needed to be worked out.

70. See Telecom Regulatory Authority of India (2007: 47–9).

71. Ibid.: 38, 50.

72. See Swamy (2011: 60, 83–4, 87). The source of the first come, first served idea seems to be the decision of a Union cabinet meeting held on 24 November 2003.

73. Former communications minister Shourie has defended his decision before the Central Bureau of Investigation based on the fact that the first come, first served principle was in-vogue even before him. It was deployed to engender a speedy resolution of the WLL crisis, an act that cleared a litigation-ridden regulatory environment and fostered a boom in the sector. The source of this information wishes to remain anonymous.

74. See Comptroller and Auditor General of India (2010: 20). A substantial amount of the official documents reported in this chapter was found in Patil (2011: Annexure). Henceforward, I will call it the *Shivraj Patil Committee Report*. See Press Note F. No. 20-100/2007-AS-I (pt), *Cut-off Date for Applications for Unified Access Services Licenses* (New Delhi: Department of Telecommunications, September 24, 2007), Source: *Annexure 35 - Shivraj Patil Committee Report*, 568; Press Release, *Capping Applications till September 25, 2007* (Department of Telecommunications, January 1, 2008), Source: *Annexure 49 – Shivraj Patil Committee Report*, 678.

75. Communications minister Raja to Prime Minister Singh, 26 December 2007 (Patil 2011: Annexure 48, pp. 672–7).

76. See Comptroller and Auditor General of India (2010: 28–50).

77. Ibid.: 44–5.

78. See Swamy (2011: 202–4).

79. See Comptroller and Auditor General of India (2010: 53–6).

80. Prime Minister Singh to communications minister Raja on 2 November 2007 (Swamy 2011: 129).

81. Communications minister Raja to Prime Minister Singh, 2 November 2007 (Swamy 2011: 131–3). This position was further reinforced by another letter, Raja to Singh, 26 December 2007 (Patil: Annexure 48, pp. 672–7). This letter was written just a couple of weeks before the infamous press release of 10 January 2008.

82. See Swamy (2011: 224–9).

83. See DoT file number 20-100/2007-AS-I: 18/N-19/N (Patil: Annexure 47, pp. 639–40).

84. See Swamy (2011: 144–5).

85. Ibid.: 50–2.

86. Ibid.: 54–6. Finance secretary D. Subba Rao reports that he engaged in substantial oral exchanges with his counterpart D.S. Mathur in DoT, and did not officially convey the matter to finance minister Chidambaram.

87. Finance secretary D. Subba Rao to telecom secretary D.S. Mathur on 22 November 2007 (Patil: Annexure 45, p. 619).

88. See Swamy (2011: 144–5).

89. Telecom secretary D.S. Mathur to finance secretary D. Subba Rao on 29 November 2007 (Patil: Annexure 46, p. 620).

90. Finance minister Chidambaram to Prime Minister Singh (Swamy 2011: 61–4). The Department of Economic Affairs, Ministry of Finance, had prepared a *Position Paper on Telecom Policy* on 3 January 2008, which was critical of DOT's approach (Swamy 2011: 71–6).

91. K. Sridhara, member of the Telecom Commission, to the secretary, Department of Legal Affairs,on 26 October 2007 (Patil: Annexure 43, pp. 610–5).

92. The Department of Legal Affairs opined that issues needed to be refined substantially and that the opinion of an Empowered Group of Ministers needed to be sought. See law secretary T. K .Vishwanathan (*Opinion of the Department of Legal Affairs—Ministry of Law and Justice*, 1 November 2007) in Patil (2011: Annexure 44, pp.616–8).

93. See Comptroller and Auditor General of India (2010: 21–2).

94. Ibid.: 46–8.

95. See Singh (2011).

5 Reforms Challenged

The Power Sector in Andhra Pradesh

IF THE TELECOMMUNICATIONS SECTOR in India has spurred economic growth despite its various scandals, the power sector faces a grave financial situation in India's current era of reforms. Unmetered or unaccounted sales of electricity constitute 35 per cent of India's electricity generation, and the losses accrue to the state electricity boards. These losses add up to 1 per cent of India GDP annually. India is now in its Eleventh Five-year Plan (2007–12), but the eighth, ninth, and tenth five-year plans only added 50.5 per cent of the targeted capacity in electricity generation. The gap between revenue and the cost of supply is growing. The private sector is not playing a significant role, contributing only about 16 per cent of power generation in India.[1] If one wants to find the sector of the Indian economy where reforms have made the least impact, it is the power sector—and the impact of electricity provision on economic growth cannot be underestimated. This chapter explores why the sector is locked in an old equilibrium of losses and a dearth of private sector competition. It does so by probing into the example of one relatively well-governed state—Andhra Pradesh.

In June 2011, V.K. Shunglu, a former comptroller and auditor general of India, drafted a report on the financial condition of companies that distribute power to consumers in India. These are the worst-performing public utilities in the power sector, and their economic malaise arises largely from the provision of free electricity to farmers and from theft. Distribution companies often do not submit their annual revenue requirements and tariff revision proposals to the government. Shunglu's report urges regulators to allow the utilities to make up for the tariff gap between the cost of service and revenues by allowing the utilities to raise tariffs. This has been the practice in relatively well-governed states such as AP and Maharashtra. The report also recommends penal action be taken against distribution companies with audited accounts, where losses have amounted to Rs 1 trillion (USD 20 billion). Given the scale of the problem, Prime Minister Manmohan Singh urged India's state power ministers to act on the draft report.[2]

India's national and state governments share responsibility for administering the country's power sector, with the states playing a significant role. Even though each state faces its own particular problems, this chapter focuses on AP, which is considered one of the better-governed states in India. AP has been regarded as a progressive state since the days of chief minister Chandrababu Naidu (1995–2004), who was a committed reformer.[3] The AP government's policy ideas pertaining to power sector reforms were considerably evolved even before the state entered into a relationship with the World Bank in 1998. The World Bank was also keen on showcasing a few progressive states as role models for emulation by other states around that time.[4] The AP government implemented reforms with remarkable zeal by unbundling the state electricity board into generation, transmission, and distribution companies, and by making a significant political commitment to competent and independent regulation. The AP Power Generation Company (APGENCO) is among the most efficiently run generation companies in India. It was awarded the Fourth India Power Award for 'overall utility performance' in 2011.[5] The vigilance department within the AP Transmission Company has won nationwide awards for catching theft.[6]

Yet, even a well-governed state like AP under Naidu (1995–2004) and subsequently under Y.S. Rajashekhar Reddy (2004–9) has not produced a financially viable power sector. Despite these markers of success, the accumulated unpaid losses owing to theft and the provision of free electricity to be subsidized by the state government was Rs 101.5 billion (USD 2 billion) through July 2011.[7] This amount constituted the uncompensated loss of the public sector utilities in AP. Why does a relatively well-governed state suffer losses in the power sector? Is it because the electricity sector is intrinsically difficult to govern in India?

This chapter discusses one important consequence of mass politics in India: how the political power of farmers has led to the policy of providing free electricity to agriculture in AP. The argument about mass politics suggests that in areas where the number of people mobilized against an electorally potent issue is significant, policy reforms will encounter greater obstacles.[8] While agriculture paid for itself in the 1970s, industry had to subsidize agriculture beginning in the 1980s.[9] As with reforms in India's industrial policies and telecommunications, 1991 represented the tipping point for institutional change in the country's power sector. Reform ideas pertaining to the generation, transmission, and distribution of electricity were consolidated around 1995 in AP,[10] just a year after an influential report of the National Development Council.[11] Yet, the power sector in AP continues to be in a grave financial condition. The private sector, with only 16 per cent of the installed power capacity, is unable to perform the positive role it plays in the telecom sector.[12] In addition, if agriculture and industry are both subsidized beyond a point where there is little scope for a cross-subsidy, it is impossible for the market mechanism to work. Private power producers work for profit and efficient public sector utilities want a decent rate of return. India's Electricity Act (2003) has introduced open access, where surplus producing state and national utility companies can feed electricity into the national grid, the price of which is determined by supply and demand conditions. This leads to expensive purchases of power during the summer months when demand outpaces supply in a rapidly growing state such as AP.[13] It has become difficult for the AP government to fill the revenue–expenditure gap in its power sector, which has assumed alarming proportions.

This chapter examines the politics behind the farmers' demand for free electricity in AP, which has singularly scuttled power sector reforms in the state. The first section of this chapter elaborates on the ideas and politics of Chandrababu Naidu and the dominant developmental ideas in AP since the mid-1990s. Reform ideas and politics driven by a fiscal crisis formed the basis of power sector reforms in AP. Section II will describe the roots of populism in AP, which became the basis for chief minister Y.S. Rajashekhar Reddy's political strategy starting in 2004. The issue of free electricity and its impact on the reform process will be discussed in some depth. Section III will conclude with reflections on the obstacles to reform in parts of Indian society, where mass politics plays a major role. Can utility companies in AP begin charging farmers higher prices in return for higher quality of electricity, possibly cross-subsidizing electricity for poorer farmers? And will the tipping point for further reform arise?

Chandrababu Naidu: Reform Ideas and Politics (1995–2004)

Chandrababu Naidu was very aware of both the political power of populism and the deep-rooted financial crisis when he became chief minister of Andhra Pradesh in 1995. His predecessor and mentor—the charismatic film actor N.T. Rama Rao of the newly formed Telugu Desam Party (TDP)—had displaced the ruling Congress party in AP with a populist political agenda in January 1983. Rao had founded the TDP in 1982 at the age of 65, and it was a significant development in Indian politics. AP was one of the few states with uninterrupted Congress party rule from 1957 to 1982. Congress setbacks in the national elections of 1967 and 1977 had not affected the party in AP.[14] The TDP's historic victory in AP during 1983 depended on significant support of backward caste groups and the *kamma* caste group. Congress party rule and the national government's tight political control over the state were hurting the pride of the Telugu-speaking populace in AP, who accounted for over 80 per cent of the population. This became an important element in opposition politics. The TDP government was voted to power on the basis of populist pledges. These included promises to keep the price of rice at Rs 2 per kilogramme and to provide free meals for schoolchildren. Rao also passed a legislation to improve the inheritance rights of women and reserved 20 per cent of the seats in district-level government for women.[15]

Chandrababu Naidu succeeded Rao as chief minister of AP in 1995.[16] Naidu is an educated and intellectually curious politician with rural roots, who was a bit of a maverick. He is the son of a middle-class farmer from the Chittoor district of AP who earned a Master's degree in economics from the Sri Venkateshwara College of Arts located in the small town of Tirupati. He began his political life as a rebellious member of the Congress party, known for his organizational ability. He was expelled from the party when he supported someone other than the party's official candidate in a local election in 1978, and had to plead with Indira Gandhi to be reinstated within the Congress. He became a young minister in the Congress government later that same year.[17]

Naidu had met the charismatic actor and TDP leader N.T. Rama Rao in the late 1970s, and impressed him enough for Rao to propose the marriage of his daughter Bhuvaneshwari to Naidu. Even though Naidu was married to the TDP leader's daughter, he contested the historic 1983 elections on the Congress ticket and lost. When Naidu was preparing to retire from politics in 1983, Rao persuaded his son-in-law to join the newly founded and victorious TDP. Naidu would later become known for building up the TDP organization, and did not contest elections for some time.[18] Even though the party was consolidated on the basis of Telugu pride, anti-Congressism, and populism (which had earned a substantial backward caste vote), Naidu strived to replace populism with good economic governance during his tenure as AP's chief minister between 1995 and 2004.

Naidu's background in economics and his experience as finance minister under Rao (in 1994) had convinced him that the pattern of governance had to change in AP. The state could not sustain the fiscal weight of populist expenditures and was riddled with administrative failures. A number of white papers pertaining to the state's financial position were published around this time.[19] The TDP had been voted out of power in 1989, despite its provision of a rice subsidy. As finance minister, Naidu was not entirely convinced about the merit of the subsidy, which Rao reintroduced in 1994.[20] In addition, the power sector was a significant drain on the exchequer. Whereas the cost of generating electricity was Rs 1.83 (6 cents) per unit, the revenue realized was only Rs 0.03 (0.1 cent) per unit. AP's subsidy bill for electricity alone was Rs 15.3 billion (USD 487.1 million) in 1995. In addition, there was the housing subsidy, the non-recovery of loans from cooperative banks, and a variety of other government expenditures. The state was faced with the double tragedy of high expenditures and low growth for many years. Sluggish growth and low tax collection left very little room for the development of infrastructure in AP.[21]

It was under these circumstances that Naidu successfully sought a loan from the World Bank in 1997. He was convinced that deficit reduction was good for the state, and that it needed to direct more funds towards physical infrastructure and human development. Furthermore, India's central government was facing a fiscal crisis, which forced it to withdraw state-level funding.[22] Under these circumstances, the terms of the World Bank loan were generous. The loan would increase AP's debt, but Naidu was convinced that as a proportion of the state's net domestic product, the debt amount was less onerous than what most other Indian states were facing.[23] The World Bank's AP Restructuring Project in 1998, worth USD 543 million, was followed by the AP Power Sector Restructuring Project of USD 210 million. By 2004, when Naidu lost the elections, the World Bank's total commitments to AP added up to USD 1.59 billion.[24]

Under these circumstances, Naidu understood good governance had to replace populism. Raising funds for development involved lobbying both the central government and private and foreign investors. Naidu convinced Bill Gates to visit Hyderabad and pledge investment in the state—investment that materialized on 28 February 1999 in Hi-Tec City. Naidu proclaimed that the state of AP had graduated from India's twenty-second state in terms of investor perception in 1995 to the third spot in 2000. He was fascinated by economic development in East and Southeast Asia, and noted that countries such as Singapore, South Korea, Malaysia, and China registered more rapid GDP growth than India. He was enthralled by Mahathir Mohamad's Vision 2020 for Malaysia. AP, Naidu believed, needed good governance in order to catch up. It was important for him to understand management and engage with managers and thinkers such as Peter Drucker and Jack Welch. Professionals should be in politics and needed to be trained in management. Naidu was in favour of higher salaries and better infrastructure for government functionaries and clean official sources of party funds.[25] It is for these reasons that Naidu has been called a 'CEO' in politics and an icon of state-level economic reforms in India.[26]

Despite a clear commitment to good governance, Naidu could not ignore electoral imperatives on the eve of AP's state assembly elections in 1999. Populism had won elections for the TDP in 1983 and in 1994. If Naidu wanted to consolidate his power, he could not ignore the politics of competitive populism. One scholar who found Naidu to be a 'self-conscious populist' reported that his populism had even outclassed the populism of N.T. Rama Rao in 1999. Astounded by the AP government's torrent of welfare schemes, the Election Commission urged the government to stop a scheme for women's welfare. Naidu, on the other hand, accused the Congress party of using the Election Commission to obstruct the welfare of women in AP.[27]

What did all this mean for power sector reforms in AP? Naidu's governance strategy was akin to walking on two legs. One was the leg of good governance, rationalizing government expenditure and finding a way to reduce unnecessary subsidies, attracting investment and development funds, and promoting social welfare. The other leg was the politics of competitive populism, where governments sought to win elections by giving more and more to the people without considering the constraints of the exchequer.

Given Naidu's reform mindset that we just discussed, he was keen to run the power sector along commercially viable lines. The government produced a paper on the AP State Electricity Board in 1996. Naidu was worried about the rapid growth in agricultural power consumption that was powered by a growing number of electrically fired pump sets. Canals, tanks, and diesel pumps had been the backbone of agricultural development in AP in the past. Agricultural energy consumption in AP had risen from 23 per cent of total consumption in 1985 to 51 per cent in 1995. According to his estimates, the same figures for industrial consumption were 51 per cent and 26 per cent, respectively. While the Congress party clamoured for free electricity for farmers, Naidu proposed placing a greater emphasis on subsidized but uninterrupted power supply. He was worried about the profligate consumption of power due to the unmetered flat rate. In addition to the problem of free power, there was the scourge of power theft.[28] The mounting losses of the state electricity board occurred despite the excellent performance by the state's generating plants. In the next section, we turn to the valiant attempts at power-sector reforms in AP, and the reasons why the mass politics of free electricity interfered with this transformation.

Reform Ideas

Naidu had the benefit of excellent technocratic assessments of the challenges that the power sector was facing in AP. The *Report of the High Level Committee: Guidelines on Restructuring and Privatization of Power Sector and Power Sector Tariff* (1995) was written just a year after the *Report of the National Development Council Committee on Power* (1994), which was sponsored by the Planning Commission. The *Report of the High Level Committee* was chaired by eminent economist Hiten Bhaya.[29] It utilized the expertise available at the prestigious Administrative College of India, located in AP's capital city of Hyderabad. The college was instrumental in drafting another influential report in 1997 on the establishment of regulatory institutions in the power sector.[30] The *Report of the High Level Committee* highlighted all the salient problems facing the power sector before the World Bank engaged with the state in 1998.

This report noted the problem of agricultural power consumption and electricity theft. It made many significant recommendations in light of the fiscal crunch, including the establishment of private independent power producers in order to spur investment and competition;[31] the unbundling of the AP State Electricity Board into separate generation, transmission, and distribution companies;[32] the need for a regulator for setting tariffs;[33] and on the technology to deal with electricity theft.[34] The report noted that public sector power generators in AP had an exemplary performance record and that private sector participation may not turn out to be the appropriate avenue for increasing efficiency in the sector. Rather than reducing costs, private sector participation could escalate costs due to foreign collaboration, technical fees, and imported equipment. The committee was averse to providing any guarantees to the private sector, and argued that independent power producers needed to take responsibility for transmitting and distributing power.[35] The report thus held a mixed view about allowing private sector participation in AP's power sector. The fiscal crisis necessitated it, but the efficiency of public sector utilities meant that such investment should be introduced with caution.

Electricity theft was also a major concern. For this reason, the report recommended that AP use a high-voltage distribution system rather than a low-voltage distribution system. It was opined that India, like the US, had a scattered load with low-load density, unlike the European system with its concentrated loads of high-load density. The high-voltage system would reduce energy loss, transformer failure, theft, and voltage fluctuation. A pilot study of 117 pump sets showed that capital investment in the high-voltage system would be cost-effective.[36]

The report also maintained that industry needed to cross-subsidize electricity for agriculture and should, therefore, purchase power from public utilities. The agricultural sector was paying 6 paise (0.1 cent) per unit when the cost of service was Rs 1.26 (4 cents) per unit, creating a subsidy burden that added up to Rs 10 billion (USD 318 million). It was important, therefore, to either charge more for agricultural consumption or retain industrial consumers who could cross-subsidize agriculture.[37] It would be tragic if private producers could cherry-pick the consumers who paid for electricity but did not take on the responsibility for helping support the subsidy for agricultural consumers.

Regulation of power utilities and the unbundling of the electricity board into generation, transmission, and distribution companies were complimentary institutional roles. The distribution sector was to be broken into smaller companies. The regulator would need to take an objective view of the tariff burden to be shared by different classes of consumers. The report realized the challenge of trying to regulate a sector where 40–45 per cent of consumers did not pay their bills, and it pointed out that free electricity was the single most important challenge facing the power sector.[38]

AP's power reform programme was built on a solid foundation of political commitment and technocratic knowledge about what ailed the sector. Naidu was quick to approach World Bank president James Wolfensohn when the bank had just begun considering lending directly to Indian states sometime in 1996. Wolfensohn was so impressed by Naidu's presentation that he urged Ed Lim, the World Bank's country director for India, to approach the issue of a loan to AP as soon as possible. The bank wanted to create reform champions in the Indian states and was approaching the states directly rather than funding projects through the central government. The team led by Lim took a holistic view and emphasized privatization, reducing public sector losses for utilities, and increased investments in physical and human infrastructure. Lim was keen to both push this agenda and to include AP as part of World Bank's portfolio. The bank pledged USD 543 million in June 1998 on the Andhra Pradesh Economic Restructuring Project, followed by another USD 210 million for the Andhra Pradesh Power Sector Restructuring Project in 1999. It was also patient about Naidu's populist appeals in 1999 on the eve of his election campaign.[39]

Power Sector Reforms

AP pursued power sector reforms with remarkable zeal. The AP Electricity Reform Act was enacted in 1998 and the AP State Electricity Board was unbundled into APGENCO and the Transmission Corporation of Andhra Pradesh Limited (APTRANSCO) in 1999. The APERC was established in 1999 and held its first public hearings in the same year. Public hearings have allowed consumers to express their grievances before the commission, and it is remarkable how journalists, scholars, and citizens hold the government accountable at these hearings in AP. APERC submitted its first tariff order in 2000, which increased the tariff for urban domestic consumers and led to widespread protest. APTRANSCO was unbundled into four distribution companies during the same year.[40]

Restructuring the electricity board faced significant opposition. The Congress party, which had initiated the reform programme at the national government level (as discussed in Chapter 3), opposed the same types of reform in AP. It joined hands with the CPI, the CPM, and other smaller parties in an attempt to stall the proceedings in the assembly. It was only because of the TDP's majority that the AP Electricity Reform Act was passed in 1998. The two main issues that raised the ire of the opposition were the influence of the World Bank and the possibility that private companies could enter the transmission, distribution, and generation segments in AP.[41]

Even Naidu was pragmatic about agricultural consumers. Though APERC raised the rates for 400,000 domestic consumers—who used more than a certain quantity of electricity—and for 300,000 commercial and industrial consumers, he finally decided not to raise the tariff for agricultural consumption. The tariff hike affected the middle class, small businesses, and industrial consumers. Rather than raise the agricultural tariff, he deployed agricultural extension services to encourage the nurturing of less water-intensive crops among the rural population. Naidu had raised the agricultural tariff in 1995 upon becoming chief minister, and this had aroused widespread opposition. He would, therefore, not risk raising the electricity tariff on the eve of the assembly elections in 1999.[42]

How did the story of tariff setting in AP unfold? Naidu urged legislators to explain to the citizens the rationale behind raising the electricity tariff. He lent political weight behind setting up APERC, which had explicit tariff-setting powers. APERC raised domestic tariffs for all classes of consumers, but raised them to the greatest extent for residential consumers. The average tariff increase was 50 per cent, but for those with the lowest monthly consumption, it amounted to an 80 per cent increase. The subsidized tariff for farmers was to be 25 paise (0.001 cent) per unit. APERC argued that the cross-subsidy burden for agricultural tariffs, which had been shouldered exclusively by industrial and commercial consumers, should be shared by domestic users as well.[43]

Widespread opposition to the tariff hike began in June 2000 and reached a peak on 30 August when the police killed two people at a protest. The Congress party led the opposition, and groups on the extreme Left of the political spectrum turned violent in their protests. The World

Bank initially viewed higher electricity tariffs, when accompanied with a better quality of power, as beneficial even to the marginal farmer. But the bank subsequently acknowledged that while tariffs had been raised, the quality of supply had not. It held that the quality of supply for farmers needed to improve in order justify a higher tariff. Electricity in rural AP was available for only a few hours during the day, and the poor quality of supply increased the incidence of transformer burnouts. The bank indicated that this low quality of service was not commensurate with the recent electricity tariff hike.[44]

The Congress party in AP spearheaded the free electricity movement and received significant support from the CPM.[45] In June 2002, the Congress party's national general secretary demanded free electricity. Dr Y.S. Rajashekhar Reddy,[46] the Congress party's leader of the opposition in the AP assembly, advocated free electricity for farmers to reduce the disparity between the farmer's incomes in irrigated and non-irrigated areas. He committed the party to free electricity for farmers if it ever came to power. In 2003, Reddy and his compatriots in the Congress party walked across 11 districts in AP and reaffirmed their commitment to free electricity. The People's Monitoring Group on Electricity Reforms, an independent advocacy group, complained that electricity tariff hikes had hurt small farmers and the urban poor, and that these segments of society did not find a voice in APERC's public hearings.[47]

Regulation of tariffs in AP, therefore, represented the single-most challenging issue for the governance of the power sector in a state where farmers had become accustomed to highly subsidized electricity. In fiscal 2001, the state government paid an estimated subsidy of Rs 16.2 billion (USD 300 million) to the AP government's generating company for subsidizing electricity to farmers. It would pay another Rs 8 billion (USD 150 million) to fully offset the price increases of the middle-class consumers.[48]

Chief minister Naidu's commitment to independent electricity regulation was not a hollow one. The respect for the founding figure of power regulation in the state, G.P. Rao, had grown among those concerned with the sector over the years. Rao was a reform-minded officer of the elite Indian Administrative Services from the AP cadre who had engineered a financial turnaround in the publicly owned Singareni collieries (coal mines). These mines provided the essential fodder for the thermal power plants in AP. Rao had retired as a senior civil servant in

Delhi and was looking forward to relaxed life in Hyderabad when Naidu approached him and asked for his help. Rao had no previous interaction with Naidu, but Naidu was looking for a competent, honest, and an independent regulator rather than a close confidant.[49]

APERC performed its regulatory duties under difficult circumstances. It is to APERC's credit that it blocked a power-purchasing agreement with the British Physical Laboratories (BPL) when it found that the deal was not in the consumers' interest. APERC developed substantial regulatory competence in the area of tariff setting and calculating the subsidy that the government had to pay owing to its social commitments. Even though agricultural energy consumption was highly subsidized, Naidu and APERC were able to charge for this usage and developed a way to calculate the government's subsidy burden. The revenue realized from this effort may have been less than Rs 2 billion (USD 40.2 million), but it established the principle that there could be no free lunch and that waste would be minimized. This required considerable political will on the part of Naidu. APERC also developed substantial competence in the area of tariff setting, based on the principle of cost to serve.[50]

APERC institutionalized regular public hearings all over AP in order to solicit the views of civil society organizations—a legacy that has endured and contributed positively towards the regulation of the power sector in AP. Civil society organizations have become deeply involved with the governance of power sector reforms in the state. People who do not belong to the power sector have become well-informed and spend considerable time and energy preparing for these annual hearings in various regions.

Critical Left-wing vernacular newspapers such as *Prajashakti* and its special correspondent M. Venugopal Rao kept a close watch on power purchase agreements, tariff setting, and consumer welfare. He and others contended that AP's public utility APGENCO, one of the most efficient public utilities in the nation, should not be neglected in an era of privatization. The state government sought to address this situation in 2003 by arranging a more generous financial package for APGENCO. To give another example, Venugopal Rao raised several objections about utilities in AP at a public hearing in May 2010. He criticized distribution companies for not presenting their annual revenue requirements and for not explaining how they would bridge their Rs 61 billion (USD 1.2 billion) gap between expenses and revenues. In June 2010, Rao argued against allowing distribution companies to enter into a power purchasing agreement with BPL without a competitive bidding process.[51] In addition to monitoring efforts from crusaders like Rao, Prayas—a non-governmental organization overseeing power sector reforms in India—posted a representative in Hyderabad who provided valuable inputs during these hearings and wrote articles in scholarly journals such as the *Economic and Political Weekly*.[52] Public action kept APERC and utility companies on their toes in AP.

Even a conscientious regulator like G.P. Rao, however, has had to bow down to the farmers' lobby. Rao was unable to direct the government to install meters for accurately measuring agricultural consumption. Agricultural consumption was carefully metered till 1984. When the TDP's N.T. Rama Rao came to power for the first time, he decided to charge agricultural consumption based on the power of an electric pump-set rather than the quantity of electricity consumed. The farmer, therefore, had no incentive to conserve the electricity used for irrigation, and meters for measuring agricultural consumption were promptly removed to the satisfaction of farmers. This was perhaps the biggest mistake in the governance of AP's power sector, as electricity consumption in agriculture has never been measured accurately ever since.

The removal of meters for measuring agricultural consumption was a substantial setback for power sector reforms in AP. Even though the process of installation was later resumed, only around 55 per cent of agricultural energy used was metered.[53] This has lead to a peculiar dilemma. On the one hand, APTRANSCO claimed that transmission and distribution losses owing to technical reasons and theft had been drastically reduced from 36.9 per cent of the electricity generated in 1999 on the eve of the reforms to 21.42 per cent in 2004.[54] Farmers, on the other hand, claimed that it was impossible to assess these claims because only about half of the agricultural consumption was metered. Since there was no way to accurately calculate agricultural consumption, farmers argued that APTRANSCO was adding the theft and transmission loss figure to agricultural consumption. According to the farmers, these fudged figures were a good way to convince the government and the World Bank about improved governance of the power sector.[55]

The farmers' contention on this point is not without some merit. The transmission and distribution loss figure was reported by the government as being less than 20 per cent until 1995, but it shot up to 38 per cent in

1998. Were these figures inflated on the eve of the reforms in 1998 in order to make it easier to demonstrate progress in an era of reforms? Since agricultural consumption was not metered, no one could confirm or refute these figures. APERC had invited the Indian Statistical Institute in 2006 to conduct a sample survey that would assess agricultural consumption in the absence of substantial metering, but this report remained a well-kept secret within APERC.[56]

If the failure to meter farm consumption was a setback for governance, Naidu also erred in neglecting the financial health of an efficient public utility—APGENCO. Under the influence of the World Bank, Naidu may have gone overboard with the idea of private-sector participation and neglected to support APGENCO to the fullest extent. The *Report of the High Level Committee* had pointed out that the publicly owned generators were an asset for AP. APGENCO maintained a plant-load factor higher than 85 per cent between 2000 and 2006, and produced power at a per unit cost of Rs 1.44 (4 cents) between 1998 and 2004, which was much lower than independent power purchasers' producing costs.[57] In 2008, when the average purchase cost from APGENCO was Rs 1.94 (4 cents) per unit, private power producers who used naphtha as fuel—such as GVK, LANCO, and Reliance—were producing power at Rs 7.09 (15 cents) per unit, and independent power producers as a whole were generating power at Rs 3.80 (8 cents) per unit.[58] The introduction of the expensive naphtha-based plants had occurred when Naidu was chief minister. These developments lend credibility to the view that the state should have done more to encourage expansion of APGENCO when the AP State Electricity Board was unbundled in 1999, as it could have reduced the subsidy burden on the state.

The problem was discussed thoroughly in a 13 May 2005 letter from J. Parthasarathy, the chairman and managing director of APGENCO, to the state's principle secretary (energy) Jannat Hussain, who was the senior civil servant dealing with energy issues. In this letter, Parthasarathy alleged that a highly performing government asset—APGENCO—was made to suffer financial hardship because the government needed to decrease its subsidy burden. APGENCO's operation and maintenance expenses were kept well below the normal permissible expenditure entitlements, although a 3 per cent rate of return on equity was granted. The government agreed to a 3 per cent return, but took a stingy view of what constituted equity.[59]

APGENCO was undermined in a variety of ways. First, it was not able to treat the depreciation of plant and equipment between 1999 and 2002 as part of its costs. Second, APGENCO's wage revisions, amounting to Rs 400 million (USD 9.1 million), were not properly accounted as expense. Third, APERC did not permit APGENCO to report the expenses it incurred in constructing the left bank of the Sri Sailam Dam as a fixed cost until full-fledged pump mode operations had begun. Fourth, interest on loans for capital expenditure, such as the construction of the Sri Sailam Dam, was not charged to the tariff. The left and right bank of this scenic dam amid forest and hills represent the most significant hydroelectric project in the state, and it contributes to more than 10 per cent of installed capacity as of July 2011.[60] Finally, APGENCO was not allowed to treat expenditures incurred on interest payments for its pension and provident fund as part of its costs. APGENCO contended that in other states, liabilities pertaining to employees' terminal benefits rest with the state government rather than with utilities, and that this should also be the practice in AP. APGENCO's managing director argued that the government should calculate a return on Rs 21 billion (USD 481.9 million) rather than the suggested Rs 7.8 billion (USD 179 million), if all the costs of APGENCO were appropriately accounted for.[61]

APGENCO could have internally generated resources for generation capacity-expansion, such as the Sri Sailam Dam, if it did not have to meet legitimate costs from its return on an artificially created lower equity. According to Parthasarathy's calculations, APGENCO was denied Rs 16 billion (USD 367.2 million) in revenues between March 1999 and March 2002.[62] If, however, APGENCO's return on equity were calculated according to Indian government guidelines, there would be no need for separate investment in capacity addition. The view that APGENCO had faced unnecessary hardship was subsequently respected by the AP government, and a more generous view of APGENCO's costs was taken into account after 2003. In India's telecom sector, promoting private sector competition had benefited consumers (as discussed in Chapter 4). The same could not be said for power sector reforms in AP, where efficient public utilities were forced to suffer financial hardship in the early years of reform.

How should we assess Naidu's period as chief minister of AP from 1995 to 2004? He had a number of significant achievements. First, Naidu was committed to establishing a capable and independent regulator.

Granting the regulator substantial independence, and the regulator's decision to hold regular public hearings, paved the way for competent tariff setting and better oversight of power purchase agreements. There were no Enron-type scandals with respect to power purchase agreements in AP.[63] Second, the government charged the agricultural sector a subsidized tariff for electricity, despite furious opposition from the Congress and the Left parties. This was a significant achievement, which curbed unnecessary and wasteful consumption of free power. If Naidu had remained in power in AP beyond 2004, he would perhaps have deployed his leadership and charisma to arrange cross-subsidization of poorer farmers' electricity consumption with the richer farmers and industrialists, rather than let loose the genie of free power that haunts the sector to this day. But all in all, Naidu can claim significant achievements in reforming AP's power sector.

Despite these achievements, the Naidu years were plagued by a number of governance setbacks. First, N.T. Rama Rao's populist legacy could not be overcome. During Naidu's tenure, neither the chief minister nor the electricity regulator succeeded in installing meters to measure farm consumption to a significant extent. It was, therefore, impossible to precisely assess the farmers' electricity consumption levels, and this consumption did not earn any revenue. Second, while competition from private companies usually requires public utilities to become efficient, Naidu's government was, perhaps, unfair to APGENCO, which was an efficiently run public utility. Had the government's financial support to APGENCO been more generous, it might have reduced the state's dependence on more expensive sources of power. In the next section of this chapter, we turn to the period when Y.S. Rajashekhar Reddy made populism the hallmark of his electoral strategy in AP.

Free Power for Agriculture: The Populism of Y.S. Rajashekhar Reddy and Beyond

Naidu—the chief minister of AP—lost the state assembly elections in 2004 and again in 2009. The new chief minister in 2004—Y.S. Rajashekhar Reddy of the Congress party—made several populist decisions immediately thereafter, which included the provision of free power for the agricultural sector. It is not easy to discount the contention that after 2004, populism won over the fiscal restraint and economic reforms in AP. The TDP, which was in alliance with the BJP, may have been hurt by the new chief minister's populist pledges. The Congress party won the assembly elections again in 2009, and Reddy continued as chief minister until a helicopter crash took his life in September 2009. The legacy of Reddy's policy of free electricity to farmers looms large over AP. This section will briefly discuss the relationship between the politics of populism and the defeat of the TDP in AP. It will then address the issue of free electricity to the agricultural sector.

Politics after Naidu

The Congress party under Y.S. Rajashekhar Reddy launched a campaign critical of Naidu's image as a reformer. Naidu was portrayed as being closer to captains of industry and multilateral funding organizations like the World Bank than to the rural people of AP. Reddy launched a highly visible 1,500 km walking campaign in May 2003, alleging that Naidu was a stooge of the World Bank who would lead the state into a debt trap. Foremost among the pledges Reddy made during the campaign was free electricity to farmers, subsidies on crop loans, funds for irrigation projects, and relief for families of farmers where someone had committed suicide. Reddy's campaign strategy was to indicate that he would correct the urban orientation of Naidu's policies.

Naidu, on the other hand, did not make populist gestures on the eve of the 2004 elections. There was a sharp contrast in Naidu's behaviour between the elections of 1999 and 2004. Naidu may have believed that his model of good governance could win elections in AP and that he did not have to resort to populism. He announced that elections would be held soon after the radical Left outfit People's War Group attempted to kill him in Tirupati in early 2004. However, the Election Commission refused to oblige him with an early election in February 2004, and the election was finally held during the summer months. The Congress party and its allies, including the Left parties, won 226 seats in these elections, whereas the Naidu's TDP could garner only 47, a dramatic decline from its 180 seats in 1999 election.[64]

It is not easy to assess the relationship between populism and election results, because various factors play a role in producing a particular electoral outcome. Even though the victorious Congress party won many more seats in 2004 (185) than in 1999 (91), its vote share came down from 40.61 per cent in 1999 to 38.5 per cent in 2004. TDP's vote share in 2004 came down by an even greater extent, from 43.87 per cent in 1999 to 37.5 per cent in 2004. Even though this was only one percentage point below the Congress's vote share, TDP lost substantial vote share among the majority of the poor voters and agricultural workers, who voted for the Congress party and its allies.[65] Scheduled Caste (SC) groups voted for the Congress alliance, backward castes voted equally for the Congress alliance and the TDP–BJP alliance, and upper castes voted for the TDP–BJP alliance.[66] Considering these results, a serious scholar of AP politics has argued that the TDP's decision to campaign without making any populist appeals may have hurt the party.[67]

In addition, Naidu's partnership with the Right-wing Hindu nationalist Bharatiya Janata Party (BJP) may have cost the TDP dearly in 2004. Naidu opined that TDP's alliance with BJP had cost the party Muslim votes in the state assembly elections in the aftermath of a terribly violent episode in Gujarat in February 2002. The violence erupted after Narendra Modi, a BJP leader and the chief minister of Gujarat, had turned a blind eye towards attacks against Muslim families in the aftermath of a tragic situation when Muslims set fire to a rail wagon carrying 58 Hindu activists travelling from the holy town of Ayodhya on 27 February 2002. Modi took a long time to stop well-organized Hindu mobs that were perpetrating atrocities on Muslims. It is reported that about 800 Muslims were killed. As a result, the BJP and its allies were denied the Muslim vote in the parliamentary and state assembly elections held in 2004.[68] During the assembly elections in AP, the Congress party and its allies garnered 64 per cent of the Muslim vote, while the TDP–BJP alliance together won merely 34 per cent of that vote. Muslims constituted more than 9 per cent of AP's population in 2001.[69]

The Congress party's promise to provide free electricity to farmers and welfare programmes for the poor may have helped it retain its position as AP's largest party in the 2009 assembly elections, albeit by a more slender majority than in 2004. The Congress party's vote share came down to 36.5 per cent in 2009, but the party retained 156 of the state's assembly seats. TDP's vote share dipped once again to 28.03 per cent, but it won more seats this time (92).[70] The Centre for the Study of Developing Societies' National Election Survey showed that voters in AP were less concerned about whether the government was corrupt than if the government was able to deliver basic needs to the people.[71] The survey showed that there was a widespread opinion among the electorate that programmes such as free electricity, education, and housing for socially backward classes had helped the Congress party. In addition, programmes sponsored by the central government, such as the Mahatma Gandhi National Rural Employment Act (MGNREGA), were implemented more successfully in AP than in other states. Thanks to jobs created by MGNREGA, agricultural workers demanded a higher wage than farmers.[72] It appears that everyone benefited from these programmes, even though the Congress party workers may have benefited more than others.

In the next section, we examine the politics surrounding free electricity for farmers in AP. Going by the region's political track record, it appears there can be no reversing such a measure. Is free electricity a populist measure that helps every section of society? Can there be a politics that discriminates in favour of the marginal and the poor farmer, who should benefit from free electricity? Or have power sector reforms, with substantial fiscal consequences, stalled because of the influence of the powerful farming community?

Farmers and Free Electricity in AP

This section reviews the evidence on whether or not free electricity benefited richer farmers in AP. Where does the demand for free electricity come from? After all, Reddy implemented free electricity immediately after assuming the office of chief minister on 14 May 2004. The annual revenue loss to the exchequer caused by this programme amounted to Rs 4 billion (USD 90.6 million).[73] This section briefly reviews the secondary literature on the provision of free electricity in AP, reports the findings of interviews conducted with the farmers' leaders in the state capital of Hyderabad since 2007, and documents a survey of three villages in June 2010. The first village is Siddinki in the Warrangal district of the Telengana region, which is a dry part of AP. The water level in this village is low and pump-set irrigation is widespread. The other two villages surveyed are in the Kurnool district. The village of Pamulapadu is canal-irrigated and the village of Karivena is not. The aim of this survey was to assess whether the presence of a canal systematically affected the demand for free electricity. Even though a review of three villages has its limitations, it provides useful insights, especially when combined with

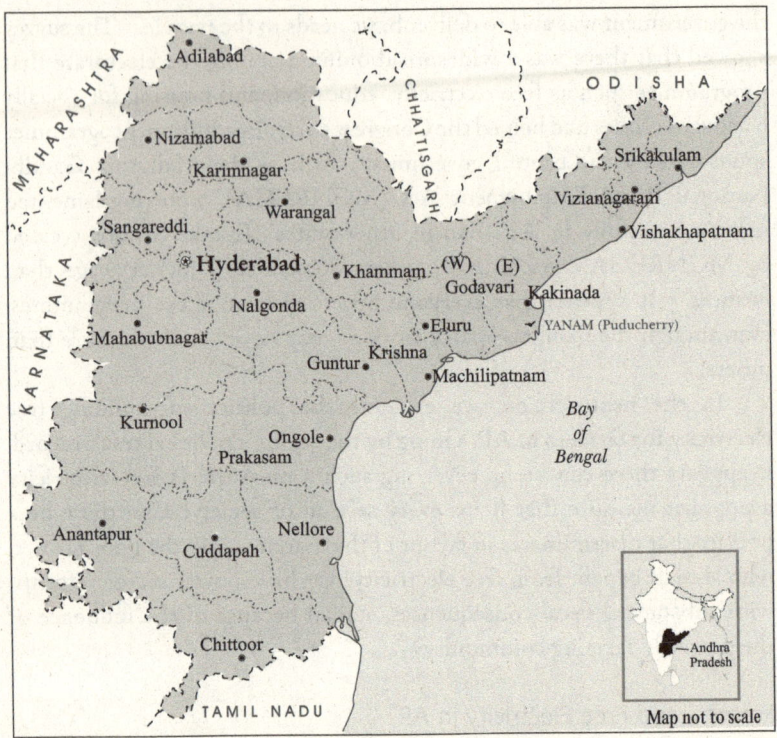

FIGURE 5.1   District Map of Andhra Pradesh

findings in the secondary literature and interviews with farmers' leaders in Hyderabad.

Studies have reported that richer farmers benefited more than the poorer ones from free electricity in AP. According to one study, the gross annual income of electric pump owners was higher (Rs 112,000) compared with those who used diesel pumps (Rs 91,000).[74] It is reported that poorer farmers in AP have historically depended on tanks and water bodies rather than electric or diesel pumps.[75] When Y.S. Rajashekhar Reddy announced farmers would receive free electricity in 2004, the majority of the farmers' leaders in Hyderabad reported that this did more harm than good for a variety of reasons. First, the quality of power supply deteriorated with the removal of the tariff, as there were more pump motor burnouts owing to transformer failures. This produced productivity losses because the cost of these burnouts was absorbed by the farmer. The quality of electricity distribution service also declined after 2004. AP was replacing distribution transformers more swiftly than Haryana before 2004, but could no longer match Haryana's pace after it announced free electricity. The rapid burnout of motor pumps constituted a tax on the farmer.[76]

Second, farmers' representatives in Hyderabad reported that Reddy had not delivered on his promise of seven hours of free electricity per day. Reddy wanted to distribute electricity to farmers for free, but publicly owned distribution companies were under pressure from the government to reduce the quantity of free electricity supplied due to fiscal considerations. Consequently, only four hours of electricity were available, usually in the dead of night. This was a substantial inconvenience for farmers who normally went to bed early and woke up early. In addition, the poor quality of electricity delivered at night increased the extent of electrocutions of both humans and animals.[77] According to APTRANSCO, there were 892 fatal accidents in 2010, 103 of which occurred at night. Consequently, 158 families were compensated to the tune of Rs 10.54 million (USD 212,000) that year.[78]

Third, the government asked farmers to install expensive equipment such as high-density polyethylene pipes (HDPEs) and superior quality motors in order to save power by using superior equipment. These constituted a substantial cost to the poorer farmers. Free electricity, given the vagaries of monsoon rains and the demands of a paddy harvest, led to a surge in the number of borewells that were dug, despite these considerations. Electricity consumption exploded. The exact figures, however, are difficult to assess because agricultural consumption is not substantially metered in AP.[79]

Many farmers' leaders interviewed in Hyderabad in December 2007 and in June 2010 said that free electricity was not good for farmers in AP. Key functionaries of the Federation of Indian farmers and the non-governmental organization Lok Satta also held this view.[80] A leader of the All Indian Kisan Sabha, which is a unit of the CPM, also favoured the subsidized but higher quality of electricity that the TDP government had provided prior to 2004. The World Bank, secondary literature, and Hyderabad farmers' views on the problems of free electricity provision were perplexing. They were contrary to Reddy's policies, which had invested political capital in free electricity and seemed to be succeeding politically. Reddy had no illusions about the fact that free electricity would benefit all.[81]

This puzzle is what drove me to explore the question at the village level. The first surveyed village was Siddinki in Warrangal district in the dry Telengana region. It is 6km away from the small town of Jangam, which is about 120 km from Hyderabad. In this dry land area, the water table in the village is 250–300 ft below the ground. Dr J. Prashanthi helped conduct the survey. She had written a doctoral dissertation in political science at the University of Hyderabad based on extensive rural fieldwork in AP.[82] Prashanthi and I were assisted by the All India Kisan Sabha, which is a unit of the CPM.[83] The CPM had been an ally of the TDP until the 1999 elections, when TDP aligned itself with the Hindu nationalist party—the BJP. The CPM was a part of the Congress alliance in 2004, but left the Congress bloc on the eve of the 2009 elections. The All India Kisan Sabha was respected in the villages we surveyed, but did not have an elected village headman in any of the villages. We made a sincere attempt to conduct a survey where the sample would not be biased by any party's position.

We interviewed 39 people over a period of three days in Siddinki during June 2010. They included 12 people from the SC group, 15 from among the backward castes (BCs), and 12 from the upper castes (UCs). Caste made an impact on individuals' economic well-being through the extent of land holdings, even though some BCs owned a substantial amount of land in the village. There were four (40 per cent) large farmers (owning 10 acres or more of land) among the BCs in our sample, five (56 per cent) among the UCs, and none among the SCs. Among farmers with medium-sized holdings owning between 5 and 10 acres of land, and at least 3 acres of irrigated land, there were four (40 per cent) UCs and four (40 per cent) BCs, respectively, but only two (20 per cent) SCs. There were 10 (50 per cent) SCs and seven (35 per cent) BCs, which owned less than 5 acres of land, but only three (15 per cent) UCs in that category (see Table 5A.1).

We asked farmers whether the subsidized power the Naidu government supplied was superior to the free power distributed by Reddy's Congress government after 2004. More than half (58 per cent) of SCs preferred Naidu over Reddy, saying they preferred the continuous electricity supply provided by the TDP government under Naidu over the intermittent free supply of power supply after 2004. In addition, the money spent on bribing officials to replace transformers had risen. At the same time, however, 83 per cent of UCs and 67 per cent of BCs preferred Reddy over Naidu (see Table 5A.2). A slim majority of the small farmers (55 per cent) and the vast majority of the middle farmers (90 per cent) preferred Reddy's free power, while a slim majority of the large farmers (56 per cent) favoured Naidu's subsidized, uninterrupted power supply (see Table 5A.3). Four respondents did not take any position on this issue. Overall, 33 per cent of the survey respondents supported Naidu, 62 per cent supported Reddy, and 5 per cent remained neutral.

In this village that was hungry for more electricity in June 2010, there was some support for Naidu's previous system of subsidized power, but the majority of respondents favoured the free power distributed by Reddy's Congress government since 2004. The use of electric pump-sets was universal in the village, and given the low water table, farmers needed 5 hp pumps. This support for Reddy's system endured, despite concerns about the lack of a continuous electricity supply under the Congress regime in AP. In addition, farmers commented on one facet of Naidu's governance that may have undermined his regime. They detested the fact that the TDP government was very particular about collecting electricity bills, and that farmers were either heavily penalized or were even imprisoned for failing to pay. This was a humiliating experience for farmers.

We next moved to village Karivena in the Kurnool district of AP, which is around 70km from the district town of Kurnool. We interviewed 73 people in Karivena. Like Siddinki, Karivena is not irrigated by a canal. Caste and landownership were intimately connected in this village. A total of 27 of the 47 small farmers were SCs. There were five middle farmers each among the BCs and UCs (76 per cent) and three SCs (24 per cent) in that category. There were nine rich farmers (69 per cent) among the UCs, four (31 per cent) among the BCs, and no SC rich farmers in our sample (see Table 5A.4). The overwhelming majority of the farmers in this village supported free power being supplied by the Reddy government. These supporters of free electricity included 36 small farmers (77 per cent), 10 middle farmers (77 per cent), and 12 rich farmers (92 per cent), who were interviewed (see Table 5A.5). Of those surveyed, 17 BCs (81 per cent), 17 UCs (77 per cent), and 24 SCs (80 per cent) also expressed the same preference (see Table 5A.6).

Ultimately, there was overwhelming support for Reddy in Karivena. Perhaps the village's greater dependence open wells (its water table was much higher than Siddinki's water table) reduced the importance of an uninterrupted electricity supply. In this sense, Karivena was rather unlike the water-deprived Siddinki, where support for Naidu, though less than a majority, was still significant.

Finally, we moved to the village of Pamulapadu in the same district (Kurnool), where we interviewed 46 people. Even though SCs dominated the small farmer population (55 per cent interviewed), BCs constituted a substantial number (39 per cent) of middle farmers, and UCs (36 per cent) and BCs (43 per cent) were almost equally split among the large farmers in our sample (see Table 5A.7). The water table in this village was low, even though half of the village land was irrigated by a canal. There was a higher incidence of borewells in this village compared with Karivena. Reddy's support was most significant among the SCs (53 per cent), followed by the BCs (45 per cent). A total of four UCs and four BCs each supported Naidu in our sample (see Table 5A.8). More smaller and middle farmers favoured Reddy, while rich farmers were evenly split between Naidu and Reddy (see Table 5A.9). People in Pamalupadu, like people in Siddinki, preferred Reddy (48 per cent), even though the support for Naidu (25 per cent) was more significant in these villages than in Karivena. These findings point to the possibility that the value of uninterrupted power supply generated at a subsidized cost may increase as one gets to the dryer parts of AP. It is worth exploring whether the support for Naidu is greater in places where the water table is lower.

We interviewed 158 people in the three villages of Siddinki, Karivena, and Pamulapadu in June 2010. More than half the small farmers were SCs (55 per cent) and there were a substantial number of BCs in that category. The majority of the middle farmers were BCs (43 per cent). The middle farmer category had a substantial number of UCs and SCs as well. Among the large farmers in our sample, it was the UCs that was the dominant group (53 per cent), but BCs had a substantial presence as well (39 per cent). To the extent that our sample was representative of the population, it appears that there had been upward mobility among the BCs as a result of land reforms in AP (see Table 5A.10).

The majority of the farmers (66 per cent) supported Reddy's free electricity, while support for Naidu was much less (20 per cent). But 23 people (14 per cent) in our sample were undecided (see Table 5A.11 and Table 5A.12). This exercise suggests that it is easy to build political support around any public utility that comes for free. Building a coalition that will progressively subsidize electricity—and provide better quality and uninterrupted supply of power in rural areas—will need to incorporate those who prefer Naidu's system of a subsidized, nine-hour uninterrupted supply of electricity, and those who are undecided about the benefits of free electricity.

These village interviews, which were conducted over a period of two weeks in June 2010, indicate that views suggesting that only rich farmers demand free electricity—views that are encountered at the World Bank, expressed in secondary literature, and held by a majority of farmer's leaders in Hyderabad—need to be amended. Reddy was correct in assessing that the demand for free electricity was rather more widespread. He would have discovered this in his 1,500km walking campaign in May 2003. It is no coincidence that the free electricity was the policy Reddy implemented in his first days as the chief minister of AP in May 2004. Reddy went ahead with this decision, despite counsel against it from his senior civil servants.[84] A policy that has support from a majority of farmers is a classic case where mass politics trumps good economics.

Conclusion: The Dilemma of Mass Politics

These findings, based on interviews in Hyderabad and a survey of three villages in June 2010, highlight the power of mass politics as an obstacle to the economic reform process in India. It is difficult not to conclude that Naidu's strategy of good governance, while it may have erred in neglecting APGENCO, struggled hard to rationalize its policy of charging for electricity, even if it was heavily subsidized for farmers. AP, therefore, stood an as an excellent candidate for power sector reform, if someone could reduce the state's subsidy burden. In hindsight, competent and independent regulation of the power sector was a commendable achievement of the Naidu era. If Naidu had been re-elected in 2004, he could have used the mandate to rationalize the subsidy burden owing to agricultural consumption.

The populism of Reddy, however, paid rich electoral dividends, and it has unleashed a vicious cycle of subsidies begetting electoral victories. The Congress party was elected in 2004 and re-elected again in 2009. The subsidy burden owing to subsidized free agricultural consumption of electricity is a worrisome phenomenon in India's political economy. There can be no question that small farmers deserve free electricity, and power consumption in the agricultural sector should be subsidized. However, free power to all engenders excessive waste, and comes with its own agonies for both farmers and utility companies. Under the Reddy government's system, electricity is supplied at odd hours, cannot be supplied continuously, and electrocutes people and animals at an alarming rate.

Free electricity presents a challenge to economic reforms in India and in AP. Despite the economic tipping point that existed during India's 1991 balance of payments crisis, efforts to reform the agricultural sector's consumption of electricity and to promote private participation have all came to a naught, even in one of the best governed states in India. Will AP produce a political entrepreneur who will separate the majority of the small and middle farmers from the larger ones and rationalize the subsidy burden? This preliminary survey shows that while there is some support for subsidized and continuous supply of electricity in AP, crafting a winning political coalition around that issue will require astute statesmanship. It is not clear, however, whether economic problems such as these will find political solutions.

In the final analysis, the power sector was vastly different from the telecom sector in India. The previous chapter on telecoms is the story of private-sector participation, promotion of competition, and a boom in telecommunications during an era of economic reforms. Dealing with telecom unions and the Department of Telecommunications proved much easier than dealing with farmers in AP. Even with a political will for change and technocratic capacity in AP, power sector reforms failed. This chapter suggests that despite the electricity sector's potential, the demands of mass politics, as reflected in the farmers' demand for free electricity, has the capacity to stall the reform process. AP can be viewed as a typical case that demonstrates the challenges facing the power sector in many Indian states today.

Appendix

TABLE **5A.1** Caste and Land Ownership in Siddinki

Acres	Castes			Total
	Backward Caste (BC)	Upper Caste (UC)	Scheduled Caste (SC)	
1*	7 (35%)	3 (15%)	10 (50%)	20
2**	4 (40%)	4 (40%)	2 (20%)	10
3***	4 (44%)	5 (56%)	0 (0%)	9
Total	15 (38%)	12 (31%)	12 (31%)	39

Source: Data collected and tabulated by author.

Notes: *1 = Small farmer with 1–5 acres of land but less than 3 acres of irrigated land.
**2 = Small farmer with 5–9 acres of land but with 3 or more acres of irrigated land.
***3 = Large farmer with 10 or more acres of land.

TABLE **5A.2** Caste and the Preference for Naidu/Reddy in Siddinki

Caste	Naidu/Reddy			Total
	Naidu	Neutral	Reddy	
BC	4 (26%)	1 (7%)	10 (67%)	15
UC	2 (17%)	0 (0%)	10 (83%)	12
SC	7 (58%)	1 (8%)	4 (34%)	12
Total	13 (33%)	2 (5%)	24 (62%)	39

Source: Data collected and tabulated by author.

TABLE **5A.3** Class and the Preference for Naidu/Reddy in Siddinki

Acres	Naidu/Reddy			Total
	Naidu	Neutral	Reddy	
1	7 (35%)	2 (10%)	11 (55%)	20
2	1 (10%)	0 (0%)	9 (90%)	10
3	5 (56%)	0 (0%)	4 (44%)	9
Total	13 (33%)	2 (5%)	24 (62%)	39

Source: Data collected and tabulated by author.

TABLE 5A.4   Caste and Land Ownership in Karivena

Acres	Caste			Total
	BC	UC	SC	
1	12 (26%)	8 (17%)	27 (57%)	47
2	5 (38%)	5 (38%)	3 (24%)	13
3	4 (31%)	9 (69%)	0 (0%)	13
Total	21 (29%)	22(30%)	30 (41%)	73

Source: Data collected and tabulated by author.

TABLE 5A.5   Class and the Preference for Naidu/Reddy in Karivena

Acres	Naidu/Reddy			Total
	Naidu	Neutral	Reddy	
1	2 (4%)	9 (19%)	36 (77%)	47
2	3 (23%)	0 (0%)	10 (77%)	13
3	1 (8%)	0 (0%)	12 (92%)	13
Total	6 (8%)	9 (12%)	58 (80%)	73

Source: Data collected and tabulated by author.

TABLE 5A.6   Caste and the Preference for Naidu/Reddy in Karivena

Caste	Naidu/Reddy			Total
	Naidu	Neutral	Reddy	
BC	1 (5%)	3 (14%)	17 (81%)	21
UC	4 (18%)	1 (5%)	17 (77%)	22
SC	1 (3%)	5 (17%)	24 (80%)	30
Total	6 (8%)	9 (12%)	58 (80%)	73

Source: Data collected and tabulated by author.

TABLE 5A.7   Caste and Land Ownership in Pamulapadu

Acres	Caste			Total
	BC	UC	SC	
1	7 (39%)	1 (6%)	10 (55%)	18
2	7 (50%)	3 (21%)	4 (29%)	14
3	6 (43%)	5 (36%)	3 (21%)	14
Total	20 (43%)	9 (20%)	17 (37%)	46

Source: Data collected and tabulated by author.

TABLE **5A.8** Caste and the Preference for Naidu/Reddy in Pamulapadu

Caste	Naidu/Reddy			Total
	Naidu	Neutral	Reddy	
BC	5 (25%)	6 (30%)	9 (45%)	20
UC	4 (44%)	1 (12%)	4 (44%)	9
SC	3 (18%)	5 (29%)	9 (53%)	17
Total	12 (26%)	12 (26%)	22 (48%)	46

Source: Data collected and tabulated by author.

TABLE **5A.9** Class and the Preference for Naidu/Reddy in Pamalupadu

Acres	Naidu/Reddy			Total
	Naidu	Neutral	Reddy	
1	3 (17%)	9 (50%)	6 (33%)	18
2	2 (14%)	3 (31%)	9 (64%)	14
3	7 (50%)	0 (0%)	7 (50%)	14
Total	12 (26%)	12 (26%)	22 (48%)	46

Source: Data collected and tabulated by author.

TABLE **5A.10** Caste and Land Ownership in Siddinki, Karivena, and Pamalupadu

Acres	Caste			Total
	BC	UC	SC	
1	26 (31%)	12 (14%)	47 (55%)	85
2	16 (43%)	12 (33%)	9 (24%)	37
3	14 (39%)	19 (53%)	3 (8%)	36
Total	56 (36%)	43 (27%)	59 (37%)	158

Source: Data collected and tabulated by author.

TABLE **5A.11** Caste and Preference for Naidu/Reddy in Siddinki, Karivena, and Pamalupadu

Caste	Naidu/Reddy			Total
	Naidu	Neutral	Reddy	
BC	10 (18%)	10 (18%)	36 (64%)	56
UC	10 (23%)	2 (5%)	31 (72%)	43
SC	11 (19%)	11 (19%)	37 (62%)	59
Total	31 (20%)	23 (14%)	104 (66%)	158

Source: Data collected and tabulated by author.

TABLE **5A.12**   Class and the Preference for Naidu/Reddy in Siddinki, Karivena, and Pamalupadu

Acres	Naidu/Reddy			Total
	Naidu	Neutral	Reddy	
1	12 (14%)	20 (24%)	53 (62%)	85
2	6 (16%)	3 (8%)	28 (76%)	37
3	13 (36%)	0 (0%)	23 (64%)	36
Total	31 (20%)	23 (14%)	104 (66%)	158

Source: Data collected and tabulated by author.

Notes

1. See Ministry of Finance (2011: 260–1); Planning Commission (2011: 313–15).

2. The details of the report have been shared by senior civil servants who will remain anonymous. The report is still in draft form as the final report has not been submitted. See also http://articles.economictimes.indiatimes.com/2011-06-02/news/29613100_1_power-sector-power-theft-electricity-act (accessed 14 October 2011).

3. See Rudolph and Rudolph (2007: 231–64).

4. See Kirk (2007: 265–99).

5. See the APGENCO website, http://www.apgenco.gov.in/inner.asp?frm =viewcontents&filename=HomePgCategory.xml&Tagname=HP_Cat501& subhname=NewsandEvents (accessed 12 October 2011).

6. See Vigilance Study Circle (2011: III,V, VII, 76–8).

7. This figure was shared by officials of the Transmission Corporation of Andhra Pradesh Limited (APTRANSCO) in September 2011 in Hyderabad.

8. See Varshney (2007: 158–64). The impact of mass politics is more significant in an era of rising fuel costs. This chapter takes the position that while rising fuel costs have increased the cost of power generation, the root cause for the rising subsidy burden is the inability of the state in AP to charge farmers for the power they consume. On power purchase, see Special Stories (2011: 14–18).

9. On the relationship between the rising power of farmers and agricultural subsidy, see Dubash and Rajan (2001: 3,369–70); Kale (2004: 471–3, 478–9); Tongia (2007: 125–7); Patel and Bhattacharya (2010: 57–61). On the rise of agrarian power from the 1970s, see Varshney (1998: 81–145); Omvedt (2005: 185–90); Gupta (1998: 62–101).

10. See Bhaya (1995).

11. See Planning Commission (1994).

12. This data was shared by APTRANSCO in September 2011.

13. See Planning Commission (2011: 325).

14. On the Congress rule in AP, see Reddy (1989: 280–7); Suri (2002: 17–24).

15. On the reasons for the rise of the TDP, see Reddy (1989: 286–92); Suri (2002: 25–36, 2006: 283–7).

16. On the messy politics of succession, see Srinivasulu and Sarangi (1999: 2,449–58).

17. See Naidu (2000: xiv–xvi).

18. Ibid.: xv–xvii.

19. Chandrababu Naidu (author interview, Hyderabad, 8 September 2011). See also, Suri (2005: 139–41).

20. See Naidu (2000: 115–17).

21. See Naidu (2000: 185–96).

22. On the relationship between the withdrawal of the central government state-level funding and the importance of state-level initiatives to secure funding, see Rudolph and Rudolph (2007: 231–64). On the reasons why the World Bank began lending to the states in India, see Kirk (2007: 265–99).

23. See Naidu (2000: 127–30). These views expressed benefited from a personal interview with Naidu (Hyderabad, 8 September 2011).

24. See Kirk (2005: 298–9).

25. See Naidu (2000: 3–16).

26. See Mooij (2007: 34–56); Rudolph and Rudolph (2007: 231–5). Naidu (2000: 20–1) himself acknowledged that a chief minister needed to be like a CEO in politics.

27. See Kirk (2005: 299–303); Suri (2002: 40–1). For a background on the political situation that may have inspired populism, see Srinivasulu and Sarangi (1999: 2,449–58).

28. See Naidu (2000: 189–96).

29. See Bhaya (1995); Planning Commission (1994).

30. See Sankar (1997).

31. Ibid.: 43–5.

32. Ibid.: 64–9.

33. Ibid.: 72–3, 105–14.

34. Ibid.: 53–4.

35. Ibid.: 16–23.

36. Ibid.: 54–9.

37. Ibid.: 51–2.

38. Ibid.: 70–114.

39. For the relationship between the World Bank and Naidu, see Kirk (2005: 297–9).

40. See Pani *et al.* (2007: 11); Tongia (2007: 147–8).

41. For an excellent account of this opposition culled from various news sources, see Kale (2007: 248–50).

42. See Kale (2007: 250–8).

43. Ibid.: 255–6.

44. See Rajeev (2002).

45. AP enjoyed a respectable history of communist politics before the consolidation of Congress dominance since 1957. See Reddy (1989: 279–83); Suri (2002: 13–20).

46. From now on, Dr Y.S. Rajashekhar Reddy will be referred to as Y.S. Rajashekhar Reddy or Reddy.

47. See Sukumar (2003).

48. See Kale (2007: 257).

49. Meetings with G.P. Rao in Hyderabad on 12 December 2007 and June 2010.

50. Meetings with G.P. Rao in Hyderabad on 12 December 2007 and June 2010. Also see, Dubash and Reddy (2007: 47–100).

51. Venugopal Rao shared materials and insights in December 2007 and June 2010 during a number of meetings in Hyderabad. For example, the petition filed by him before APERC on 29 May 2010 on the annual revenue requirements and the tariff proposals of the four publicly owned distribution companies makes fascinating reading. He filed another petition regarding the power purchase agreement between BPL and the distribution companies on 3 June. Also see, Rao (2007: 311–18).

52. N. Sreekumar of Prayas has actively participated in critically evaluating the power sector in AP. See, for example, Sreekumar *et al.* (2007: 24–7). I benefited from meetings with N. Sreekumar (Hyderabad, 16 December 2007) and M. Thimma Reddy (Hyderabad, 30 June 2010).

53. Insights about metering agricultural consumption were provided by Rachel Chatterjee, the chairman and managing director of APTRANSCO, in Hyderabad on 12 December 2007.

54. These figures were provided by APTRANSCO in June 2010.

55. I interviewed a number of farmer's leaders in December 2007 and June 2010. Persons who held this view included D. Ramakrishna Reddy, M. Balarama Reddy, and P.V. Subbaiah Choudary of the Federation of Indian Farmers. I was made sensitive to this issue by one of the stalwarts of power sector reforms in India, T.L. Sankar, now an honorary professor in the Administrative Staff College of India in a meeting in Hyderabad (13 December 2007).

56. Even though the chairman of APERC promised to share this report in a meeting in Hyderabad on 17 December 2007, this commitment was not fulfilled. I was visiting the state at that time as an independent consultant of the World Bank.

57. Figures pertaining to the performance of APGENCO were shared by A.P. Jain, the managing director of APGENCO, on 14 December 2007.

58. These figures were shared by APTRANSCO in June 2010 in Hyderabad. I am grateful to Sutirtha Bhattacharya (power secretary, AP government, in June 2010 and infrastructure secretary in September 2011) and Umesh Sharraf (joint managing director of APTRANSCO) for their insights and for requesting colleagues to share these and other figures with me. Such individuals make researching on governance a real pleasure.

59. This revealing letter was shared in Hyderabad. It details the manner in which APGENCO was systematically discriminated against—which is described in the next paragraph. I have learned much about APGENCO from K.P. Rao, a retired civil servant who never failed to call a spade a spade.

60. See APTRANSCO (2011: 20).

61. See the letter from J. Parthasarathy, chairman and managing director of AP GENCO, to power secretary Jannat Husain (13 May 2004). The figures are on Page 8 of the letter's annexure.

62. See p. 3 of the letter from J. Parthasarathy, chairman and managing director of AP GENCO, to power secretary Jannat Husain (13 May 2004).

63. For an insight into the scandal regarding the power purchase agreement between the Maharashtra State Electricity Board and the Dhabol Power Corporation financed by Enron, see Prayas Energy Group (2001: 2,063–8); comment in , 'Lessons from Dhabol', Economic and Political Weekly 36:5-6 (February 3-10,, 2001): 427–8 (AQ 6); Kannan and Pillai (2002: 416–24). There was vigorous debate on power purchase agreements in the public hearings of APERC, which curbed the greed of the private sector as it approached power purchase agreements in AP. Some informed people in AP believe that the agreement with LVS Energy in the early years was a flawed one.

64. See Suri (2009: 65–72).

65. Ibid.: 70–5.

66. Ibid.: 75. There are four caste groups in the Hindu society. The backward caste groups form the largest proportion of the population (35 per cent) than the scheduled castes or Dalits, who are socially even more oppressed and constitute around 17 per cent of the population. On the relationship between caste and politics in India, see Chandra (2004); Ganguly and Mukherji (2011: 109–40); Jaffrelot (2003); Pai (2010); Subramanian (1999); Swamy (2010: 268–7). On caste and politics in AP, see Reddy (1989: 282–92).

67. See Suri (2002).

68. This view was expressed by a senior TDP politician in Hyderabad in September 2011.

69. For more on the carnage in Godhra, see Ganguly and Mukherji (2011: 146–8). The figure about the Muslim population is reported from the 2001

Census. See http://censusindia.gov.in/Census_Data_2001/Census_data_finder/C_Series/Population_by_religious_communities.htm (accessed 21 December 2013).

70. See Suri (2009: 70–3).

71. See Suri *et al.* (2009: 111).

72. See Aiyar (2010: 204–29); Suri, Rao, and Reddy (2009: 111–12). This was also evident from the village surveys in AP in June 2010, which have been detailed subsequently. The MGNREGA, by providing a decent wage to the unemployed, raised the wages of farm workers. An agricultural worker could be paid around Rs 180 (USD 3.50) per day for eight-hours of farm work during the harvest season in 2010 in AP.

73. Pani *et al.* (2007: 46).

74. See World Bank (2001: 15–17).

75. See Reddy (2006: 199–211).

76. See Dossani and Ranganathan (2005: 51–6); World Bank (2001: 15–17).

77. From discussions with Sarampally M. Reddy of the All India Kisan Sabha (All India Farmer's Union) in December 2007 and in June 2010; and P. Chengal Reddy, Balaram Reddy, D. Ramakrishna Reddy, and P.V. Subbaiah Choudary of the Federation of Indian Farmers in Hyderabad in December 2007.

78. These figures were shared by APTRANSCO in September 2011.

79. The farmers' leaders in endnote 76 also shared these views.

80. I had discussions with P. Madan Mohana Rao of Lok Satta in December 2007. He was working on a franchisee model, where an external franchisee would work with the villagers to maintain the distribution set of the public utility. Farmers, according to Rao, were not averse to metering electricity consumption in the villages where he was operating.

81. Y.S. Rajashekhar Reddy, the former chief minister of AP, (author interview, Hyderabad, 17 December 2007).

82. My friend Prof. Prakash Sarangi from the Department of Political Science at the University of Hyderabad had pointed me in the direction of his PhD student, Prashanthi.

83. Sarampally M. Reddy of the All India Kisan Sabha made excellent arrangements for us in the villages that were surveyed. We would meet certain people in the villages who would then explain the villagers about our mission. The villagers were keen to share their views and were drawn from varied class, caste and political orientations. Such was the response that it sometimes became difficult to accommodate all those who wished to share their views with us.

84. Three senior civil servants in Reddy's administration have shared this view with me in Hyderabad.

Conclusion

The Ideational Tipping Point and Institutional Change in India

INDIA'S TRANSITION FROM AN over-regulated, import-substitution economic model to a framework based on deregulation and globalization does not have many parallels in the developing world. The Introduction to this book pointed out that India poses a puzzle for the developmental state literature, which stresses that hard authoritarian states were necessary to deal effectively with vested interests in developing countries, as opposed to subjecting their economic activities to the discipline of global competition. There could be no Lee Kuan Yew, Park Chung Hee, or Deng Xiaoping in a country like India, where powerful social forces—such as the industrial class, farmers, and a variety of other interest groups—had a vested interest in over-regulation. If the developmental state was to be the model, then India's gradual path of moderation between the state and market was doomed to be a developmental muddle that could never achieve rapid economic growth. How, then, did the silent revolution favouring rapid economic growth occur in India, rising out of the country's gradual processes of economic and political change?

This book discussed four separate paths of economic change and provided historical evidence that supports these trajectories. The punctuated equilibrium model emphasizes the importance of a drastic change at a critical juncture, which makes a quick impact during the exogenous shock to the system. In this scenario, the powerful appeal of new economic ideas to policymakers during a crisis, such as a depression or a balance of payments shock, could facilitate a transformation. Under these circumstances, it is the appeal of an idea rather than a rational assessment of its utility that drives change. Alternatively, new economic ideas can be introduced somewhat coercively by multilateral institutions during a balance of payments shock. In these situations, it is the vulnerable countries' dependence on organizations that can provide financing, rather than the policymakers' beliefs, that propels change. This book suggests that neither of these paths proffer a good explanation for the Indian case.

Chapter 1 suggested that the tipping-point model is another framework for understanding economic change. This model of gradual economic change characterizes a situation where pressures for change build up to a tipping point because of the ways a system has been undermined over a long period of time. Change occurs because a certain threshold has been reached. For example, water suddenly begins to boil at a certain temperature, but it requires that heat be continuously supplied to reach that stage. What looks like a sudden phenomenon has actually been building up over a period of time. Endogenous processes are important for understanding such changes, but an exogenous shock can also make a greater impact in the direction of change if it builds on the existing internal processes of change. In other words, if endogenous and exogenous forces work together, substantial and abrupt change is possible in the tipping-point model.

The chapter also discussed two variants of the tipping-point model. Some scholars show that a conflict between interest groups over a period of time can be the reason for a system reaching the tipping point. In Chapter 1, I discussed the work of Kathleen Thelen, which shows how the relationship between the state and the master craftsmen in Germany sowed the seeds of skill-based employment training in Germany. Douglass North, likewise, tells us how the rise of the capitalist class in Britain over a period of time created checks and balances for the monarch. The Glorious Revolution and the birth of the Bank of England in the seventeenth century were consequences of conflicts between the monarch and the capitalist class represented in Parliament.

This book garners historical evidence for a second variant of the tipping-point model. It draws on the model in Peter Hall's account of the rise of neo-liberal policies in Britain and seeks to go beyond it. Chapter 1 showed that Hall has an endogenous story of gradual ideational and economic policy changes at the first- and second-order levels that are relatively minor policy and institutional shifts. The big bang paradigm shift subsequently occurs with the political ascendancy of Margaret Thatcher. Her arrival is the exogenous element in the historical path. Mark Blyth and I find that Hall's classic paper, however, is not clear about which part of the story—gradual ideational change or Thatcher's emergence—is more important and whether or not they are related.

This book suggests that one has to consider ideas and interests simultaneously to understand the causes of economic change in India. The availability of various ideas was important for shaping the interests of the policy community that pursued different agendas during different periods in India's post-independence history. The Introduction described how the movement of ideas favouring regulation and deregulation in the West and in India arose out of developmental needs and puzzlement with the results of previous policies. Chapter 2 described the ideational mood within the Indian government in 1966, when the country devalued the rupee, but only under pressure from foreign donors. Changes in the dominant paradigm among India's economic technocrats, which started taking shape in the mid-1970s, suggest a great deal about why India did not embrace globalization and deregulation in 1966, but did so in 1991.

Ideational change evolved gradually during the Indian historical cases presented in this book, and was significantly affected by the results of over-regulation and import substitution. The Introduction detailed how over-regulation had produced its critics in the West in the 1970s, owing to the inability of the regulation to solve the problem of market failure. Indian economists such as Jagdish Bhagwati and T.N. Srinivasan were two pioneers who shaped economic thought on these issues. Chapter 3 detailed how these ideas grew in importance within the Indian technocracy in the 1980s, when the senior leadership began toying with ideas of economic change. These ideas were largely home-grown, given the nature of the problems that Indian policymakers had sought to resolve. The home-grown nature of these policy changes are evident when one examines the ideas that begin to emerge in Indian government reports starting in the late 1970s.

The international demonstration effect of the rise of Asia and the decline of the Soviet Union in the 1980s were also significant in the Indian case. China's export-led model of economic growth was especially appealing because even die-hard critics of globalization could not argue that China was a stooge of American imperialism. The demonstration effect helped Indian policymakers evaluate the results of their own policies. India's 3.5 per cent rate of average annual economic growth in the 1970s far surpassed the country's colonial experience, but was considered paltry compared with the East Asian economic boom. In addition, the decline and subsequent demise of the Soviet Union was a setback for those who had been inspired by Soviet planning, which had made a significant impact on India's development policy in the country's first decades after independence.

Since India is replete with social actors with a vested interest in the political process, the conversion of economic ideas into economic policy was a gradual and painstaking process. It involved a significant dose of politics, which meant dealing with rent-seeking, import-substituting industrialists and farmers. Chapter 3 described how the Indian state had been reduced to a balancer of class interests in the 1980s. Industrialists demanded deregulation and production benefits, but were not keen to be disciplined by economic globalization. As the backward farming castes were mobilized, the state took a benevolent view of subsidies on items such as water, electricity, fertilizer, and food grain. Loans were also waived. The balance of class power shifted towards the agriculture sector in the national budget of 1990, when the Janata Dal coalition called for an agricultural policy resolution. The political coalition of farmers favouring more investment in agriculture demanded that the sector enjoy the same benefits as industry. Neither the industry nor the agricultural sector in India was willing to submit to economic discipline, and the country's fiscal deficit became unsustainable in the context of India's substantial dependence on foreign commercial banks for financing its economic growth.

Yet, policy ideas favouring deregulation were gradually embedded within India's political economy, despite the resistance of the dominant coalition. Consequently, there was significant, though not dramatic industrial deregulation in the 1980s (and only sparse engagement with globalization during that period). The MRTP Act was diluted, the necessity of seeking production permissions or industrial licences was waived for some industrial sectors, and direct taxes were reduced. These were clear benefits for industry and the middle class, but did not subject them to the discipline of global competition through trade or foreign investment. These benefits infuriated the farmers, who subsequently obtained numerous benefits of their own after the Congress party was toppled in 1989.

India's telecom saga, like the country's industrial deregulation, also validates the proposition about the move toward gradual deregulation during the 1980s (as has been discussed in Chapter 4). Telecom unions and the communications ministry fiercely opposed Prime Minister Rajiv Gandhi's efforts to de-monopolize the sector. A new Department of Telecommunications (DoT) was born within the Ministry of Communications; a publicly owned utility—Mahanagar Telecom Nigam Limited (MTNL)—was given autonomy from the ministry and treated like a corporate actor; and an autonomous Centre for the Development of Telematics (C-DOT) was charged with technological development. C-DOT's switch technology for rural areas was hailed as a major success, and licensed to private manufacturers of telecom equipment. Despite these developments, opposition from the DoT ensured that MTNL would operate only in two cities, and there were no private telecom service providers in India throughout the 1980s.

The economic history of India during the 1980s provides evidence to demonstrate the power of the tipping-point model of economic change. This model emphasizes the importance of gradual processes of change that build pressures over a period of time. Change can be dramatic after the accumulation of a certain amount of internal pressure that undermines the old system, or can occur when an exogenous event triggers large-scale changes in the system, building on processes that had undermined old institutions. Domestic ideational and political processes that drove India in the direction of paradigm change favouring deregulation and globalization in 1991 were clearly at work in the 1980s. But the country's dominant political coalition posed a formidable obstacle to change. Still, a growing number of Indian technocrats and policymakers were convinced that India had to seize any opportunity for change if it was ever going to resemble the more rapidly growing parts of Asia.

The dramatic change in Indian economic policies and institutions that occurred between May and July 1991 happened both because of new ideas and because politics had brought India to a tipping point where endogenous changes had considerably undermined the county's import-substitution regime. The tipping point was a balance-of-payments shock, which was comparable to the country's balance of payments shock in 1966. In 1991, the crisis empowered India's leaders and the technocrats to transform the country's institutions of economic governance.

Chapter 3 detailed how India's committed executive technocratic team seized the political opportunity to demolish the four pillars of regulation on 24 July 1991. These included an overvalued exchange rate, intrusive industrial controls, aversion to foreign investment, and excessive regulation of large companies. The technocrats exploited Indian industry's dependence on imports and foreign exchange from the International Monetary Fund (IMF) during a financial crisis to persuade industrialists to accept deregulation and competition. The national budget in 1991 passed smoothly, because the principal opposition parties abstained from voting. Once the writing on the wall was clear, sections of Indian industry—especially the Confederation of Indian Industry—actively supported deregulation and globalization. Industrial licensing—the requirement that industrialists had to obtain government permissions regarding production location and scale, which had existed since 1956—was almost totally abolished during this period. The rupee was significantly devalued and tariffs reduced. The devaluation meant that the effective rate of protection was much higher than tariff reduction, and signalled the salience of export promotion as a policy goal over import substitution. Foreign investment was now considered a good source of financing.

India's executive-technocratic team was able to negotiate a favourable set of terms with the IMF at the time of the crisis, terms that reflected the Indian policymakers' own sets of priorities. The fact that India's democracy was not a classic authoritarian developmental state and had to take social actors seriously was well known to the multilateral organizations that wanted India to embark on politically sustainable economic change. This reality meant the scope of change in India would be limited: labour laws were not rewritten, fiscal deficit contraction lasted only for one year, and the deficit grew quite significantly after that. The IMF's respect for India's qualified technocracy augurs well for IMF programmes—a significant lesson considering the legacy of IMF programmes briefly discussed in Chapter 1. In India, deficit reduction has been a function of domestic conviction rather than external imposition.

The simultaneous importance of ideas and politics in India's economic transition is further evident in the country's telecom transformation. The Prime Minister's Office (PMO) and the finance ministry supported the entry of private service providers into the telecom sector in 1991. These ministries were convinced that the private sector was a source of investment and competition that would likely make the public utilities more efficient. This introduction of competition hurt the interests of the DoT housed within the communications ministry, which had no intention of renouncing its monopoly position. DoT did not accept World Bank funding and only relented to private cellular service provision in the four metropolitan cities—Delhi, Mumbai, Chennai, and Kolkata. In 1991, DoT viewed cellular telephony as an elite service that would serve a small niche market. They had not realized that this technology would revolutionize Indian telecommunications' potential for growth.

Chapter 4 detailed the political and layered nature of change in India's booming telecommunications sector. First, the government placed DoT, which was India's telecom policymaker and service provider throughout the 1980s, in charge of governing competition between public and private telecom companies as well. Quite predictably, this arrangement led to a conflict of interest for DoT—why would an organization enable its competition? This conflict of interest generated substantial governance dilemmas since DoT consistently tried to undermine rather than create competition. Such actions produced a litigious environment, and inspired the Indian Supreme Court to suggest the need for a new telecom regulator in a landmark judgement in 1996. Parliament subsequently passed an Act establishing the Telecom Regulatory Authority of India (TRAI) in 1997. TRAI performed its duties, but its limited powers initially rendered it incapable of either promoting competition or staving off a bankruptcy situation for private service providers in 1999. The Indian government went further in its attempts to promote competition in the telecom sector in 2000 by establishing a special telecom appeals court. This layered process involved setting up new institutional rules favouring competition within an old institution and allowing the new rules to overtake the old one (favouring monopoly) over a period of time.

Chapter 4 showed that deregulation is fundamentally different from regulation. Promoting competition is not only about freeing up private companies from the excesses of state intervention. It is also about creating institutions that can deal with the monopolistic propensities of private companies and public sector entities that can scuttle competition. Yet, TRAI has demonstrated meaningful progress in regulating the telecom sector in recent years. It has created transparent procedures, such as consultations and recommendations, which can be viewed on its website. It supported private-sector participation and competition in telecommunication when DoT was averse to it. It dealt admirably with a crisis when the cash-rich Indian company Reliance Infocomm tried to secure cheap cellular licences for CDMA technology to challenge GSM[1] cellular operators in India. Reliance Infocomm would have been the major beneficiary of cheap licences that were awarded for mobile phone activities within a limited area for the price of a cheap fixed-service licence. If Reliance had succeeded, this story would resemble the classic regulatory capture scenario described in the Introduction. The most recent case of selling spectrum below market price in the 2G scam (described in Chapter 4) constitutes yet another attempt of companies attempting to obtain regulatory privileges cheaply. All manner of standards were violated during India's allocation of the 2G spectrum. The communications minister in charge of this process was sent to prison after the country's comptroller and auditor general blew the whistle. This was a case where the telecom regulator was neither proactive nor found to be compromised.

The 2G scam should inspire further regulatory evolution in India's telecom sector. Prime Minister Manmohan Singh has suggested endowing the country's regulators with greater powers and accountability. Reducing the cabinet ministers' discretionary powers could reduce the rent-seeking opportunities that arise for politicians when they are granted regulatory powers. The United States and United Kingdom have followed this approach when establishing their telecom regulatory agencies.

This tipping-point model of economic change, which suggests that new ideas can create situations that bring economic actors into conflicts, offers possibilities for understanding various other arenas of economic reform in India. First, India's stock market experienced gradual and perceptible reform during the 1980s, but was also impeded by the powerful brokers of the Bombay Stock Exchange. This all changed after the country's balance of payments crisis in 1991. India needed a well-regulated stock market to attract the savings of Indians and foreigners, which could be used to fund productive investments in the corporate sector. Regulatory evolution in India's stock market, like the evolution in the country's telecoms, was a layered process driven by investment crises beyond 1991.[2] Second, India's civil aviation sector was gradually deregulated in the 1980s when air taxis were allowed. The major boost for commercial air travel, however, came when a law was enacted allowing private airlines to enter the Indian market in 1994. Airline deregulation ensued over the course of the 1990s, but unlike the case with telecoms or stock markets, deregulation of airlines in the absence of an independent regulator has created challenges for the profitability of commercial operators. Moreover, the government-owned airline Air India remains a classic case of how a corporate entity should not be governed.[3]

Let us now turn to a more significant challenge to the process of reform. Ideas that stimulate interests favouring economic reform have been significantly challenged in many parts of Indian society (as has been discussed in Chapter 3). Ashutosh Varshney has noted that mass politics has defeated the best intentions of politicians and policymakers who wanted to restructure the Indian power sector. This scenario involved a large number of organized voters whose short-term interests are ranged against the reformers. Mass politics characterized by the farmers' voting power in rural India has perpetuated a regime of free electricity for farmers in many states. In India's attempts at economic reform, it was easier to deal with telecom unions and DoT than with the collective power of the farmers' lobby.

Free electricity to farmers is a hazard to economic development. While there is a case for subsidizing electricity to all farmers—especially the poorest farmers—free electricity harms everyone. First, it is fiscally unsustainable. Second, it engenders waste. Third, the quality of supply of a utility that is being supplied free of cost cannot be satisfactory. We found a large number of human and animal electrocutions owing to the poor maintenance of the infrastructure needed for distributing power in Andhra Pradesh (AP). Healthy competition and the market cannot be introduced to a sector when a large number of consumers are unwilling to pay.

In Chapter 5, we discussed the power sector in AP, which appeared to be a perfect candidate for reform. AP's chief minister Chandrababu Naidu was considered a reform icon. He was aided in his efforts by a qualified technocracy that had a sophisticated knowledge about what ailed the power sector even before the World Bank was invited to finance a restructuring programme in AP's power sector. The chief minister put his political weight behind a competent electricity regulatory institution that was granted substantial autonomy. In addition, the generating companies in AP were among the best-performing public utilities in the country. Naidu battled politics and began charging a nominal electricity tariff to farmers in AP.

The Congress party's chief minister in AP, the late Y.S. Rajashekhar Reddy, turned populist immediately after the 2004 elections, when he defeated Naidu's party and came to power with a majority of seats in the state legislature. His government's first public announcement was that it intended to deliver on its election promise of providing free electricity to farmers. This policy proved popular, and Reddy was re-elected in 2009. While the World Bank and many farmers' leaders in the state capital have opined that free electricity to farmers would benefit only rich farmers, our survey of three carefully selected villages demonstrates that overall support for Reddy was greater than for Naidu across all economic groups. If something is offered free of cost, citizens are unlikely to realize that paying is better than obtaining a service free of cost in the long term.

There is a significant constituency of farmers in AP who complain about the quality of free electricity. But AP's power sector reforms demonstrate clearly that mass politics can be an obstacle to the reform process. It was easier for reformers to deal with telecom unions and the industrial class than with farmers of AP. And it is difficult to find a political entrepreneur who can build a constituency around subsidized electricity tariffs and a superior quality of power supply.

Future research can tell us whether mass politics debilitates other types of reform as well. Why, for example, do India's rigid trade union laws protect less than 10 per cent of its workforce? This is a major cause for concern, because the lack of unionization leads to the exploitation of workers. And, an employer's inability to deal effectively with lazy workers creates the incentive for firms to discourage unionization. Entrepreneurs indulge in small-scale exploitative operations. India is a labour-abundant country with a large and youthful workforce that has not gained a foothold in labour-intensive manufacturing to the same extent as workers in China have.

The case of economic change in India highlights the simultaneous importance of ideas and political interests in driving economic change in a rapidly growing and democratic country. The impact of these two forces for change cannot easily be separated. Ideational change—based on an evaluation of past policies—is a gradual process. Chapter 1 pointed to an ideational basis for deregulation in the West and in the developing world. There was an uncanny similarity between the economic literature critical of regulation and the literature on rent-seeking industrialization in the developing world in the 1970s. In addition, two of the world's leading economists who criticized over-regulated rent-seeking industrialization and advocated for greater globalization and trade were Indian. It is not surprising that the Indian government began taking note of over-regulation and slow growth in the country during the mid-1970s. However, the agents of change encountered powerful parties with vested interests in the existing system that fought against them during crises and during normal economic times. Yet, the introduction of new economic ideas and gradual policy changes in India during normal times undermined the country's prevailing economic system. Exogenous shocks built upon slow-moving processes of endogenous ideational and political change, inspiring a shift in the economic policy paradigm in India.

This book makes the case for a tipping-point model of economic change, where slow-moving endogenous economic and political processes were the real drivers of change in India. This is in stark contrast to the punctuated-equilibrium model, where an exogenous event dramatically disrupts prevailing institutions. The tipping-point model is path-dependent, whereas the punctuated equilibrium model is not. The tipping-point model suggests that even an exogenous shock that precipitates what appears to be a cataclysmic change succeeds because it builds on a historical legacy that had undermined the old system to a considerable extent. The tipping-point model's potential for explaining economic change is rather underutilized in political economy. Would Peter Hall's 1993 analysis about the rise of neo-liberalism in Britain be more compelling if it were narrated more explicitly as a case where gradual endogenous changes were the critical drivers of economic change rather than the exogenous political change associated with the arrival of Margaret Thatcher?

Notes

1. GSM stands for Groupe Spécial Mobile, or as it is currently known—Global System for Mobile communications.
2. See Echeverri-Gent (2007: 300–27).
3. See Mukherji and Kankanhalli (2009).

Bibliography

Acemoglu, Daron and James A. Robinson. 2006. *Economic Origins of Dictatorship and Democracy*. New York: Cambridge University Press.

———. 2012. *Why Nations Fail: The Origins of Power, Prosperity and Poverty*. London: Profile Books.

Acharya, Shankar. 1988. 'India's Fiscal Policy', in Robert E.B. Lucas and Gustave F. Papanek (eds), *The Indian Economy*. New Delhi: Oxford University Press.

Acharya, Shankar and Rakesh Mohan. 2010. 'Introduction', in Shankar Acharya and Rakesh Mohan (eds), *Indian Economy: Performance and Challenges*. New Delhi: Oxford University Press.

Agence-France Press. 1991. 'Standard and Poor's Affirms India's Long-term Credit Rating' (26 September).

Aggarwal, Vinod K. and Rahul Mukherji. 2008. 'India's Shifting Trade Policy', in Vinod K. Aggarwal and Min Gyo-Koo (eds), *Asia's New Institutional Architecture*. Heidelberg: Springer-Verlag.

Ahluwalia, Montek S. 1974. 'The Scope For Policy Intervention', in Holis B. Chenery, Montek S. Ahluwalia, C.L.G. Bell, John H. Duloy, and Richard Jolly (eds), *Redistribution With Growth*. London: Oxford University Press, World Bank, and Institute of Development Studies.

———. 1986. 'Balance-of-Payments Adjustments in India, 1970–71 to 1983–84', *World Development* 14(8): 937–62.

Aiyar, Yamini. 2010. 'Invited Spaces, Invited Participation: Effects of Greater Participation on Accountability in Service Delivery', *India Review* 9(2): 204–29.

Alexander, P.C. 1978. *Report of the Committee on Import-Export Policies and Procedures*. New Delhi: Ministry of Commerce.

Amsden, Alice H. 1989. 'The State and Taiwan's Economic Development', in Peter Evans, Dietrich Rueschemeyer, and Theda Skocpol (eds), *Bringing the State Back In*. New York: Cambridge University Press; pp. 107–68.

Amsden, Alice H. 1989. *Asia's Next Giant: South Korea and Late Industrialization.* New York: Oxford University Press.

APTRANSCO. 2011. *Performance Report—White Paper* (July). Hyderabad: Government of Andhra Pradesh.

ASSOCHAM. 1995. *Partnership for Progress: The ASSOCHAM Story 1920–1995.* New Delhi: ASSOCHAM.

———. 1966. *Forty-Seventh Annual Report: Being that for the Year Ended 31st October 1966.* New Delhi: ASSOCHAM.

———. 1967. *Forty-Eighth Annual Report: Being that for the Year Ended 31st October 1967.* New Delhi: ASSOCHAM.

Athreya, M.B. 1996. 'India's Telecommunications Policy', *Telecommunications Policy*, 20(1): 11–7.

Bajpai, Manjul and Anjali Hans. 2005. *Report: Overview of the Indian Experience Regarding Fixed Line Operators Acquiring Mobility via Wireless in Local Loop (WLL).* New Delhi: Cellular Operators Association of India.

Bajpai, Rajendra. 1991. 'Rough Road to Free-market Prosperity for New Delhi', *Straits Times*, 20 August.

Baldwin, David A. 1980. 'Inter-dependence and Power: A Conceptual Analysis', *International Organization*, 43(4): 471–506.

Bannerjee, Abhijit and Lakshmi Iyer. 2005. 'History, Institutions, and Economic Performance: The Legacy of Colonial Land Tenure Systems in India', *The American Economic Review*, 95(4): 1,190–213.

Bardhan, Pranab. 1984. *The Political Economy of Development in India.* Oxford: Basil Blackwell.

Baru, Sanjaya. 1991. 'The Value of Dissent', *The Economic Times*, 14 July.

Becker, Gary S. 1983. 'A Theory of Competition Among Pressure Groups For Political Influence', *Quarterly Journal of Economics*, XCVIII(3): 371–400.

Beland, Daniel. 2009. 'Ideas, Institutions, and Policy Change', *Journal of European Public Policy*, 16(5): 701–18.

Bell, Bernard R. 1965. *Report to the President of the International Bank for Reconstruction and Development and the International Development Association On India's Economic Development Volume 1* (1 October). Washington: World Bank.

Bentall, Jim and Stuart Corbridge. 1996. 'New Agrarianism and Northwest India: The Bharatiya Kisan Union', *Transactions of the Institute of British Geographers*, 21(1): 27–48.

Bhaduri, Amit and Deepak Nayyar. 1996. *The Intelligent Person's Guide to Liberalization.* New Delhi: Penguin Books.

Bhagwati, Jagdish N. 1958. 'International Trade and Economic Expansion', *American Economic Review*, 48(5): 941–53.

Bhagwati, Jagdish N. 1969. 'Optimal Policies and Immiserizing Growth', *American Economic Review*, 59(5): 967–70

———. 1986. 'Rethinking Trade Strategy', in John P. Lewis and Velleriana Kallab (eds), *Development Strategies Reconsidered*. New Brunswick, NJ: Transaction Books.

———. 1993. *India in Transition: Freeing the Economy*. Oxford: Clarendon Press.

———. 1998. 'The Design of Indian Development', in Isher J. Ahluwalia and I.M.D. Little (eds), *India's Economic Reforms and Development: Essays for Manmohan Singh*. New Delhi: Oxford University Press.

———. 2007. 'What Went Wrong', in Rahul Mukherji (ed.), *India's Economic Transition: The Politics of Reform*. New Delhi: Oxford University Press.

Bhagwati, Jagdish and Padma Desai. 1970. *India: Planning For Industrialization*. London: Oxford University Press.

Bhagwati, Jagdish and T.N. Srinivasan. 1975. *Foreign Trade Regimes and Economic Development: India*, for the National Bureau of Economic Research. New York: Columbia University Press.

———. 1980. 'Revenue-Seeking: A Generalization of the Theory of Tariffs', *Journal of Political Economy*, 88(6): 1,069–87.

Bhattacharya, A.K. 1991. 'Getting Down to Brasstacks', *The Economic Times*, 30 June.

———. 2011. 'Two Months that Changed India', *Business Standard* (2 July). New Delhi. See http://www.business-standard.com/india/news/two-months-that-changed-india/441198/ (accessed 15 November 2011).

Bhaya, Hiten. 1995. *The Report of the High Level Committee: Guidelines on Restructuring and Privatisation of Power Sector Tariff*. Hyderabad: Government of Andhra Pradesh.

Bird, Graham. 1996. 'The International Monetary Fund and Developing Countries', *International Organization*, 50(3): 477–511.

Bjorkman, James Warner. 1980. 'Public Law 480 and the Policies of Self-Help and Short-Tether: Indo-American Relations, 1965–68', in Lloyd I. Rudolph and Susanne H. Rudolph (eds), *The Regional Imperative: The Administration of U.S. Foreign Policy towards South Asian States under Presidents Johnson and Nixon*. Atlantic Highlands, NJ: Humanities Press.

Blyth, Mark. 2002. *Great Transformations: Economic Ideas and Institutional Change in the Twentieth Century*. New York: Cambridge University Press.

———. 2006. 'When Liberalisms Change: Comparing the Politics of Deflations and Inflations', in Arthur T. Denzau, Thomas C. Willet, and Ravi K. Roy (eds), *Neoliberalism, National, and Regional Experiments with Global Ideas*. London: Routledge.

Blyth, Mark. 2007. 'Powering, Puzzling, or Persuading? The Mechanisms of Building Institutional Orders', *International Studies Quarterly*, 51(4): 761–77.

———. 2011. 'Peter's Perfect Paradox—or—How to Write the Complete Article: Policy Paradigms', Unpublished MS (January). Providence, RI: Brown University.

Boughton, James M. 2003. 'Who's in Charge? Ownership and Conditionality in IMF Supported Programs', *IMF Working Paper 03/191* (September). Washington: International Monetary Fund.

Brecher, Michael. 1961. *Nehru: A Political Biography*. New York: Oxford University Press.

Bronckers, Marco C.E.J. and Pierre Larouche. 1997. 'Telecommunications Services and the World Trade Organization', *The Journal of World Trade* 31(3): 5–45.

Buira, Ariel. 2003. 'Introduction', in Ariel Buira (ed.), *Challenges to the World Bank and IMF*. London: Anthem Press.

Bureau of Industrial Costs and Prices. 1998. *BICP Study on the Cellular Phone Services*. New Delhi: Government of India.

Butler, David, Ashok Lahiri, and Prannoy Roy. 1997. 'India Decides: Elections 1952–1995', in Partha Chatterjee (ed.), *State and Politics in India*. New Delhi: Oxford University Press.

Byres, Terence J. 1998. 'The Creation of "The Tribe of Pundits Called Economists": Institutions, Institution-Builders and Economic Debate', in Terence J. Byres (ed.), *The Indian Economy*. New Delhi: Oxford University Press.

Campbell, John L. 2004. *Institutional Change and Globalization*. New Jersey: Princeton University Press.

Cappoccia, Giovanni and R. Daniel Kelemen. 2007. 'The Study of Critical Junctures: Theory, Narrative, and Counterfactuals in Historical Institutionalism', *World Politics* 59(3): 314–69.

Chandra, Kanchan. 2004. *Why Ethnic Parties Succeed*. New York: Cambridge University Press.

Chand, Vikram K. (ed). 2007. *Reinventing Public Services in India*. Washington and New Delhi: World Bank and Sage.

Chatterjee, Partha. 2011. 'Democracy and Economic Transformation in India', in Sanjay Ruparelia, Sanjay Reddy, John Harriss, and Stuart Corbridge (eds), *Understanding India's New Political Economy*. New York: Routledge.

Chellaney, Brahma. 1991. 'India Opens Doors to Capitalism', *The Washington Post*, 29 July.

Chibber, Vivek. 2003. *Locked in Place*. Princeton: Princeton University Press.

Chibber, Vivek and Adaner Usmani. 2013. 'The State and the Capitalist Class in India', in Atul Kohli and Prerna Singh (eds), *Routledge Handbook of Indian Politics*. New York: Routledge.

Chhibber, Pradeep. 1995. 'Political Parties, Electoral Competition, Government Expenditures and Economic Reform in India', *The Journal of Development Studies* 32(1): 74–96.

Chidambaram, Palaniappan. 2007. *The View from The Outside*. New Delhi: Penguin Books.

Choudhry, Praveen K., Vijay L. Kelkar, and Vikash Yadav. 2004. 'The Evolution of "Homegrown Conditionality" in India–IMF Relations', *Journal of Development Studies*, 40(6): 59–81.

Choudhuri, Sachindra. 1966. *Why Devaluation* (5 June). New Delhi: Publications Division, Ministry of Information and Broadcasting.

Choudhury, Sachin. 1968. 'Finance Minister's Broadcast: 5 June 1966', in L.M. Singhvi (ed.), *Devaluation of the Rupee: Its Implications and Consequences*. New Delhi: S. Chand and Company.

Chowdari, J.P. 1990. *Address by JP Chowdari* (18 April). New Delhi: National Conference on India's Economic Strategy for the 1990s.

Chowdary, T.H. 2000. 'Telecom Demonopolization: Policy or Farce?' *Economic and Political Weekly*, 35(6): 428–39.

Chua, Beng Huat. 2010. 'Disrupting Hegemonic Liberalism in East Asia', *Boundary*, 37(2): 199–216.

Chwieroth, Jeffrey. 2007. 'Testing and Measuring the Role of Ideas: The Case of Neoliberalism in the International Monetary Fund', *International Studies Quarterly*, 51(5): 5–30.

———. 2010. 'How Do Crises Lead to Change? Liberalizing Capital Controls in the Early Years of New Order Indonesia', *World Politics*, 62(3): 496–527.

Clark, Ephraim and Geeta Lakshmi. 2003. 'Controlling the Risk: A Case Study of the Indian liquidity Crisis 1990–92', *Journal of International Development*, 15(3): 288–9.

Coase, Ronald H. 1998. 'The New Institutional Economics', *American Economic Review*, 88(2): 72–4.

Comptroller and Auditor General of India. 2010. *Performance Audit Report on the Issue of Licences and Allocation of 2G Spectrum by the Department of Telecommunications—Ministry of Communications and Information Technology*. New Delhi: Comptroller and Auditor General of India.

Confederation of Indian Industry. 1994. *Report on Competitive Advantage of India*. New Delhi: Confederation of Indian Industry.

Cowhey, Peter. 1990. 'The International Telecommunications Regime: The Political Roots of International Regimes for High Technology', *International Organization*, 44(2): 169–99.

Cullather, Nick. 2007. 'Hunger and Containment: How India Became Important in US Cold War Strategy', *India Review*, 6(2): 59–90.

———. 2010. *The Hungry World: America's Cold War Battle Against Poverty in Asia*. Cambridge, MA: Harvard University Press.

Dagli, Vadilal. 1979. *Report of The Committee on Controls and Subsidies*. New Delhi: Ministry of Finance.

———. 1979a. *Report of the Committee on Controls and Subsidies*. New Delhi: Government of India.

Damodaran, Harish. 2008. *India's New Capitalists*. New Delhi: Permanent Black.

Dasgupta, Ajit K. 1974. *Economic Theory and the Developing Countries*. London: Macmillan.

Dasgupta, Ashim. 1991. 'There is an Alternative', *Frontline* (20 July–2 August): 151–2.

David, Paul. 1985. 'Clio and the Economics of Qwerty', *American Economic Review*, 75(2): 332–7.

Delhi High Court. 1998. *Union of India v. TRAI. Judgment of Usha Mehra*. New Delhi: High Court.

Denoon, David B.H. 1986. *Devaluation under Pressure: India, Indonesia, and Ghana*. Cambridge: The MIT Press.

———. 1988. 'Cycles in Indian Economic Liberalization', *Comparative Politics*, 31(1): 51–2.

Department of Telecommunications. 2011. *Annual Report 2010–2011*. New Delhi: Government of India.

———. 2005. *Annual Report 2003–2004*. New Delhi: Ministry of Communications.

Derthick, Martha and Paul J. Quirk. 1985. *The Politics of Deregulation*. Washington, DC: The Brookings Institution.

Desai, Ashok V. 2003. *India's Telecommunications Industry: History, Analysis and Diagnosis*. New Delhi: Sage Publications.

Dhar, P.N. 1990. *Constraints on Growth: Reflections on the Indian Experience*. New Delhi: Oxford University Press.

Dixit, Avinash K. 1996. *The Making of Economic Policy: A Transactions-Cost Approach*. Cambridge: The MIT Press.

Division of the Humanities and Social Sciences. 1986. *A Conversation with J. Burke Knapp: Conversations About George Woods And The World Bank* (5 September). Portola Valley: California Institute of Technology.

Dokeniya, Anupama. 1999. 'Reforming the State: Telecom Liberalization in India', *Telecommunications Policy*, 23(2): 111–22.

Dossani, Rafiq and V.R. Ranganathan. 2005. 'Farmers' Willingness to Pay for Power in India', in Joel Ruet (ed.), *Against the Current, Vol. III*. New Delhi: Manohar.

Dreze, J. and Amarta Sen. 2011. 'Putting Growth in Its Place' (14 November), *Outlookindia.com*. New Delhi: http://www.outlookindia.com/article.aspx?278843 (accessed 11 November 2013).

Dubash, Navroz and Sudhir C. Rajan. 2001. 'Power Politics: Process of Power Sector Reform in India', *Economic and Political Weekly*, 36(35, 1 September): 3,369–70.

Dubash, Navroz and D. Narasimha Reddy. 2007. *The Practice and Politics of Regulation: Regulatory Governance in Indian Electricity*. New Delhi: National Institute of Public Finance and Policy.

Echeverri-Gent, John. 2007. 'Politics of Market Micro-Structure: Towards a New Political Economy of India's Equity Market Reform', in Rahul Mukherji (ed.), *India's Economic Transition*. New Delhi: Oxford University Press.

Eckestein, Harry. 1975. 'Case Study and Theory in Political Science', in Fed I. Greenstein and Nelson W. Polsby (eds), *Handbook of Political Science*. Reading: Addison-Wesley.

Economist Intelligence Unit. 1998. 'MTNL Plans Cellular Service in Delhi', *EIU ViewsWire*, 7 January, London.

———. 1999. 'New Telecoms Policy in Pipeline', *EIU ViewsWire*, 13 January, London.

———. 1999a. 'Government Passes New Telecom Policy', *EIU ViewsWire*, 10 May, London.

———. 1999b. 'A Telecom Truce is Called', *EIU ViewsWire*, 30 June, London.

———. 1999c. 'Government Intent on Telecoms Bailout Package', *EIU ViewsWire*, 23 July, London.

Evans, Peter. 1995. *Embedded Autonomy: States and Industrial Transformation*. Princeton: Princeton University Press.

FICCI. 1966. *Correspondence and Relevant Documents Relating to Important Questions Dealt with by the Federation During the Year 1966*. New Delhi: Federation House.

———. 1991. *Correspondence and relevant documents relating to important questions dealt with by the FICCI from January 1990 to March 1991*. New Delhi: Federation House.

Frankel, Francine R. 1978. *India's Political Economy: The Gradual Revolution*. Princeton, NJ: Princeton University Press.

———. 1997. 'Decline of a Social Order,' in Sudipta Kaviraj (ed.), *Politics in India*. New Delhi: Oxford University Press.

———. 2005. *India's Political Economy, 1947–2004: The Gradual Revolution*. New Delhi: Oxford University Press.

Gandhi, Mohandas K. 1977. 'Address to the Fourth Annual Session of the Federation', in H. Venkatsubbiah (ed.), *Enterprise and Economic Change: 50 Years of FICCI*. New Delhi: Vikas Publishing House Private Limited.

Ganguly, Sumit. 2002. *Conflict Unending: India–Pakistan Tensions Since 1947*. New Delhi: Oxford University Press.

Ganguly, Sumit and Rahul Mukherji. 2011. *India since 1980*. New York and New Delhi: Cambridge University Press.

Garret, Geoffrey. 1998. *Partisan Politics in the Global Economy*. Cambridge: Cambridge University Press.

George, Alexander L. and Andrew Bennett. 2004. *Case Studies and Theory Development in the Social Sciences*. Cambridge: The MIT Press.

Gerschenkron, Alexander. 1962. *Economic Backwardness in Historical Perspective*. Cambridge: Harvard University Press.

Goldstone, Jack A. 1991. *Revolution and Rebellion in the Early Modern World*. Berkeley: University of California Press.

Gould, Stephen Jay and Niles Eldridge. 1977. 'Punctuated Equilibria: The Tempo and Mode of Evolution Reconsidered', *Paleontological Society*, 3(2): 115–51.

Gourevitch, Peter A. 1986. *Politics in Hard Times: Comparative Responses to International Economic Crises*. Ithaca: Cornell University Press.

Government of India. 1980. *Statement on Industrial Policy*. New Delhi: Department of Industrial Development, Ministry of Industry.

———. 1986. *Economic Survey 1985–86*. New Delhi: Ministry of Finance.

———. 1991. *Statement on Industrial Policy*. New Delhi: Ministry of Industry.

———. 1995. *Silver Jubilee (1970–1995): Compendium of Sectorial Studies*. New Delhi: Bureau of Industrial Costs and Prices, Ministry of Industry.

Gowda, M.V. Rajeev and E. Sridharan. 2007. 'The Consolidation of India's Democracy: The Role of Parties and the Party System', in S. Ganguly, L. Diamond, and M. Plattner (eds), *The State of India's Democracy*. Baltimore: Johns Hopkins University Press.

Grief, Avner and David D. Laitin. 2004. 'A Theory of Endogenous Institutional Change', *American Political Science Review*, 98(4): 633–52.

Grief, Avner. 2006. *Institutions and the Path to the Modern Economy*. New York: Cambridge University Press.

Gupta, Akhil. 1998. *Post-colonial Developments: Agriculture in the Making of a Modern Nation*. Durham: Duke University Press.

Gupta, Rajni. 2002. 'Telecommunications Liberalization: Critical Role of Legal and Regulatory Regime', *Economic and Political Weekly*, 37(17): 1,668–75.

Gupta, Surajeet Das. 2004. 'The WLL Letters', *Business Standard*. New Delhi.

Gwin, Cathrine and Lawrence A Veit. 1985. 'The Indian Miracle', *Foreign Policy*, 58(Spring): 79–98.

Haas, Peter. 1992. 'Introduction: Epistemic Communities and International Policy Coordination', *International Organization*, 46(1): 1–35.

Hacker, Jacob. 2005. 'Policy Drift: The Hidden Politics of U.S. Welfare State Retrenchment', in Wolfgang Streeck and Kathleen Thelen (eds), *Beyond Continuity: Institutional Change in Advanced Political Economies*. Oxford: Oxford University Press.

Haggard, Stephan. 1990. *Pathways from the Periphery: The Politics of Growth in Newly Industrializing Countries*. Ithaca, NY: Cornell University Press.

Haggard, Stephan and Sylvia Maxfield. 1996a. 'The Political Economy of Financial Internationalization in the Developing World', *International Organization*, 50(1): 35–68.

———. 1996b. 'The Political Economy of Financial Internationalization in the Developing World', in Robert O. Keohane and Helen V. Milner (eds), *Internationalization and Domestic Politics*, New York: Cambridge University Press: 209–39.

Hall, Peter. 1993. 'Policy Paradigms, Social Learning, and the State: The Case of Economic Policymaking in Britain', *Comparative Politics*, 25(3): 275–96.

———. 2010. 'Historical Institutionalism in Rationalist Sociological Perspective', in James Mahoney and Kathleen Thelen (eds), *Explaining Institutional Change: Ambiguity, Agency, and Power*. New York: Cambridge University Press.

Hall, Peter A. and David Soskice. 2001. 'An Introduction to Varieties of Capitalism', in Peter A. Hall and David Soskice (eds), *Varieties of Capitalism: The Institutional Foundations of Comparative Advantage*. New York: Cambridge University Press.

Hankla, Charles R. 2006. 'Party Linkages and Economic Policy: An Examination of Indira Gandhi's India', *Business and Politics*, 8(3): pp. 1–29, Article 4.

Hanson, A.H. 1966. *The Process of Planning*. London: Oxford University Press.

Hazari, R.K. 1967. *Industrial Planning and Licensing Policy: Final Report*. New Delhi: Planning Commission.

———. 1969. *Report of the Industrial Licensing Policy Inquiry Committee: Main Report*. New Delhi: Department of Industrial Development, Government of India.

———. 1985. *Essays on Industrial Policy*. New Delhi: Concept Publishers.

Hazarika, Sanjoy. 1990. 'New India Budget Stresses Farming and Export Push', *The New York Times* (20 March).

———. 1991. 'India Retreats From Socialist Past', *The New York Times* (25 July).

Herring, Ronald J. 1999. 'Embedded Particularism: India's Failed Developmental State', in Meredith Woo-Cummings (ed.), *The Developmental State*, Ithaca, NY: Cornell University Press.

Hill, Hal. 2000. *The Indonesian Economy*. Cambridge: Cambridge University Press.

Hirschman, Albert O. 1945/1980. *National Power and the Structure of Foreign Trade*. Berkeley: University of California Press.

———. 1980. *The Strategy of Economic Development*. New Haven: Yale University Press.

———. 1989. 'How the Keynesian Revolution was Exported from the United States, and Other Comments', in Peter A Hall (ed.), *The Political Power of Economic Ideas: Keynesianism Across Nations*. Princeton: Princeton University Press.

Hussain, Abid. 1984. *Report of the Committee on Trade Policy*. New Delhi: Ministry of Commerce.

ICICI. 1998. *Draft Report to the Department of Telecommunications: State Cellular Projects—Assessment of Viability*. Mumbai: Government of India.

International Monetary Fund. 1991. *Minutes of Executive Board Meetings 91/7* (18 January). Washington, DC: International Monetary Fund.

———. 1991a. *Minutes of Executive Board Meeting 91/28* (27 February). Washington, DC: International Monetary Fund.

———. 1991b. *Minutes of Executive Board Meeting 91/97* (22 July). Washington, DC: International Monetary Fund.

———. 1991c. *Minutes of Executive Board Meeting 91/121* (12 September). Washington, DC: International Monetary Fund.

———. 1991d. *Minutes of Executive Board Meeting 91/145* (31 October). Washington, DC: International Monetary Fund.

———. 1992. *Minutes of Executive Board Meeting 92/145* (4 December). Washington, DC: International Monetary Fund.

Jabko, Nicolas. 2006. *Playing the Market: A Political Strategy for Uniting Europe—1985–2005*. Ithaca, NY: Cornell University Press.

Jaffrelot, Christophe. 2000. 'The Rise of the Other Backward Classes in the Hindi Belt', *The Journal of Asian Studies*, 59(1): 86–109.

———. 2003. *India's Silent Revolution: The Rise of Lower Castes in Northern India*. London: Hurst and Company.

Jenkins, Rob. 1999. *Democratic Politics and Economic Reform in India*. New York: Cambridge University Press.

Jha, Lakshmi Kant. 1986. *Report of the Economic and Administrative Reforms Commission on Accountability*. New Delhi: Department of Administrative Reforms and Public Grievances.

Johnson, Harry G. 1967. 'The Possibility of Income Losses from Increased Efficiency or Factor Accumulation in the Presence of Tariffs', *Economic Journal*, 77(305): 151–4.

Joshi, Vijay and I.M.D. Little. 1994. *India: Macroeconomics and Political Economy*. New Delhi: Oxford University Press.

Kale, Sunila. 2004. 'Current Reforms: The Politics of Policy Change in India's Electricity Sector', *Pacific Affairs*, 77(3): 471–9.

———. 2007. *Power Steering: The Politics of Utility Privatization in India*, PhD Dissertation. Austin: University of Texas.

Kannan, K.P. and N. Vijaymohan Pillai. 2002. *Plight of the Power Sector in India* Thiruvanthapuram: Centre for Development Studies.

Kantha, Sharmila and Subhajyoti Ray. 2006. *Building India with Partnership: The Story of CII 1895–2005*. New Delhi: Penguin Books.

Kapur, Devesh and Pratap B. Mehta (eds). 2005. *Public Institutions in India: Performance and Design*. New Delhi: Oxford University Press.

Katyal, K.K. 1991. 'We Had to Take Hard Decisions: PM', *The Hindu* (10 July).

Kaul, Man Mohini. 2005. 'ASEAN–India Relations during the Cold War', in Frederic Grare and Amitabh Mattoo (eds), *India and ASEAN*. New Delhi: Manohar.

Kaviraj, Sudipta. 1997. 'A Critique of the Passive Revolution', in Partha Chatterjee (ed.), *State and Politics in India*. New Delhi: Oxford University Press.

Khan, Mohsin S. and Sunil Sharma. 2003. 'IMF Conditionality and Country Ownership of Adjustment Programs', *The World Bank Research Observer*, 18(2): 227–48.

Khosla, Shyam. 1991. 'Budget Adopted Amid Walkouts', *Tribune* (15 September).

Khusro, A.M., Montek Singh Ahluwalia, Raja J. Chelliah, Ashok V. Desai, P N Dhar, Mrinal Dutta-Chaudhury, K.N. Kabra, K. Krishnamurthy, N.S. Siddharthan, and A.N. Verma. 1990. *Industrial Policy: A Panel Discussion*. New Delhi: Institute of Economic Growth and Vikas Publishing House.

King, Gary, Robert O. Keohane, and Sidney Verba. 1994. *Designing Social Inquiry: Scientific Inference in Qualitative Research*. Princeton: Princeton University Press.

Kirk, Jason A. 2005. 'Banking on India's States: The Politics of World Bank Reform Programs in Andhra Pradesh and Karnataka', *India Review*, 4(3/4): 298–9.

———. 2007. 'Economic Reform, Federal Politics, and External Assistance: Understanding New Delhi's Perspective on the World Bank's State-Level Loans', in Rahul Mukherji (ed.), *India's Economic Transition: The Politics of Reforms*. New Delhi: Oxford University Press.

Kochanek, Stanley. 1974. *Business and Politics in India*. Berkeley: University of California Press; pp. 289–320.

———. 1995–6. 'The Transformation of Interest Politics in India', *Pacific Affairs*, 68(4): 529–50.

———. 2007. 'Liberalization and Business Lobbying in India', in Rahul Mukherji (ed.), *India's Economic Transition*. New Delhi: Oxford University Press.

Kohli, Atul. 1989. 'The Politics of Economic Liberalization in India', *World Development*, 17(3): 305–28.

———. 1991. *Democracy and Discontent*. New York: Cambridge University Press.

———. 2004. *State Directed Development: Political Power and Industrialization in the Global Periphery*. New York: Cambridge University Press.

———. 2006. 'Politics of Economic Growth in India, 1980–2005, Part-I'. *Economic and Political Weekly*, 41(13): 1,251–9.

———. 2009. *Democracy and Development in India*. New Delhi: Oxford University Press.

Krasner, Stephen D. 1984. 'Approaches to the State: Alternative Conceptions and Historical Dynamics', *Comparative Politics*, 16(2): 223–45.

———. 1991. 'Global Communications and National Power', *World Politics*, 28(3): 336–66.

Krishnan, R. 1991. 'We Saw it Coming', *Frontline*, 20 July–2 August.

Krueger, Anne O. 1974. 'The Political Economy of the Rent-Seeking Society', *American Economic Review*, 64(3): 291–303.

———. 1993. *Political Economy of Policy Reform in Developing Countries*. Cambridge: The MIT Press.

———. 1997. 'Trade Policy and Economic Development: How We Learn', *American Economic Review*, 87(1): 1–22

Kudaisya, Medha M. 2002. 'Reforms by Stealth', *South Asia*, 25(2, August): 216–20.

———. 2003. *The Life and Times of GD Birla*. New Delhi: Oxford University Press.

———. 2009. '"A Mighty Adventure": Institutionalising the Idea of Planning in Post-Colonial India', *Modern Asian Studies*, 43(4): 960–8.

Kumar, Nirmallya. 2009. *India's Global Powerhouses: How They are Taking On the World*. Boston: Harvard Business Press.

Kumar, Nagesh. 1996. 'India: Industrialization, Liberalization, and Inward and Outward Foreign Direct Investment', in John H. Dunning and Rajneesh Narula (eds), *Foreign Direct Investment and Governments*. London: Routledge: 378.

Kumbhkarni, C.M. 1991. 'Budget Passage Boosts Cong Morale', *Tribune*, 10 September.

Kux, Dennis. 1992. *India and the United States: Estranged Democracies 1941–1991*. Washington, DC: National Defense University Press.

Lee, Kuan Yew. 2000. *From Third World to First: The Singapore Story 1965–2000*. Singapore: Singapore Press Holdings.

Levy, Brian and Pablo T. Spiller. 1994. 'The Institutional Foundations of Regulatory Commitment: A Comparative Analysis of Telecommunications Regulation', *Journal of Law Economics and Organization*, 10(2): 201–46.

Lewis, John P. 1964. *Quiet Crisis in India: Economic Development and American Policy*. New York: Anchor Books, Doubleday & Company Limited.

———. 1997. *India's Political Economy: Governance and Reform*. New Delhi: Oxford University Press.

Lewis, W. Arthur. 1978. *The Evolution of the International Economic Order*. New Jersey: Princeton University Press.

Liddle, R. William. 1991. 'The Relative Autonomy of the Third World Politician: Soeharto and Indonesian Economic Development in Comparative Perspective', *International Studies Quarterly*, 35(4): 411–16.

Lijphardt, Arend. 1971. 'Comparative Politics and Comparative Method', *American Political Science Review*, 63(3): 682–93.

Lok Sabha Debates. 1966. 57 (25 July–5 August). New Delhi: Government of India; pp. 1,653–4.

———. 1966 (9 August). New Delhi: Government of India.

———. 1991 (4 March). 9th Series, 14:6. New Delhi: Government of India: 831–5.

———. 1991a (19 July). 10th Series, 1–9. New Delhi: Government of India; pp. 1–10.

———. 1991b (24 July). 10th Series, 1–9. New Delhi: Government of India; pp. 271–315.

———. 1991c (30 July). 10th Series, 2:15/16. New Delhi: Government of India; pp. 288–305.

Mahoney, James and Kathleen Thelen. 2010. 'A Theory of Gradual Institutional Change', in Kathleen Thelen and James Mahoney (eds), *Explaining Institutional Change: Ambiguity, Power, and Agency*. New York: Cambridge University Press; pp. 1–37.

Majumdar, Sumit K. 2012. *India's Late, Late Industrial Revolution*. New York: Cambridge University Press.

Manor, James. 1983. 'Anomie and Indian Politics: Origins and Wider Impact', *Economic and Political Weekly*, 18(19, 21 May): 725–34.

———. 1987. 'Tried, Then Abandoned: Economic Liberalization in India', *IDS Bulletin*, 18(4): 30–44.

Masani, M.R. 1968. 'Round-Up of Reactions', in L.M. Singhvi (ed.), *Devaluation of the Rupee: Its Implications and Consequences*. New Delhi: S. Chand and Company.

McDowell, Stephen U. 1997. *Globalization, Liberalization and Policy Change*. New York: St Martin's Press.

Mehta, Asoka. 1968. "Answers to Some Questions in Lok Sabha Regarding Devaluation - February 17, 1966." In *Devaluation of the Rupee: It's Implications and Consequences* edited by L M Singhvi. New Delhi: S. Chand and Company.

Mehta, Ashok. 1973. 'Growth of the Public Sector as the Dominant Sector', in C.N. Vakil, (ed.), *Industrial Development in India: Policy and Problems*. New Delhi: Orient Longman.

Mill, John Stuart. 1987. *The Logic of the Moral Sciences*. London: Gerald Duckworth and Company.

Milner, Helen V. 1997. *Interests, Institutions, and Information: Domestic Politics and International Relations*. Princeton: Princeton University Press.

Milner, Helen V. and Keiko Kubota. 2005. 'Why the Move to Free Trade? Democracy and Trade Policy in the Developing Countries', *International Organization*, 59(1): 107–43.

Ministry of Finance. 2011. *Economic Survey 2010–11*. New Delhi: Government of India and Oxford University Press.

Mishra, Surendra (ed.). 1996. *Finance Minister's Budget Speeches 1947 to 1996*. Delhi: Surjeet Publications and Lok Sabha Secretariat.

Misra, K.P. Misra. 1972. 'Intra-State Imperialism: The Case of Pakistan', *Journal of Peace Research*, 9(1): 27–39.

Mitra, Subrata K. 1991. 'Room to Maneuver in the Middle: Local Elite, Political Action, and the State in India', *World Politics*, 43(3): 390–413.

Miurhead, Bruce. 2005. 'Differing Perspectives: The World Bank and the 1963 Aid-India Negotiations', *India Review*, 4(1): 1–22.

Moe, Terry. 1994. 'Power and Political Institutions', in Ian Shapiro, Daniel Galvin and Stephen Skowronek (eds), *Rethinking Political Institutions: The Art of the State*. New York: New York University Press.

Mooij, Jos. 2007. 'Hype, Skill and Class: The Politics of Reform in Andhra Pradesh, India', *Commonwealth and Comparative Politics*, 45(1): 34–56.

Moore, Barrington Jr. 1966. *Social Origins of Dictatorship and Democracy: Lord and Peasant in the Making of the Modern World*. Boston: Beacon Press.

Mukherji, Rahul. 1999. *A Path to Trade and Investment Liberalization*. New York: Columbia University unpublished dissertation.

———. 2000. 'India's Aborted Liberalization—1966', *Pacific Affairs* 73(3): 375–92.

Mukherji, Rahul. 2004. 'Managing Competition: Politics and the Building of Independent Regulatory Institutions', *India Review*, 3(4): 280–1.

———. 2006. 'Promoting Competition in India's Telecom Sector', in Vikram K. Chand (ed.), *Reinventing Public Services in India*. Washington, DC, and New Delhi: World Bank and Sage Publications.

———. 2007. 'Economic Transition in a Plural Polity: India', in Rahul Mukherji (ed.), *India's Economic Transition: The Politics of Reforms*, New Delhi: Oxford University Press.

———. 2008. 'Appraising the Legacy of Bandung: A View from India', in See Seng Tan and Amitav Acharya (eds), *Bandung Revisited*, Singapore: NUS Press.

———. 2009. 'The State, Economic Growth, and Development in India', *India Review*, 8(1): 87–8.

———. 2009a. 'India's Foreign Economic Policies', in Sumit Ganguly (ed.), *India's Foreign Policy*. New Delhi: Oxford University Press.

———. 2010. 'Regulation and Infrastructure Development in India: Comparing Telecommunications, Ports and Power', in Vikram K. Chand (ed.), *Public Service Delivery in India: Understanding the Reform Process*. New Delhi: Oxford University Press.

———. 2010a. 'India's Foreign Economic Policies', in Sumit Ganguly (ed.), *India's Foreign Policy*. New Delhi: Oxford University Press.

Mukherji, Rahul and Gaurav A. Kankanhalli. 2009. 'Civil Aviation in India', *Working Paper 97* (18 November). Singapore: Institute of South Asian Studies.

Mukerji, Siddhartha. 2007. *State and Industrial Transformation in India*, unpublished MPhil Dissertation. New Delhi: Jawaharlal Nehru University.

Murillo, Maria V. 2009. *Political Competition, Partisanship, and Policy making in Latin American Utilities*. Princeton: Princeton University Press.

Murthy, N.R. Narayana. 2011. '"India Inc": The New Face of Business-Infosys', in Medha M. Kudaisya (ed.), *The Oxford India Anthology of Business History*. New Delhi: Oxford University Press.

Naidu, N. Chandrababu (with Sevanti Ninan). 2000. *Plain Speaking*. New Delhi: Viking Penguin.

Naqvi, Jawed. 1991. 'Hardline Indian Party Drops Opposition To Defence Cuts', Reuters News (14 July).

———. 1991a. 'Indian Prime Minister Rao Faces Crisis Over Tough Budget', Reuters News (31 July).

———. 1991b. 'Bid To Defuse Indian Budget Crisis Just Angers Deputies More', Reuters News (2 August).

Narasimhan, M. 1985. *Committee to Examine the Principles of a Possible Shift from Financial to Physical Controls—Final Report*. New Delhi: Ministry of Finance.

Nassim, Nicholas Taleb and Mark Blyth. 2001. 'The Black Swan of Cairo: How Suppressing Volatility Makes the World Less Predictable and More Dangerous', *Foreign Affairs*, 90(3): 33–9.

National Taskforce on Information Technology and Software Development. 1998. *IT Taskforce—Basic Background Report*. New Delhi: Government of India.

Naughton, Barry. 1995. *Growing Out of the Plan: Chinese Economic Reform 1978–1993*. New York: Cambridge University Press.

Nayar, Baldev R. 2006. 'When Did the Hindu Rate of Growth End?', *Economic and Political Weekly*, 41(19): 1,886.

————. 2006a. 'India's Globalization: Evaluating the Economic Consequences', *Policy Studies 22*. Washington, DC: East-West Center Washington.

———— (ed.). 2007. *Globalization and Politics in India*. New Delhi: Oxford University Press.

Nelson, Joan M. (ed.). 1990. *Economic Crisis and Policy Change*. Princeton: Princeton University Press.

Nilekani, Nandan. 2008. *Imagining India: Ideas for the New Century*. New Delhi: Allen Lane; pp. 61–82.

Noll, Roger G. 1989. 'The Politics of Regulation', in Richard Schmalensee and Robert D. Willig (eds), *Handbook of Industrial Organization Volume II*. Amsterdam: North Holland.

Nooruddin, Irfan. 2011. *Coalition Politics and Economic Development*. New York: Cambridge University Press.

North, Douglass C. 1990. *Institutions, Institutional Change and Economic Performance*. New York: Cambridge University Press.

————. 1995. 'The New Institutional Economics and Third World Development', in John Harriss, Janet Hunter, and Colin M. Lewis (eds), *The New Institutional Economics and the Third World*. New York: Routledge.

————. 2005. *Understanding the Process of Economic Change*. Princeton: Princeton University Press.

North, Douglass C. and Barry R. Weingast. 1989. 'Constitutions and Commitment: The Evolution of Institutions Governing Public Choice in Seventeenth Century England', *Journal of Economic History*, 49(4): 803–32.

North, Douglass C., John J. Wallis, and Barry R. Weingast. 2009. *Violence and Social Orders: A Conceptual Framework for Interpreting Recorded History*. New York: Cambridge University Press.

Offe, Claus. 2006. 'Political Institutions and Social Power', in Ian Shapiro, Daniel Galvin, and Stephen Skowronek (eds), *Rethinking Social Institutions*. New York: New York University Press.

Oliver, Robert W. 1985. *A Conversation with Simon Aldewereld II—Conversations about George Woods and the World Bank*. Pasadena: California Institute of Technology.

———. 1995. *George Woods and the World Bank*. Boulder: Lynne Rienner Publishers.

Olson, Mancur. 1965. *The Logic of Collective Action: Public Goods and the Theory of Goods*. Cambridge: Harvard University Press.

———. 1993. 'Dictatorship, Democracy, and Development', *American Political Science Review*, 87(3): 567–76.

Omvedt, Gail. 2005. 'Farmer's Movements', in Raka Ray and Mary F. Katzenstein (eds), *Social Movements in India*. New Delhi: Oxford University Press.

Oral History Program. 1981. *Transcript of Interview with J. Burke Knapp* (6 October and 29 October). Washington, DC: The World Bank/IFC Archives.

———. 1986. *Transcript of Interview with Stanley Please* (26 August). Washington, DC: The World Bank/IFC Archives.

———. 1986a. *Transcript of Interview with Benjamin B King* (24–25 July). Washington, DC: The World Bank/IFC Archives.

Paarlberg, Robert L. 1985. *Food Trade and Foreign Policy: India, the Soviet Union and the United States*. Ithaca, NY, and London: Cornell University Press.

Pai, Sudha. 2010. *Developmental State and the Dalit Question in Madhya Pradesh: Congress Response*. New Delhi: Routledge.

Panagariya, Arvind. 2008. *India: The Emerging Giant*. New York and New Delhi: Oxford University Press.

Pani, B. Saranga, M. Thimma Reddy, and N. Sreekumar. 2007. 'Power Sector Reforms in Andhra Pradesh', Governance and Policy Spaces Working Paper #11. Hyderabad: Centre for Economic and Social Studies.

Paranjpe, H.K. 1986. 'The Monopolies and Restrictive Trade Practices Act: A Review 1970–83', in S. Guhan and Manu Shroff (eds), *Essays on Economic Progress and Welfare: In Honour of I.G. Patel*. New Delhi: Oxford University Press.

Patel, I.G. 1987. 'On Taking India into the Twenty First Century', *Modern Asian Studies* 21(2).

———. 2003. *Glimpses of Indian Economic Policy*. New Delhi: Oxford University Press.

Patel, Urjit R. and Saugata Bhattacharya. 2010. 'Infrastructure in India: The Economics of Transition from Public to Private Provision', *Journal of Comparative Economics*, 38(1): 57–61.

Patil, Shivraj V. 2011. *Report on Examination of Appropriateness of Procedures Followed by Department of Telecommunications in Issuance of Licenses and Allocation of Spectrum During the Period 2001–2009* (31 January). New Delhi: Ministry of Communications and Information Technology.

Pederson, Jorgen D. 2000. 'Explaining Economic Liberalization in India', *World Development*, 28(2): 268–71.

Pempel, T.J. 1998. *Regime Shift: Comparative Dynamics of the Japanese Political Economy*. Ithaca, NY: Cornell University Press.

Petrazzini, Ben A. 1996. 'Telecommunications Policy in India: The Political Underpinnings of Reform', *Telecommunications Policy*, 20(1): 40–1.

Pierson, Paul. 1996. 'The New Politics of the Welfare State,', *World Politics*, 48(2): 143–92.

———. 2000. 'Increasing Returns, Path Dependence, and the Study of Politics', *American Political Science Review*, 94(2): 225–52.

———. 2004. *Politics in Time: History, Institutions, and Social Analysis*. Princeton: Princeton University Press.

Pierson, Paul and Theda Skocpol. 2002. 'Historical Institutions in Contemporary Political Science', in Ira Katznelson and Helen V. Milner (eds), *Political Science: State of the Discipline*. New York: W.W. Norton.

Planning Commission. 1994. *Report of NDC Committee on Power* (September). New Delhi: Government of India.

———. 2001. *Indian Planning Experience: A Statistical Profile* (January). New Delhi: Government of India.

———. 2011. *Mid-Term Appraisal: Eleventh Five Year Plan 2007–2012*. New Delhi: Government of India and Oxford University Press.

Pop-Eleches, Grigore. 2009. *From Economic Crisis to Reform: IMF Programs in Latin America And Eastern Europe*. Princeton: Princeton University Press.

Posner, Richard A. 1974. 'Theories of Economic Regulation', *The Bell Journal of Economics and Management Science*, 5(2): 335–58.

Prass, Paul. 1993. 'Chaudhary Charan Singh: An Indian Political Life', *Economic and Political Weekly*, 28(39): 2,087–90.

Prayas Energy Group. 2001. 'Godbole Committee Report on Enron Project: Expose and Way Out', *Economic and Political Weekly*, 36(23, 9 June): 2,063–8.

Putnam, Robert D. 1988. 'Diplomacy and Domestic Politics', *International Organization*, 42(3): 427–60.

Raghavan, Vikram. 2007. *Communications Law in India*. New Delhi: LexisNexis.

Rahman, Tariq. 1996. *Language and Politics in Pakistan*. Karachi: Oxford University Press.

Rajeev, M. 2002. 'Bank Argues Small Farmers Case', *The Times of India* (January). Hyderabad.

Rajghatta, Chidanand. 1992. 'A Money-splendoured Man: Dr. Manmohan Singh', *Citi-India* (April). New Delhi.

Rangarajan, Chakravarthy. 1981. 'Strategic Issues in Industrial Development', in C. Rangarajan, Anand P. Gupta, Rakesh Khurana, H. N. Pathak, and Charan D. Wadhwa (eds), *Strategy For Industrial Development in the 1980s*. New Delhi: Oxford University Press and IBH.

Rangarajan, Chakravarthy. 1987. 'The Analytical Frame-work of the Chakravarty Committee Report on the Monetary System', *Reserve Bank of India Bulletin* (September).

———. 1991. 'Recent Exchange Rate Adjustments: Causes and Consequences', *Reserve Bank of India Bulletin* (September).

———. 2010. 'Two Episodes in the Reform Process', in Shankar Acharya and Rakesh Mohan (eds), *India's Economy: Performance and Challenges*. New Delhi: Oxford University Press.

Rao, M. Venugopal. 2007. 'Power Purchase Agreements and Legal Action', in R.S. Rao and V. Hanumantha Rao (eds), *Fifty Years of Andhra Pradesh 1956–2006*. Hyderabad: Centre for Documentation, Research and Communication.

Reddy, G. Ram. 1989. 'The Politics of Accommodation: Caste, Class and Dominance in Andhra Pradesh', in Francine R. Frankel and M.S.A. Rao (eds), *Dominance and State Power in Modern India*. New Delhi: Oxford University Press.

Reddy, Sarampally M. 2006. 'Status of Minor Irrigation in Andhra Pradesh', in R.S. Rao, V. Hanumantha Rao, and N. Venugopal (eds), *Fifty Years of Andhra Pradesh 1956–2006*. Hyderabad: Centre for Documentation, Research and Communication.

Reuters News. 1991. 'IMF Grants Cash-Strapped India 220 Million Dollar Credit' (22 July).

———. 1991a. 'India Starts Talks With IMF On Emergency Loan' (30 July).

———. 1991b. 'India, IMF Provisionally Agree Loan Terms—Paper' (17 August).

———. 1991c. 'IMF Expected to Approve Emergency $620 Million Loan for India' (3 September).

———. 1991d. 'IMF Approves $634 Million Loan To Aid Ailing Economy' (12 September).

———. 1991e. 'West Backs Rao's Reforms with 6.7 Billion Dollars Aid to India' (20 September).

Reynolds, Lloyd G. 1983. 'The Spread of Economic Growth to the Third World', *Journal of Economic Literature*, 21(3): 941–80.

Rodan, P.H. Rosenstein. 1943. 'Problems of Industrialization of Easter and South-Eastern Europe', *The Economic Journal*, 53(210/211): 202–11.

Rodrik, Dani and Arvind Subramanian. 2004. 'From "Hindu Growth" to Productivity Surge: The Mystery of Indian Growth Transition', *The IMF Working Paper 04:77*. Washington, DC: International Monetary Fund.

Rubin, Barnett R. 1985. 'Economic Liberalization and the Indian State', *Third World Quarterly*, 7(4): 942–57.

Rudolph, Lloyd I. and Susanne H. Rudolph. 1987. *In Pursuit of Lakshmi: The Political Economy of the Indian State*. Chicago: The University of Chicago Press.

———. 1997. 'Regime Types and Economic Performance', in Sudipta Kaviraj (ed.), *Politics in India*. New Delhi: Oxford University Press.

———. 2007. 'Iconization of Chandrababu: Sharing Sovereignty in India's Federal Market Economy', in Rahul Mukherji (ed.), *India's Economic Transition: The Politics of Reform*. New Delhi: Oxford University Press; pp. 231–64.

Ruggie, John Gerard. 1983. 'International Regimes, Transactions, and Change: Embedded Liberalism in the Post-war Economic Order', in Stephen D. Krasner (ed.), *International Regimes*. Ithaca, NY: Cornell University Press.

Sagar, Easwar. 1966. 'Johnson's Hold-up of Food Aid to India Causes Worry', *Hindustan Times* (23 November).

Saha, Biswatosh. 2004. 'State Support for R and D in Developing Countries: Telecom Equipment Industry in India and China', *Economic and Political Weekly*, 39(35): 3,917–21.

Sankar, T.L. 1997. *Restructuring the Regulatory System: Power Sector in India* (March). Hyderabad: Administrative Staff College of India.

Schickler, Eric. 2001. *Disjointed Pluralism: Institutional Innovation and the Development of the U.S. Congress*. New Jersey: Princeton University Press.

Sen, Amartya. 1998. 'Theory and Practice of Development', in Isher J. Ahluwalia and I.M.D. Little (eds), *India's Economic Reforms: Essays for Manmohan Singh*. New Delhi: Oxford University Press.

Sengupta, Arjun Sengupta. 1984. *Report of the Committee to Review Policy for Public Enterprises*. New Delhi: Ministry of Finance.

Sengupta, Mithu. 2009. 'Making the State Change its Mind', *New Political Economy*, 14(2 June) 208–10.

Sengupta, Nitish K. 1987. *Government and Business*. New Delhi: Vikas Publishing.

Seshan, P.A. 1991. 'Sharpest Downvaluation in Recent Years', *The Hindu* (4 July).

Sharma, Chanchal R. 2011. 'A Discursive Dominance Theory of Economic Reform Sustainability', *India Review* 10(2): 126–84.

Sharma, K.K. 1990. 'Commodities and Agriculture: Grain Support Prices Increased in India', *Financial Times* (19 June).

———. 1991. 'Farmers Threaten Action—Agricultural Concessions are Still Not Filling Landowners Pockets', *Financial Times* (16 September).

Shastri, Vanita. 1997. 'The Politics of Economic Liberalization in India', *Contemporary South Asia*, 6(1): 43–4.

Shirk, Susan L. 1993. *The Political Logic of Economic Reform in China*. Berkeley: University of California.

Singh, J.P. 1999. *Leapfrogging Development: The Political Economy of Telecommunications Restructuring*. Albany: State University of New York Press.

Singh, Manmohan. 1964. *India's Export Trends and Prospects for Self-sustained Growth*. Oxford: Clarendon Press.

———. 1996. 'India: The Unfinished Agenda of Economic Reforms', *28th Jawaharlal Nehru Memorial Lecture*, 13 November, New Delhi.

Singh, Shalini. 2011. 'Trai Says Cancel 69 Telecom Licenses, DoT Agrees to Only', *The Times of India* (31 August). New Delhi.

Singh, Vishwanath P. 1990. 'Inaugural Address', Forty-first Meeting of the National Development Council, *World Economic Forum* (9 April). New Delhi: Confederation of indian Industry.

Singhvi, L.M. 1968. 'Round-Up Of Reactions: Trade and Industry', in L.M. Singhvi (ed.), *Devaluation of the Rupee*. New Delhi: S. Chand and Company.

Sinha, Aseema. 2005. 'Understanding the Rise and Transformation of Business Collective Action in India', *Business and Politics*, 7(2): Article 2.

Sinha, Nikhil. 1996. 'The Political Economy of India's Telecommunications Reforms', *Telecommunications Policy*, 20(1): 23–38.

Sinha, Yashwant. 2007. *Confessions of a Swadeshi Reformer*. New Delhi: Penguin Viking.

Simmons, Beth A. and Zachary Elkins. 2003. 'Globalization and Policy Diffusion: Explaining Three Decades of Liberalization', in Miles Kahler and David A. Lake (eds), *Governance in a Global Economy: Political Authority in Transition*. Princeton: Princeton University Press.

Snyder, Jack L. 1984. 'Richness, Rigor, and Relevance in the Study of Soviet Foreign Policy', *International Security*, 9(3): 89–108.

Special Correspondent. 1966. 'Mehta Holds Foreign Aid Inescapable: No Pressure in Formulation of Economic Policy'. *The Hindu*, 10 May. Chennai.

Special Stories. 2011. 'Fuel Crisis Deepens: Threatens to Derail 40,000 MW of Projects', *Power Line* (August): 14–18.

Sreekumar, N., K. Raghu, and M. Thimma Reddy. 2007. 'Strengths and Challenges of Andhra Pradesh Power Sector', *Economic and Political Weekly*, 46(42, 10 November): 24–7.

Sridharan, Kripa. 1996. *The ASEAN Region in India's Foreign Policy*. Aldershot: Dartmouth Publishing Company Limited.

Srinivasan, T.N. 2000. 'The Washington Consensus a Decade Later: Ideology and the Art and Science of Policy Advice', *The World Bank Research Observer*, 15(2): 265–70.

Srinivasan, T.N. 2011. *Growth, Sustainability, and India's Economic Reforms.* New Delhi: Oxford University Press.

Srinivasulu, K. and Prakash Sarangi. 1999. 'Political Realignments in Post-NTR Andhra Pradesh', *Economic and Political Weekly*, 34(34–5, 21 August): 2,449–58.

Stallings, Barbara. 1992. 'International Influence on Economic Policy: Debt, Stabilization, and Structural Reform', in Stephan Haggard and Robert R. Kaufman (eds), *The Politics of Economic Adjustment*. Princeton: Princeton University Press.

Stigler, George J. 1971. 'The Theory of Economic Regulation', *The Bell Journal of Economic and Management Science*, 2(1): 3–21.

Stone, Randall W. 2008. 'The Scope of IMF Conditionality', *International Organization*, 62(4): 589–620.

Streeck, Wolfgang and Kathleen Thelen. 2005. 'Introduction: Institutional Change in Advanced Political Economies', in Wolfgang Streeck and Kathleen Thelen (eds), *Beyond Continuity: Institutional Change in Advanced Political Economies*. Oxford: Oxford University Press.

Streeten, Paul. Shahid J. Burki, Mahbub ul Haq, Norman Hicks, and Frances Stewart. 1981. *First Things First: Meeting Basic Human Needs in the Developing World*. New York: Oxford University Press and World Bank.

Subramaniam, C. 1966. *Devaluation: Some Implications* (June). New Delhi: Publications Division—Ministry of Information and Broadcasting.

Subramanian, Narendra. 1999. *Ethnicity and Populist Mobilization: Political Parties, Citizenship and Democracy in South India*. New Delhi: Oxford University Press.

Sukumar, C.R. 2003. 'AP Govt Asked to Review Power Agreements', *The Hindu Business Line* (17 March). Hyderabad.

Sundaram, K. 1972. Political Response to the 1966 Devaluation—2', *Economic and Political Weekly* 7(36, 19 September).

Supreme Court of India. 2002. *Cellular Operators of India versus Union of India.* Judgment of G.B. Pattanaik. New Delhi: Supreme Court of India.

———. 2006. *Delhi Science Forum v. Union of India. Judgment of N.P. Singh and K. Venkataswami*. New Delhi: Supreme Court of India.

Suri, K.C. 2002. *Democratic Process and Electoral Politics in Andhra Pradesh, India*. Overseas Development Institute Working Paper #180. London: Overseas Development Institute.

Suri, K.C. 2005. 'The Dilemma of Democracy: Economic Reforms and Electoral Politics in Andhra Pradesh', in Jos Mooij (ed.), *The Politics of Economic Reforms in India*. New Delhi: Sage Publications.

————. 2006. 'Telegu Desam Party', in Peter Ronald de Souza and E. Sridharan (eds), *India's Political Parties*. New Delhi: Sage.

Suri, K.C. 2009. 'Andhra Pradesh: Fall of the CEO in the Arena of Democracy', in Sandeep Shastri, K.C. Suri, and Yogendra Yadav (eds), *Electoral Politics in Indian States*. New Delhi: Oxford University Press.

Suri, K.C., P. Narasimha Rao, and V. Anji Reddy. 2009. 'Andhra Pradesh: A Vote for Status Quo', *Economic and Political Weekly*, 44(39, 26 September): 108–13.

Swaminathan, Rajesh. 1997. 'Functioning   Anarchy: India's National Telecommunications   Policy and the Development of Basic Telephone Services', *Columbia Journal of Asian Law* 11(2): 422–3.

Swamy, Arun R. 2010. 'Political Mobilization', in Niraja G. Jayal and Pratap B. Mehta (eds), *The Oxford Companion to Politics in India*, New Delhi: Oxford University Press.

Swamy, Subramanian. 2011. *2G Spectrum Scam*. New Delhi: Har-Anand Publications.

Swank, Duane. 2002. *Global Capital: Political Institutions and Policy Change in Developed Welfare States*. New York: Cambridge University Press.

Swank, Duane and Sven Stienmo. 2002. 'The New Political Economy of Taxation in Advanced Capitalist Democracies', *American Journal of Political Science*, 46(3): 642–55.

Tan, Tai-Yong. 2007. 'Port Cities and Hinterlands: A Comparative Study of Singapore and Calcutta', *Political Geography*, 26(7): 855–8.

Tan, Tai-Yong and See Chak Mun. 2009. "The Evolution of India-ASEAN Relations." *India Review* 8(1): 25–41.

Tarrant, Bill. 1991. 'Big Reforms to Follow India's Devaluation, Minister Says', Reuters News (5 July).

TDSAT, A. 2003. *Cellular Operators of India v. Union of India. Judgment of D.P. Wadhwa*. New Delhi: TDSAT.

TDSAT, B. 2003a. *Cellular Operators of India v. Union of India. R.U.S. Prasad and P.R. Dasgupta*. New Delhi: TDSAT.

Tendulkar, Suresh D. and T.A. Bhavani. 2007. *Understanding Reforms: Post-1991 India*. New Delhi: Oxford University Press.

Thacker, Strom C. 1999. 'The High Politics of IMF Lending', *World Politics*, 52(1): 38–75.

Thakur, Ramesh. 1994. *The Politics and Economics of India's Foreign Policy*. London: Hurst and Company.

Thakurta, Paranjoy Guha. 1991. 'Sweat, Toil and Tears: Manmohan Singh is Determined to Rejuvenate the Economy', *Sunday* (14–20 July).

Thakurta, Paranjoy Guha. 1991a. 'We Must Become Hard-boiled Businessman: Commerce Minister P. Chidambaram on His Brave New Trade Policies', *Sunday* (14–20 July).

Telecom Regulatory Authority of India. 2001. *Recommendation on Issues Relating to 'Limited Mobility' through Wireless in Local Loop in the Access Network by Basic Service Providers*. New Delhi: Government of India.

———. 2003. *Recommendations on Unified Licensing*. New Delhi: Government of India.

———. 2006. *Study Paper on Telecom Industry in India and China*. New Delhi: Government of India.

———. 2007. *Telecom Regulatory Authority of India, Recommendations on Review of License Terms and Conditions and Capping of Number of Access Providers* (28 August). New Delhi: Government of India.

———. 2011. *Highlights of Telecom Subscription Data as on 31 March 2011*, Press Release No. 35/2011 (29 April). New Delhi: Government of India.

———. 2011a. *Highlights of Telecom Subscription Data as on 30 June, 2011*, Information Note to the Press—Press Release No. 45/2011. New Delhi: Government of India.

———. 2013. *Highlights on Telecom Subscription Data as on 28th February 2013*, Press Release No. 31 / 2013 (18 April). New Delhi: Government of India.

The Economic Times Editorial. 1991. 'A Non-IMF Route for the Government', *The Economic Times*, 22 June.

———. 1991a. 'Devaluation Prepares the Ground for IMF Loan', *The Economic Times*, 14 July.

———. 1991b. 'BJP Only Opposition Party to Welcome New Policy', *The Economic Times*, 25 July.

The Hindu Editorial. 1991. 'Industrial Policy to be Approved Today', *The Hindu*, 21 July.

The Hindu Editorial. 1991a. 'The Left Package to Ease BOP Crisis', *The Hindu*, 25 July.

———. 1991b. 'Disincentives to New Investment', *The Hindu*, 26 July.

———. 1991c. 'Industry not happy with budget', *The Hindu*, 26 July.

———. 1991d. 'Differences in Congress over Economic Policies', *The Hindu*, 26 July.

The Times of India Editorial. 1991. 'Govt Comes under Fire', *The Times of India*, 6 August.

Thelen, Kathleen. 2004. *How Institutions Evolve: The Political Economy of Skills in Germany, Britain, the United States, and Japan*. New York: Cambridge University Press.

Tilly, Charles. 1985. 'War Making and State Making as Organized Crime', in Peter Evans, Dietrich Rueschemeyer, and Theda Skocpol (eds), *Bringing the State Back In*. New York: Cambridge University Press.

———. 1992. *Coercion, Capital and European States*. Cambridge: Blackwell.

Todaro, Michael P. 1981. *Economic Development in the Third World*. New York and London: Longman.

Tongia, Rahul. 2007. 'The Political Economy of Indian Power Sector Reforms', in David G. Victor and Thomas C. Heller (eds), *The Political Economy of Power Sector Reform: The Experience of Five Major Developing Countries*. New York: Cambridge University Press.

Tripathy, Dwijendra and Jyoti Jumani. 2006. *The Concise Oxford History of Indian Business*. New Delhi: Oxford University Press.

Tsai, Kellee. 2006. 'Informal Institutions and Endogenous Change: Institutional Change in China', *World Politics*, 59(1): 116–41.

Tsiang, S.C. 1985. 'Foreign Trade and Investment as Boosters for Take Off: The Experience of Taiwan', in Vittorio Corbo, Anne O. Krueger, and Fernando Oscar (eds), *Export Oriented Development Strategies*. Boulder, Colorado: Westview Press.

Vanaik, Achin. 1990. *The Painful Transition*. London: Verso.

Varam, Dev. 1991. 'Indian Business Happy with Industrial Policy, Sore at Budget', Reuters News (25 July).

Varshney, Ashutosh. 1998. *Democracy, Development and the Countryside: Urban–Rural Struggles in India*. New York: Cambridge University Press.

———. 2000. 'Is India Becoming More Democratic', *The Journal of Asian Studies* 59(1): 8–10.

———. 2007. 'Mass Politics or Elite Politics: Understanding the Politics of India's Economic Reforms', in Rahul Mukherji (ed.), *India's Economic Transition: The Politics of Reforms*. New Delhi: Oxford University Press.

Venkatsubbiah, H. 1977. *Enterprise and Economic Change: 50 Years of FICCI*. New Delhi: Vikas Publishing House Private Limited.

Verghese, B.G. 2010. *First Draft: The Making of Modern India*. Chennai: Tranquebar Press.

Vigilance Study Circle. 2011. *Eighth Anniversary Celebrations of Vigilance Study Circle: Hyderabad—Souvenir* (8 July). Hyderabad: Vigilance Study Circle; pp. III, V, VII, 76–8.

Vittal, N. 2004. 'Sri N. Vittal on NTP-94', *Journal of the CTMS*, 13(5): 5–15.

Vogel, Steven. 1996. *Freer Markets, More Rules: Regulatory Reform in Advanced Industrial Countries*. Ithaca, NY: Cornell University Press.

Vreeland, James Raymond. 2003. *The IMF and Economic Development*. New York: Cambridge University Press.

Wade, Robert. 1990. *Governing the Market: Economic Theory and the Role of Government in East Asian Industrialization*. Princeton: Princeton University Press.

Wallach, Jessica S. 2003. 'Structural Breaks in Indian Macroeconomic Data', *Economic and Political Weekly*, 38(41): 4,312–15.

Wallerstein, Immanuel. 1979. *The Capitalist World Economy*. New York: Cambridge University Press.

Waltz, Kenneth N. 1979. *Theory of International Politics*. New York: McGraw-Hill Publishing Co.

Weiner, Myron. 1986. 'The Political Economy of Industrial Growth in India', *World Politics*, 38(4, July): 596–610.

Williamson, John. 2000. 'What Should the World Bank Think about the Washington Consensus?', *The World Bank Research Observer* 15(2): 251–64.

Woll, Cornelia. 2010. 'Firm Interests in Uncertain Times: Business Lobbying in Multilateral Service Liberalization', in Rawi Abdelal, Mark Blyth, and Craig Parsons (eds), *Constructing the International Economy*. Ithaca, NY: Cornell University Press.

Woo-Cummings, Meredith (ed.). 1999. *The Developmental State*. New York: Cornell University Press.

Woods, Ngaire Woods. 2006. *The Globalizers: The IMF, the World Bank, and Their Borrowers*. Ithaca, NY: Cornell University Press.

World Bank. 1991. *Report and Recommendation of the International Bank for Reconstruction and Development* (12 November). Washington, DC: World Bank.

———. 2001. *India: Power Supply to Agriculture*. Washington, DC: Energy Sector Unit, South Asia Regional Office.

———. 2010. *The World Development Indicators, Accessed through the National University of Singapore Library's eEdatabases* (January). Washington, DC: World Bank.

Index

222 • Index

About the Author

Rahul Mukherji is on the faculty of the South Asian Studies Programme, National University of Singapore. He earlier taught political economy at the Jawaharlal Nehru University, New Delhi; Hunter College, New York; and the University of Vermont, Burlington. He serves on the editorial board of *Pacific Affairs*, is a contributing editor of *India Review*, and is on the NUS Advisory Board of the *International Studies Review*. His research has appeared in the *Journal of Asian Studies*, *Review of International Political Economy*, *Journal of Development Studies*, *Pacific Affairs*, *India Review*, and *Economic and Political Weekly*. Rahul has edited *India's Economic Transition* (OIP, 2010) and co-authored with Sumit Ganguly, *India Since 1980* (2011) which is being translated into Portuguese. His most recent book is the Oxford India Short Introduction to the *Political Economy of Reforms in India*. He holds a PhD in Political Science from Columbia University.

Rahul is passionate about teaching and cooking.